Tourism and the Less Developed Countries

Tourism and the Less Developed Countries

Edited by David Harrison

Belhaven Press
London

HALSTED
PRESS

WILEY

Halsted Press
an imprint of John Wiley and Sons, Inc.
New York   Toronto

First published in Great Britain in 1992 by
Belhaven Press (a division of Pinter Publishers Limited)
25 Floral Street, London WC2E 9DS

British Library Cataloguing in Publication Data

A CIP catalogue record for this book is available from the
British Library

ISBN 1 85293 132 9

Copublished in the Western Hemisphere by Halsted Press, an imprint of
John Wiley & Sons, Inc. New York   Toronto
[605 Third Avenue, New York, NY 10158–0012]

Library of Congress Cataloging in Publication Data

A CIP catalog record for this book is available from the Library of Congress

ISBN 0 470 21906 8

Typeset by DP Photosetting, Aylesbury, Bucks
Printed and bound in Great Britain by Biddles Ltd., Guildford and King's Lynn

Contents

vi   *Contents*

List of tables

List of figures

Notes on contributors

Elizabeth Atieno Adero Onunga has worked at LTU International Airways in Germany, where she was mainly concerned with traffic rights. She completed a Management Training course with Kenya Airways, in Nairobi, and is now employed in the Marketing Department of Kenya Airways as a Passenger Tariff Officer. She obtained an MA in Development Economics at the University of Kent in 1988, having undertaken research on the international demand for Kenyan tourism

Parvin Alizadeh is a Senior Lecturer in Economics at the City of London Polytechnic. She has also been a consultant to the United Nations Conference on Trade and Development (UNCTAD) for a number of years. Her latest project for UNCTAD is focused on the 'Implications of European Integration for Developing Countries' Exports', and will appear in H. Grubel (Ed.), *The E.C. After 1992* (Macmillan, forthcoming). She has also published a number of articles on industrialisation in developing countries.

Glenn Bowman is a social anthropologist employed by the University of Kent as Lecturer in Communications and Image Studies. His doctoral research for Oxford University focused on Christian Pilgrimage to the Holy Land, and he has published a number of articles on that topic. He is currently researching issues relating to the interplay of sectarian identity and nationalism in the contexts of the Israeli Occupied Territories and the communities which made up Yugoslavia.

Sylvia Chant lectures in the Department of Geography, London School of Economics. She has researched and published widely on gender and development and has particular interests in women's employment and household survival strategies among the urban poor in Mexico, Costa Rica and the Philippines. Dr Chant is author of *Women and Survival in Mexican Cities* (Manchester University Press, 1991), co-author (with Lynne Brydon) of *Women in the Third World* (Edward Elgar, 1989) and editor of *Gender and Migration in Developing Countries* (Belhaven, 1992). Since 1987 she has been joint editor of the journal *Bulletin of Latin American Research*.

Malcolm Crick is Senior Lecturer in Social Anthropology at Deakin University, Australia. He studied social anthropology at the Universities of Sussex and Oxford and is author of *Explorations in Language and Meaning: Towards a Semantic Anthropology*

(Malaby Press, 1976). He conducted fieldwork on international tourism in Sri Lanka in 1982 and has subsequently published several articles in this field, including 'Representations of International Tourism in the Social Sciences: Sun, Sex, Savings and Servility', in the *Annual Review of Anthropology* (1989).

C. Michael Hall is Senior Lecturer in Tourism and Heritage Management in the Department of Management Systems, and Senior Research Fellow, New Zealand Natural Heritage Foundation, Massey University, New Zealand. He is author of *Introduction to Tourism in Australia: Impacts, Planning and Development* (Longman Cheshire, 1991), co-editor of *Special Interest Tourism* (Belhaven, 1992) and has research interests in sustainable development, event tourism, politics of tourism and leisure, environmental history and heritage management.

Derek R. Hall is Head of Geography at Sunderland University and convenor of the Tourism and Leisure Enterprises Unit. He edited the companion Belhaven text, *Tourism and Economic Development in Eastern Europe and the Soviet Union* (1991), and has published several works on tourism and on Cuba, including a chapter on that country in R.B. Potter (Ed.), *Urbanization, Planning and Development in the Caribbean* (Mansell, 1989). His current projects include advising on ecotourism development in Romania.

David Harrison lectures in Sociology in the School of Cultural and Community Studies, University of Sussex. Author of *The Sociology of Modernization and Development* (Unwin Hyman, 1988), he has carried out anthropological and sociological research on tourism in the Caribbean, southern Africa and Eastern Europe and is currently covenor of the Tourism Working Group of the European Association for Development and Research Institutes.

Vera Mackie is a Lecturer in Japanese History at the University of Melbourne, Australia. She has research interests in gender relations in Japan and the history of feminism in Japan. Her publications include 'Feminist Politics in Japan', *New Left Review,* 1988, and 'Division of Labour' in G. McCormack and Y. Sugimoto (eds), *Modernization and Beyond: The Japanese Trajectory* (Cambridge University Press, 1988).

Linda K. Richter is Professor of Political Science at Kansas State University where she teaches public policy, developing nations and public administration. She is an associate editor of *Annals of Tourism Research,* a member of the National Travel and Tourism Advisory Board, and a member of the International Academy for the Study of Tourism. Author of over forty articles on tourism, as well as *The Politics of Tourism in Asia* (University of Hawaii Press, 1989), she is currently writing a second edition of *Land Reform and Tourism Development: Policy-making in the Philippines* (Schenkman, first published 1982).

M. Thea Sinclair is Director of the Tourism Research Centre and Senior Lecturer in Economics at the University of Kent. She completed a study of Tourism Development in Kenya for the World Bank (whose support is acknowledged but who bear no responsibility for the chapter in this book) and has also undertaken tourism research for the United Nations, Spain's National Research Plan and various local organisations. She has recently edited a book on *The Tourism Industry* (CAB International, 1991) and is an active member of Tourism Concern.

Preface

Generally speaking, tourists have a bad press. A short while ago, I was preparing for a cycle ride with my son, then ten years old. Thinking we might venture off the beaten track, I tucked a map into my belt, only to elicit the horrified request that I leave the map at home. Why? 'Because people might think we're tourists.' Later, when walking through Brighton, I asked what he had against tourists, and he replied that they took up a lot of room on the pavement.

A month or two after the above incidents, we took a family holiday in the Mediterranean, where my son was mortified to be frequently mistaken for a local resident. Here, at least, he preferred the status of a tourist.

A similar amibivalence is displayed by many older critics of tourism, especially international tourism. The position taken by contributors to this book is more balanced, and it is hoped their work will prompt more research into the social, economic and political consequences of what is undeniably one of the world's most significant industries. Unfortunately, its importance is not always recognised. Funding for research is difficult to obtain, except perhaps for economists, and applications are frequently treated by funding bodies, and others who should know better, as unnecessary, even as something of a joke. That said, even though the British Overseas Development Association is now proud to have no in-house tourism specialist, in 1974 it funded a research fellowship for me to study the consequences of tourism in the Eastern Caribbean. More recently, short visits to Swaziland (1987) and Bulgaria (1989 and 1990) were generously funded by the British Council, and I gladly acknowledge such assistance.

Some thanks are due: Greta Bowman continued to tolerate living with a tetchy academic and maintains (probably correctly) that she deserves all the thanks I can offer. I hope she will feel the result is worthwhile. More muted thanks are due to Asha and Ian, who were often denied use of the computer for their games. In general, the human cost of academic texts is unrecognised but heavy. Marc Williams and Mike Barrow, colleagues at the University of Sussex, read parts of the first two chapters, Rob Benfield was supportive, and Iain Stevenson of Belhaven Press was extraordinarily tolerant and helpful. As editor, I must accept the blame for any shortcomings in the following pages, and I especially regret that space did not allow detailed consideration of the environmental implications of tourism. However, all the contributors deserve my thanks, especially those who came late into the project. Everyone responded positively (albeit through gritted teeth) to my pedantic comments and I think we all deserve a holiday.

David Harrison
Brighton, December 1991

1 International tourism and the less developed countries: the background

David Harrison

Introduction

This book is the third in a series and was to have been entitled *Tourism in the Third World*. The first of its predecessors focused on tourism in Western Europe (Williams and Shaw, 1988) and the second on tourism in the Soviet bloc (Hall, 1991). However, even as chapters were being written for the latter publication, Soviet influence was in decline and Eastern Europe entering a period of ferment. States which for forty years had been highly centralised around a dominant communist party, with pervasive state monopolies and non-market economic systems, suddenly welcomed capitalism, entrepreneurship, market forces and political pluralism, and rejected their previous economic and political institutions.

As Eastern Europe changes, those features that distinguished it from 'the Third World', always a problematic concept (Worsley, 1980 and 1984; Harrison, 1988), become increasingly less marked. The emphasis on civil society, new economic and political institutions, even on national identities, is reminiscent of the 'new nations' of the 1950s and 1960s and, arguably, the nations of Eastern Europe are only now emerging from a period of colonialism. In fact, as well as in terminology, the disappearance of the Second World entails the disappearance of the Third World, and we are increasingly dealing with 'a heterogeneous yet hierarchical and inegalitarian structure of capitalist states, each with increasingly polarised internal class divisions (Cliffe and Seddon, 1991, p. 9). When discussing issues of development, it is no longer possible to regard Albania, Romania and Bulgaria, for example, as obviously different from Egypt, Zambia or Pakistan. The whiff of convergence is in the air. More than was originally intended, this book is a sequel to the volume dealing with Eastern Europe.

Although contributors to this volume follow their preferred classification, in this chapter reference will be made to less developed countries (LDCs), rather than to the 'Third World', which is no longer deemed appropriate, for reasons already given, or to 'developing' or 'underdeveloped' societies, terms now closely identified with competing perspectives on development, which will be discussed later in this chapter.

Mere reference to LDCs does not indicate which countries should be placed in that category. In fact, whether we refer to LDCs, the Third World, or to Low- and Middle-Income economies, the list will be much the same and most countries of the world will be on it. However, LDC here refers to countries not regarded by the World Bank in 1990 as High Income Economies, as well as about a dozen oil-rich states and a few island economies with relatively high GNP per capita (the Bank's sole and inadequate criterion) but nevertheless considered by the UN or their own governments as 'developing' (World Bank, 1990, pp. 178–9 and 243). By contrast, territories or groups in or under the control of developed countries, American Samoa, Puerto Rico, or the North American Indians, for example, may evidence some characteristics associated with a lack of development. There will always be anomalies and incongruities, and the addition of (possibly) a few countries in Western Europe, Turkey, and most of the former Eastern bloc (subjects of earlier volumes) makes an already heterogeneous collection of nation states even more varied. Clearly, some states are closer to 'development' than others, and reference may still be made to 'Newly Industrialising Countries' (NICs), which could number up to thirty-one, depending on who is doing the classifying (O'Neill, 1984, pp. 711–2).

There are good reasons for focusing on tourism to LDCs, in particular. Their governments are anxious to promote economic growth and tourism – especially *international* tourism – is one means to this end. However, it necessarily involves visitors from rich countries visiting the poor – but not necessarily the poorest – thus highlighting disparities in wealth and raising their expectations. In such circumstances, the welcome to tourists may become ambivalent and tourism becomes a political as well as a social, economic and moral issue.

The growth of international tourism

The provision of statistics is not an end in itself. Indeed, the problems of defining and measuring tourism have been discussed in the two earlier volumes in this series (Williams and Shaw, 1988, pp. 10–11; Hall, 1991, pp. 12–17), and by numerous other commentators (Bhatia, 1986, pp. 97–110; Withyman, 1985; Allard, 1989; Latham, 1989; Witt, Brooke and Buckley, 1991, pp. 2–5). The definition used by the World Tourism Organisation (WTO) is extremely broad and figures provided by nation states are not always directly comparable. Criteria for inclusion vary from state to state (for example, visiting nationals residing overseas and workers commuting across borders are not uniformly treated), data are collected in different ways, and double counting and important omissions are common.

According to the WTO, a tourist is a temporary visitor staying at least twenty-four hours in any country not their normal place of residence, whereas excursionists, the second category of visitor, do not spend the night in the destination country. Such a definition includes people visiting for leisure purposes and business visitors, and incorporates most visitors not paid from within the country being visited (Mathieson and Wall, 1982, p. 11; Witt, Brooke and Buckley, 1991, p. 3). The very comprehensiveness of this definition has prompted others to provide more specific typologies (Cohen 1974 and 1979; Hamilton-Smith, 1987; Smith, 1989, pp. 11–14). Nevertheless, there is a case for an overall classification: in the course of a journey, a traveller may fulfil several different tourist 'roles', even if on a 'business' trip, and tourist impact may sometimes have less to do with tourists' motivation than with residents' perceptions.

Even greater problems are encountered in assessing tourist expenditures and receipts, which rarely include air fares but may include travel by public transport on road or rail. Data provided by banks, the usual source of information (Allard, 1989, p. 422) do not exhaust tourist transactions and tourist expenditure which is, in any case, spread over a wide range of goods and services. Whilst it has been argued that

Table 1.1 International tourist arrivals, 1950–1990 (excluding excursionists)

Date	No.	Date	No.
1950	25,282,000	1984	312,434,000
1960	69,296,000	1985	322,723,000
1970	159,690,000	1986	330,527,000
1980	284,841,000	1987	356,787,000
1981	288,848,000	1988	381,946,000
1982	286,780,000	1989	414,223,000
1983	284,173,900	1990	425,000,000

Source: WTO, 1991a, p. 11

broader measures of tourist expenditures and receipts are needed (Baretje, 1982), others have suggested that even existing estimates are highly suspect (White and Walker, 1982, p. 53).

Despite such reservations, however, the published figures indicate broad trends. Most obvious of all, as a result of higher standards of living in the West and improvements in the speed and carrying capacity of air transport, over the last forty years there has been a phenomenal growth in international tourism. By 1990, about 425 million international tourist arrivals were being recorded, as indicated in Table 1.1, a sixteenfold increase since 1950 and of more than 600 per cent since 1960. Indeed, over the forty-year period, tourist arrivals have increased annually, except over the period 1981–1983, when there was a slight decline. Growth continued in the 1980s, despite variations in its rate as a consquence of the unstable international economic situation.

Table 1.2 World's top tourism earners and spenders, 1986 (in US $ million)

Country	International tourist receipts	Rank	International tourist expenditure	Rank	Share of world total (%) Receipts	Expenditure	International tourist arrivals (000s)	Rank
USA	34,432	1	34,977	1	16.4	15.1	36,604	2
France	16,500	2	10,292	5	7.9	4.4	50,199	1
Spain	16,174	3	3,080	15	7.7	1.3	35,350	3
Italy	11,984	4	6,772	7	5.7	2.9	25,935	4
U.K.	11,182	5	15,111	4	5.3	6.5	17,338	6
Austria	9,317	6	5,027	9	4.5	2.2	18,202	5
Germany	8,658	7	23,727	2	4.1	10.2	14,653	8
Switzerland	5,568	8	4,907	10	2.7	2.1	12,600	10
Canada	5,014	9	7,370	6	2.4	3.2	15,111	7
Mexico	4,794	10	4,247	13	2.3	1.8	6,297	17
Hungary							14,236	9
Japan			22,490	3		9.7		
Netherlands			6,454	8		2.8		

Source: WTO, 1991b, pp. 130–2

Even at first sight, international tourism represents an immense, temporary migration of population. Furthermore, it is now the third largest item in world trade, accounting for more than 7 per cent of all world exports, and a level of expenditure exceeding the GNP of all countries but the USA, which itself contributes about a quarter of all spending on domestic and international travel (Waters, 1988, p. 4; WTO, 1991b, Vol. 1, p. 24; Hall, 1991, p. 24). Together, international and domestic tourism account for 12 per cent of world GNP. Tourism is big business.

A regional survey

As in the early 1970s (Hoivik and Heiberg, 1980, pp. 70–1), international tourism is dominated by developed countries, as indicated in Table 1.2. Of the ten countries which earned most from international tourism in 1986, for example, including the USA and Canada, seven are in Europe and only Mexico might be regarded as an LDC; indeed, it is often classified as a Newly Industrialised Country (NIC) (O'Neill, 1984, p. 710). As expected, too, earnings are related to tourist numbers, and of the top ten earners from tourism, nine are in the top ten destination areas. Only Mexico attracts a significantly higher proportion of earnings than of its international arrivals. Indeed, the top ten earners attract almost 60 per cent of world tourist earnings and almost half of all international arrivals.

Although international tourist arrivals have increased in all regions, some have performed better than others, as indicated in Tables 1.3 and 1.4. Europe remains the

Table 1.3 International tourist arrivals, by region: selected years, 1950–1990* (in 000s of arrivals)

	Africa	Americas	East Asia/ Pacific**	Europe	Middle East	South Asia
1950	524	7,485	–	16,808	–	47
1960	1,035	16,705	–	50,117	–	180
1970	2,842	36,648	–	112,008	–	912
1980	7,070	53,703	19,967	196,000	5,821	2,280
1981	8,046	53,464	23,446	195,289	6,160	2,443
1982	7,826	50,799	20,067	197,759	7,907	2,422
1983	8,210	51,014	22,318	192,828	7,316	2,487
1984	8,916	59,390	26,561	207,628	7,473	2,466
1985	9,805	58,728	29,408	214,263	7,979	2,540
1986	9,488	62,894	33,128	215,396	6,890	2,731
1987	9,986	67,986	38,372	230,752	6,984	2,707
1988	12,646	74,991	44,703	239,347	7,379	2,880
1989	13,604	78,456	44,387	266,946	7,775	3,055
1990	14,000	84,000	46,500	271,250	6,000	3,250

*   This includes international travel within the region
**   Tourist arrivals for China, included in this region, are calculated differently in other WTO publications, where they are much lower e.g. Yearbooks of Tourism Statistics.

Source: WTO, 1991a, p. 11; WTO, 1991b, Vol. I, pp. 4–21

Table 1.4 International tourist arrivals for selected years, 1950–1990: percentage share by region

	Africa	Americas	East Asia/ Pacific**	Europe	Middle East	South Asia
1950	2	30	–	66	–	0.1
1960	1.5	24	–	72	–	0.3
1970	1.8	23	–	70	–	0.6
1980	2.5	19	7	69	2	0.8
1985	3.0	18	9	66	2.5	0.8
1989	3.3	19	11	64	1.9	0.7
1990	3.3	20	11	64	1.4	0.8

Source: WTO, 1991a, p. 11; WTO, 1991b, Vol. I, pp. 4–21

dominant destination and sending area in tourism but, since 1950, its share of international arrivals has declined slightly, having peaked in 1970.

Within Europe, arrivals have been distributed unevenly. In 1989, the top five countries (France, Spain, Italy, Austria and the UK, in that order) took almost 149 million, or some 55 per cent of all European arrivals, with France, Spain and Italy together taking more than 40 per cent (WTO 1991a, p. 16). Turkey (categorised by the WTO as part of Southern Europe, and here considered an LDC). has been one of the fastest growing destination areas in recent years. From 1985 to 1990, its tourist arrivals went from 2.23 million to 5.4 million, an increase of 140 per cent (WTO, 1991a, pp. 5 and 16).

The share of the Americas – the USA and Canada, Latin America and the Caribbean – has declined even more noticeably than Europe, from 30 per cent of international arrivals in 1950 to 20 per cent in 1990. Again, changes have not been uniform. The proportion of international arrivals to Canada and the USA fell from almost 83 per cent in 1950 to under 70 per cent in 1989. By contrast, the region's LDCs have increased their share of the regional market, as indicated in Table 1.5, maintaining their position in the world market. In 1970, the Caribbean territories,

Table 1.5 International tourist arrivals to the Americas, and percentage share of the regional market: selected years, 1950–1989

Date	Tourists to the Americas (000s)	The Caribbean*	Central America**	South America	USA and Canada	Total
		(% share over the period)				
1950	7,485	6.7	5.2	5.5	82.6	100
1960	16,705	9.2	4.5	2.5	83.8	100
1970	36,648	10.7	8.0	6.6	74.7	100
1980	53,703	12.9	10.5	10.7	65.9	100
1985	58,728	13.4	9.4	11.5	65.7	100
1989	78,456	13.5	10.2	10.4	65.9	100

*   The Bahamas and Bermuda are included by WTO in the Caribbean region
**   Mexico is included by the WTO in Central America

Source: from WTO, 1991a, p. 14; WTO, 1991b, Vol. I, pp. 6–14

for example, attracted four and a quarter million tourists (excluding cruise ship passengers and excursionists), amounting to 2.65 per cent of all international tourist arrivals, increasing to almost eleven million tourists, or 2.7 per cent of all international arrivals, by 1989. Of these tourists, at least two thirds, and usually a far greater proportion, were holidaymakers. Noteworthy, too, is the increase in arrivals from Europe, which had doubled between 1984 and 1989 (Caribbean Tourism Organisation, 1990, pp. 5, 7 and 75).

Apart from the Caribbean states, in which the Bahamas (included by the WTO), Puerto Rico and the Dominican Republic are prominent, Mexico and Argentina are important receiving societies. In 1989 they attracted more than six million and almost two and a half million tourists respectively (WTO, 1991b, Vol. 1, pp. 136–7). Within the Americas, the further south one moves, the smaller proportion of arrivals are from the USA. In 1989, 87 per cent of Mexico's international tourists were from the USA, as were 81 per cent visiting Canada, 86 per cent the Bahamas, 84 per cent Bermuda and 67 per cent Jamaica. By contrast, US arrivals to the Caribbean islands of St Kitts, St Lucia and St Vincent were 39 per cent, 29 per cent and 25 per cent respectively (WTO, 1991b, Vol. II). The USA is less important to Central American tourism and of almost minimal significance to South America. In 1988, for example, 14 per cent of Brazil's tourists were from the USA, with 29 per cent from Europe and nearly half from other Latin American countries. The corresponding figures for Chile and Argentina were 8 per cent and 3.6 per cent, with 80 per cent of tourists to both coming from their Latin American neighbours (WTO, 1990, Vol. II). However, whilst Argentina, the most popular South American destination country, has increased its tourist arrivals in recent years, from one and a half million in 1985 to two and a half million in 1989, mainly from Uruguay, Brazil and Chile, Brazil's tourist arrivals have decreased. In 1989, they were one and a quarter million, a reduction of half a million on the 1985 figure (WTO, 1991a, p. 14).

In recent years rapid growth has also been recorded in the region classified by the WTO as East Asia and the Pacific, as indicated in Table 1.3. From 1980 to 1990, tourist arrivals increased by some 120 per cent. Although the rate of growth declined over the period 1985–1989, it was still almost twice as high as the world average of 28 per cent, as shown in Table 1.6. It is worth noting, too, that even before 1985, seven of the most successful countries in the region – Thailand, South Korea (boosted by the Seol Olympic Games in 1988), Singapore, Hong Kong, the Philippines, Taiwan and Malaysia – were considered by some commentators to have attained the status of NICs (O'Neill, 1984, pp. 711–2). As a general rule, very poor countries tend to attract relatively few tourists.

China is a key destination area. From 1980 to 1988, its tourist arrivals went from almost six million to nearly thirty-two million, of whom more than 90 per cent were from Hong Kong, Macao or Taiwan. However, (non-Chinese) 'foreign visitors' also increased, reaching 1.8 million by 1988. All arrivals decreased by 20 per cent the following year, as a consequence of the Tiananmen Square massacre of June, 1989.

In the mid-1980s it was predicted that, by 1995, Japan would be second only to Germany as a source of international tourists (Edwards, 1985, p. 21) and the trend seems well under way. Encouraged by their government to travel, the majority go to the USA (Waters, 1988, pp. 114–115). However, in 1988, Japanese formed nearly one third of 'foreign visitors' to China, (State Statistical Bureau of the Chinese People's Republic of China, 1990, p. 618), the single most important source of tourists to South Korea (48 per cent) and Hong Kong (22 per cent) and second in Singapore (16 per cent), Indonesia (12 per cent) and Thailand (11 per cent).

Europe, North America and East Asia and the Pacific account for most

Table 1.6 Tourist arrivals in East Asia and the Pacific, 1985–1989

	1985	1986	(000s) 1987	1988	1989	% change 1985–9
E Asia and Pacific*	25,493	29,124	33,804	39,443	38,730	52
Indonesia	749	823	1,060	1,301	1,626	117
Thailand	2,438	2,818	3,483	4,231	4,810	97
South Korea	1,426	1,659	1,875	2,340	2,728	91
Singapore	2,738	2,902	3,373	3,833	4,397	61
Hong Kong	3,370	3,733	4,502	5,589	5,361	59
Philippines	755	764	781	1,023	1,076	42
Taiwan	1,452	1,610	1,761	1,935	2,004	38
Malaysia	2,933	3,027	3,146	3,374	3,954	35
China**	7,133	9,000	10,760	12,361	9,361	31
Fiji	228	258	190	208	251	100

*   Excluding Japan, Australia and New Zealand.
**   These figures should be treated with caution. If ethnic Chinese from Macao, Hong Kong and Taiwan are included, along with other 'overseas Chinese', the 1988 figure is increased to 31,694,800 (Statistical Bureau of the People's Republic of China, 1990, p. 618). Figures supplied by WTO but relating only to visitors not ethnically Chinese, are as follows:
1987: 1,727, 821
1988: 1,842,206
1989: 1,460,970

(WTO, 1990, Vol. II, p. 25; WTO, 1991b, Vol. II, p. 29. See also Waters, 1988, p. 116; State Statistical Bureau of the People's Republic of China, 1990, pp. 618–620)

Source: WTO, 1991b, pp. 5 and 15

international arrivals and, in all these regions, intra-regional tourism is vital, (WTO, 1988, p. 25). By comparison, the Middle East, Africa and South Asia attract few international tourists – a little over 5 per cent of all arrivals in 1989 (WTO, 1991a, p. 11).

Until recently, tourism in the Middle East has been dominated by Egypt and Jordan. Sometimes classified by the WTO as part of the Middle East, in 1989 Egypt attracted almost a third of the region's arrivals. Another 29 per cent went to Jordan (WTO, 1991a, p. 17). As in other Arab countries, tourism to both was severely affected by tension in the region and the Gulf War of 1991.

In Africa, holidaymakers are less than half all arrivals (WTO, 1991c, p. 5). During 1989, excluding Egypt, six countries accounted for 70 per cent all that continent's international tourists. In North Africa: Morocco, Tunisia and Algeria (55 per cent); in East Africa: Kenya and Zimbabwe (8 per cent) and, to the south, the Republic of South Africa (7 per cent) (WTO, 1991a, p. 13). Noticeably, Morocco, Tunisia and Algeria are an integral part of the European 'periphery', with nearly half of their tourists crossing the Mediterranean. Similarly, 60 per cent of Kenyan visitors are from Europe, with another 12 per cent from North America. Further south, away from the European 'centre', only 13 per cent of Zimbabwe's tourists are from Europe, whereas 35 per cent are from Southern Africa and 40 per cent from East Africa.

Finally, since 1970 South Asia has barely managed to maintain its market share, which is still less than one per cent of all international arrivals, as indicated in Table

Table 1.7   World tourism and less developed countries: international arrivals, tourism receipts and exports, 1989

	% of all arrivals to LDCs	% of all LDC receipts from tourism
Americas	31.3	31.4
Africa	17.7	9.9
West Asia	12.6	12.6
S and SE Asia	35.8	42.8
Oceania	1.6	2.6
Europe	1.0	0.7
Total	100.0	100.0

Source: WTO, 1991b, Vol. I, pp. 36–7

1.4. In terms of numbers, India is utterly dominant, from 1985 to 1989 actually increasing its share of the region's tourists from 49 per cent to 60 per cent (WTO, 1991a, p. 17). This was partly because of the poor performance of other countries, most of which are too poor and/or too small to attract tourists in large numbers. And Sri Lanka, for example, which relies on Europe for almost two thirds of its tourists, has struggled to recover ground lost since the start of its internal unrest, which first surfaced in 1983. Indeed, its tourist arrivals fell steadily from 319,000 in 1984 to 185,000 in 1989, recovering in 1990 to 298,000 (UN, 1990, p. 745; WTO, 1991a, pp. 5 and 17). India, too, partly relies on European tourists, who in 1988 accounted for more than one third of its tourist intake, with South Asia providing a slightly smaller proportion.

In global terms, then, the situation is clear. In 1989, 'developed' countries attracted 65 per cent of all international arrivals and 72 per cent of all receipts from tourism, with 'developing countries and territories' (which then excluded European and Asian socialist countries), here referred to as LDCs, attracting 21 per cent of international tourists and 26 per cent of the tourist receipts (WTO, 1991b, Vol. 1, p. 37). Europe remains the major destination area, taking 64 per cent of all international tourist arrivals, and provides almost 61 per cent of all international arrivals. A corresponding growth has occurred in East Asia, which now attracts 11 per cent of arrivals (WTO, 1991a, p. 11).

Among the LDCs, Latin America, the Caribbean, South and South-east Asia together attract 67 per cent of all tourist arrivals to LDCs, and 74 per cent of their receipts, with Oceania, West Asia and Africa lagging some way behind, as indicated in Table 1.7. It is predicted that, over the next decade, some 'exotic destinations' will increase their share of the long-haul market (Lickorish, 1988, p. 271). especially the Caribbean and South-east Asia. By contrast, the share of Africa and South America may decline and, less exotically, North America is likely to build on its existing position as the top destination for long-haul travellers from Europe (Edwards, 1991). Proof of intent, certainly, is evident in the use of President Bush in television commercials advertising holidays in the USA.

Modernisation and development

As Eastern Europe is discovering anew, modernisation is a mixed blessing and its equation with 'development' a matter of personal evaluation rather than objective verification. Broadly speaking, however, the issues have been discussed across two major perspectives: modernisation theory (MT) and underdevelopment theory (UDT), both of which have been debated at length elsewhere (Worsley, 1984, pp. 16–60; Harrison, 1988; Barnett, 1988, pp. 3–50; Hunt, 1989; Hulme and Turner, 1990, pp. 34–67).

Modernisation theory focuses on the process of Westernisation, whereby the internal structures of 'developing' societies become more like those of the West, allegedly by emulating Western development patterns. Economically, there is a shift from agriculture to industry (and from rural to urban), and a central role for money and the money market. Socially, the influence of the family and other collectivities declines, institutions become more differentiated, and a pivotal role is played by 'modernising' elites and other 'change agents' in introducing modern values and institutions, often in the face of hostile or resistant tradition. Such changes are matched at the cultural and psychological levels, and modern consciousness involves greater autonomy for the individual.

Modernisation theory (MT) has an evident 'fit' with neoclassical economics, with its emphasis on prices, the market, and maximisation of self-interest (Little, 1982, pp. 25–6). If investment capital, entrepreneurial skills, technological knowledge and values necessary for modernity are absent from societies which are 'developing' (a term clearly implying a process of evolution or improvement), possibly because of the conservative nature of tradition, they can be diffused from outside, perhaps as some form of aid, provided there are sufficient, and sufficiently powerful, indigenous change agents to act as catalysts and carry the rest of society with them, albeit unwillingly.

Underdevelopment theory (UDT), articulated in explicit opposition to MT, considers development and underdevelopment (as opposed to a *lack* of development) to be linked elements in the same process. Here, development in one part of the world system occurs only at the expense of another part. 'Centres or 'metropoles' exploit 'peripheries' or 'satellites' through the mechanism of unequal exchange, thus transferring value from the relatively underdeveloped to the relatively developed regions. (Emmanuel, 1972; Mandel, 1978, p. 353; Harrison, 1988, pp. 91–2).

In UDT, 'underdevelopment' is explained by reference to the structurally subordinate position of underdeveloped societies within the world system, rather than by the dead hand of tradition, the lack of an educated élite, or the absence of values conducive to capitalist development. Furthermore, whereas MT considers that the interests of developing societies are best served by forging even closer links with developed societies, until recently UDT has advocated delinking from capitalism as a necessary first step to 'real' development (but cf. Frank, 1991, p. 25).

Although MT and UDT have been regarded as mutually exclusive paradigms (Foster-Carter, 1976), they have much in common: both are Eurocentric; both embody the notion of transition from one state to another, and both accommodate the idea of a world system – disagreeing, though, on how it is to be envisaged. Finally, both virtually ignore the wants and ambitions of those about to be developed. More recently, too, it has become widely recognised that internal factors and external linkages are significant, and that LDCs, including some following a 'socialist' path (Kitching, 1985, pp. 144–5; Brett, 1987, p. 37), may adopt questionable development strategies: an awareness undoubtedly heightened by the recent Balkanisation of Eastern Europe. All these factors provide ample ground for suggesting that, between MT and UDT, there is at least a 'limited commensurability' (Harrison, 1988, pp. 167–72). This may have been considerably enhanced by the rise of environmentalism, arguably another 'school' of development (Redclift, 1984 and 1987; Lélé, 1991). Equally Western and equally reliant on 'scientific' evidence, it focuses on change from (real?) overdevelopment to an ideal (and greener) future. With highly complex notions of a world system, environmental issues have nevertheless attracted the same degree of enthusiasm (and sometimes the same people) previously committed to other perspectives. For many, Brandt has given way to Brundtland.

This brief summary of development perspectives is no mere excursion into abstract theory. Rather, it indicates the changing framework within which all development strategies, including tourism, have been formulated over the last fifty years, and which has explicitly guided most empirical work. Of course, specific academic disciplines have their own ways of approaching international tourism, and these are detailed in numerous reviews of the tourism literature (Graburn and Jafari, 1991), but ultimately tourism in less developed countries, *or anywhere else*, is justified by its many participants, 'host' or 'guest', according to the alleged benefits it brings. And whereas modernisation is a more or less objective process, usually emanating from Western industrialised countries, with specific and describable patterns of economic, social and political change, the evaluation of costs and benefits belongs to the sphere of development. The point is worth emphasising: defining development necessarily involves assessment and evaluation. Furthermore, what specific individuals, groups or classes consider progress, or development, may or may not coincide with the empirical reality of modernisation (cf. Berger, Berger and Kellner, 1974, p. 15; Toye, 1987, pp. 10–11; Harrison, 1988, pp. 153–6).

Tourism, Modernisation and development

The previous section may seem a highly theoretical diversion. However, at face value, tourism can be seen as a form of modernisation, transferring capital, technology, expertise, and 'modern' values from the West to LDCs. Indeed, the relevance of such theoretical debates can be illustrated by reference to Boracay, a tiny island in the Philippines (Smith, 1988).

The islanders subsisted on farming and fishing until Boracay was 'discovered' by international tourists in the 1980s. The result was an intense pressure on the island's infrastructure, and the need for electricity, a central water supply and a system of sewage disposal soon became apparent. With the invasion of 'drifter' tourists, middle-class and family-oriented tourists declined in number, but the amount of garbage and other forms of pollution increased. With electricity came neon lights and discotheques; villagers sold souvenirs and rented out cottages and land values increased astronomically. And despite the reservations of older and more conservative islanders, young people 'nearly idolized' the tourists, for whom 'most of the working class . . . were willing to work literally day and night . . . for the sake of the money'. (Smith, 1988, pp. 12–13). Furthermore, drunkenness, narcotics and prostitution were imported into the island by the tourists, who also proceeded to deplete coral resources already damaged by the islanders' fishing practices (Smith, 1988, pp. 7 and 17).

At the time of Smith's paper, the government was having to decide if it could provide funds (and how to obtain them) for such necessities as a sewage treatment plant, a modern water supply and a garbage disposal system, as well as access piers and first-aid services.

At first sight, what happened to the island should occur only in a horror story. However, towards the end of the paper, Smith remarks:

Yet the people of Boracay, like all rural Filipinos, would enjoy having the infra-structure that is needed to support tourism, because it would make their lives easier, pleasanter and safer. And they certainly *want* the income generated by tourism, in the form of cash with which to buy goods and services including better education for their children. They appreciate the employment that is enabling their young people to stay on the island, or to return home to Boracay from the squalor of big cities, and be with their families. In the eyes of most villagers, tourism has been very positive – and the sins of the 'drifter' tourists can be temporarily overlooked in the face of their largesse. [Smith, 1988, pp. 15–16]

Boracay was undoubtedly being 'modernised', in the sense of being incorporated more closely into the world economic system, with the expansion of the cash economy and wage labour and the introduction of 'Western' norms and values. But was it 'development'? And who is the judge?

Population and the economic impact

The problem of tourist numbers

Several measures have been developed to contextualise the effect of tourist numbers in societies of various population sizes and land areas. In addition, there is considerable interest, especially among policy-makers and economists, in developing 'objective' measures of the economic impact of tourism (cf. Mathieson and Wall, 1982, Chapter 3; Duffield, 1982; Sutcliffe, 1985; Peppelenbosch and Tempelman, 1989; Witt, Brooke and Buckley, 1991, pp. 5–16). In general, they focus on the contribution of tourism to the balance of payments, the country's GDP, and employment.

Although useful for global comparisons, figures on tourist arrivals mean little unless situated in the context of the destination country. It is common, for example, to compare Tourist Intensity Rates (TIR) for different countries, where annual tourist arrivals are related to population size. An alternative measure, taking account of the time tourists stay in the territory, is the Tourist Penetration Rate (TPR), which relates total tourists nights to nights spent in the country by all residents. Another measurement is the Tourist Density Ratio (TDR), focusing on the ratio of tourist nights to the area of the region.

Some idea of the impact of tourist arrivals in different countries can be obtained through these measurements. Figures for important destination societies, along with several countries discussed in this book and the UK, which is included for comparative purposes, are provided in Table 1.8.

Calculation has also been made of the Concentration Ratio, which indicates the percentage of tourists received from a country's three most important sending societies (Hall, 1991, p. 18). From this, it is again clear that some receiving societies rely heavily on a few sending countries. The overwhelming reliance by neighbours of the United States on tourists from that country has already been mentioned – and explains the high concentration ratio of the Bahamas and Mexico. By contrast, like Botswana and Lesotho, Swaziland (not a major tourist destination) relies for its intake on the Republic of South Africa, its regional 'centre'.

Through the use of such measures as the TIR, TPR and TDR, it is possible to highlight major differences among countries and indicate the importance of specific variables. Length of stay is important. In 1988, for example, tourists stayed on average for eleven days in Barbados, more than twice as long as in the Bahamas or

Table 1.8 The measurement of tourist impact and concentration ratios, selected countries, 1988

Country	TIR Ratio	TIR Rank	TPR Ratio	TPR Rank	TDR Ratio	TDR Rank	CR
Bahamas	604.5	1	6.6	1	1.2	6	95
Barbados	177.8	2	5.4	2	31.6	2	75
Singapore	161.0	3	1.3	4	34.4	1	31*
U.K.**	27.6	4	0.75	5	1.8	4	41
Swaziland	27.4	5	0.13	12	0.06	11	81
Jamaica	27.0	6	0.74	6	1.6	5	92
Israel***	26.6	7	1.50	3	3.2	3	47
Costa Rica	12.2	8	0.33	7	0.18	8	60
Morocco	11.8	9	0.29	8	0.16	7	42
Thailand	7.8	10	0.15	11	0.02	15	38
Mexico	6.8	11	0.19	10	0.08	10	94
Argentina†	6.7	12	0.20	9	0.02	15	64
Egypt**	3.9	13	0.10	14	0.05	12	27
Kenya	3.0	14	0.13	12	0.05	12	41
Sri Lanka	1.1	15	0.04	15	0.09	9	40
India	0.2	15	0.02	16	0.04	14	35

Notes

TIR Tourist Intensity Rate $= \dfrac{\text{International Tourist Arrivals}}{\text{1988 population}} \times 100$

TPR Tourist Penetration Rate $= \dfrac{\text{average length of stay} \times \text{number of tourists}}{365 \times \text{1988 population}} \times 1100$

TDR Tourist Density Ratio $= \dfrac{\text{average length of stay} \times \text{number of tourists}}{365 \times \text{area in square kilometres}}$

CR Concentration Ratio = % of all tourist arrivals of top three sending countries

*   This excludes 'Other EAP' of 29 per cent (WTO, 1990, Vol. II, p. 104)
**   All visitors (WTO, 1990, Vol. II, pp. 151 and 202)
*** Average length of stay in Israel is given as 21 days. However, average length of stay in tourist-oriented establishments is only 3 days (WTO, 1990, Vol. II, pp. 46, 49 and 551). As with other countries, the former figure is used in these calculations.
†   Average length of stay in Argentina has been estimated at 11 days, based on figures given by WTO for neighbouring countries

Source: WTO, 1990, Vols I and II; IBRD (World Bank), 1990; Central Statistical Office, Swaziland.

Singapore, and for less than two days in Swaziland (which accounts for that country's relatively low TPR and TDR rating). One way of increasing receipts from tourism is to persuade people to stay longer, rather than attract more visitors. Population size is another factor. In 1988, for example, tourists to the Bahamas amounted to six times that country's population. When large numbers of people visit a relatively small territory, pressure may be increased. Barbados, for example, has 431 square kilometres compared to Kenya's 580,000, and it is the relatively small size of Singapore, with 1,000 square kilometres, along with more than four million tourists every year, that gives it one of the highest TDRs in the world.

Taking account of length of stay and land area, rather than simply the proportion of tourist arrivals to the indigenous population, produces somewhat different league tables for destination areas. Nevertheless, with such exceptions as Swaziland, where tourists stayed, on average, only 1.7 days, the ratios are fairly consistent. High TIR ranks are normally accompanied by high TPR and TDR ratings. However, such measurements ignore seasonality or concentration of tourist facilities within a country, both of which are major features of international tourism, and concentration ratios for specific regions at specified periods would clearly be very high. In addition, and of equal importance, they do not deal with socio-cultural features, which may be crucial in various assessments of the social significance of tourism. Despite their high rankings in the above measures, the Bahamas, Barbados and Singapore may cope more easily with relatively large numbers of tourists, to which they have become accustomed, than poorer countries, such as Kenya and Sri Lanka, which are lower in the rankings. And more than fifteen and a half million visitors a year to a developed country with a population of fifty-seven million (the UK) may be subjectively considered less significant than two thousand tourists to an extremely poor country of 1.4 million (Bhutan), where differences in culture and standards of living between 'host' and 'guest' are much greater. Indeed, although it is an undoubted feature of much modern tourism, increased scale alone may be a poor index of economic, social or cultural change in societies affected by tourism, either now or in the past.

The economic impact of tourism

There is considerable disagreement among economists about the economic impact of tourism. The issues have been discussed by numerous commentators (Duffield, 1982; Mathieson and Wall, 1982, pp. 64–92; Sutcliffe, 1985 and Fletcher, 1989) and it is not possible to review them here. However, in general, they focus on the contribution tourism makes to foreign exchange, to the Gross Domestic Product (GDP), and to employment.

Foreign exchange and Gross Domestic Product

Although such figures should be treated with caution, reliance on tourism clearly varies considerably, as indicated for selected countries in Table 1.9. The proportion of tourist receipts to the total exports of most countries listed is well above the world average of seven per cent (WTO, 1990, Vol. 1, p. 13). In 1984, for example, tourism in the Bahamas was said to account for more than a third of all exports and more than three quarters of the nation's GDP (WTO, 1988, p. 104), a situation undoubtedly continuing to the present. Clearly, international tourism is an important source of foreign exchange to parts of the Caribbean, for example, Barbados and Jamaica, and for Morocco, Costa Rica, Thailand, Mexico, Egypt, Kenya and India. In addition, in most countries listed in Table 1.9 – including the UK, which was placed there for comparative purposes – exports are a significant proportion of GDP (seen through the contribution of tourist receipts to GDP as a proportion of tourist receipts to exports). Where tourism is a relatively high contributor to both exports and GDP, dependence on tourism is considerable, especially in Barbados and Jamaica (where there is also a very high concentration ratio), but also in Morocco, Thailand, Egypt and Kenya. This is again the case for Singapore, which is highly export-oriented. In 1984, tourist receipts were 10 per cent of its GDP (WTO, 1988, p. 104) and by 1985 tourism was the island's third most important source of foreign exchange (Khan, Chou and Wong, 1990, p. 409). Indeed,

Table 1.9   Tourism balance in selected countries, 1988

Country	(US $ million) Tourism receipts*	Tourism expend.	Balance	Tourism as % of Exports**	GDP	Receipts per capita ($ US)
Bahamas	1,136	150	986	NA	53.0[a]	4,544
Barbados	459	29	430	60.1	29.8	1,836
Singapore	2,399	930	1,469	NA	9.7	905
UK	11,023	14,650	–3,627	5.7	1.3	193
Swaziland	18	14	4	4.1	2.9	24
Jamaica	525	45	480	33.5	16.5	214
Israel	1,343	1,130	213	8.9	3.2	305
Costa Rica	165	72	93	10.3	13.5	57
Morocco	1,102	132	970	26.3	5.0	46
Thailand	3,120	602	2,518	15.6	5.4	57
Mexico†	3,497	2,361	1,136	12.7	2.5	43
Argentina	634	975	–341	NA	0.8[b]	20
Egypt	1,784	75	1,709	36.6	4.9	34
Kenya	410	25	385	21.9	4.8	17
Sri Lanka	79	60	19	4.3	1.1	5
India††	1,390	438	952	10.3	0.6	2

*   Tourist receipts exclude payments for transport
**   Exports of all goods and services
†   1987 figures   ††   1986 figures

Source: WTO, 1990, Vol. I, pp. 127–130, 183–6
    International Monetary Fund, 1990 (Country Tables)
    [a]   Caribbean Tourism Organisation, 1990, p 4.
    [b]   IBRD (World Bank), 1990, p. 183.

figures compiled by the WTO suggest that in 1984, tourism receipts were considerably higher than those obtained for the main export product in Barbados, Bermuda, Haiti, Panama, the Philippines, Singapore, Thailand and India (WTO, 1988, p. 105).

It is no surprise that the UK and Argentina have an unfavourable tourism balance. The former is a developed country and citizens have a high level of disposable income, some of which is spent on overseas holidays; Argentina, one of the most developed countries in South America, is in a similar position within that region.

Employment

Other commentators have noted the problems of assessing the contribution made by international tourism to employment (cf. Mathieson and Wall, 1982, pp. 76–82; Witt, Brooke and Buckley, 1991, pp. 10–12). In such matters, it is usual to distinguish between direct, indirect and induced employment. Employment arising directly from tourism – for example, in hotels – may be relatively little, and such establishments also cater for at least some local residents, perhaps playing a key role in the country's class structure. Indirect employment will be created in other sectors of the economy which nonetheless do not depend on tourism for their existence. Taxis and other forms of public transport, restaurants, bars and retail outlets, theatres, cinemas and other places of entertainment, as well as a country's arts and crafts, fall into this category. For workers in these sectors, only part of their time may be spent dealing with tourists, even though the tourist industry may be crucial to the sector. Finally, induced employment is that which arises from an increased general demand for goods and services which has been prompted by an expansion in tourist expenditure.

It is because tourism cuts across sectors that it is difficult to estimate – even where data are adequate – the effect it has on employment. However, in some countries its importance is evident. In Bermuda in 1985, for example, tourism was responsible for the direct employment for almost two thirds of the labour force (Archer, 1987, p. vii), and figures from the WTO suggest that in the Virgin Islands, the Bahamas and Jamaica, direct and indirect employment in tourism accounts for 50 per cent, 35 per cent and 37 per cent of the labour force respectively (WTO, 1988, p. 74). Estimates of employment in the same region are provided by the Caribbean Tourism Organisation (CTO). Noting that the larger and more luxurious hotels tended to generate more employment than smaller hotels and self-catering establishments, the CTO recently estimated that, on the basis of 1.19 jobs per hotel room, in 1989 direct employment in accommodation establishments in the Caribbean (including Bermuda) amounted to 141,000 people. (CTO, 1989, p. 84). It went on to suggest that the total number of jobs generated by tourism was about three times this amount (1989, p. 85).

Some critics of tourism as a development strategy suggest that its contribution to employment has been exaggerated. Bachmann, for example, claims that in 1979 the Kenyan tourism industry accounted for 0.5 per cent of all Kenyan workers, and that in the modern sector it directly contributed 32,000 jobs and was indirectly responsible for a further 25,000, overall a 'modest' contribution (1988, p. 185–6). At a more local level, he arrived at similar conclusions:

Although tourism creates some new jobs, the regional unemployment problem is not resolved, because an even larger number of jobless people immigrate constantly from distant places to the tourist centre thus increasing the unemployed population of Malindi and Watamu. [Bachmann, 1988, p. 281]

His views are echoed by Summary (1987, p. 537) and Rajotte (1987, p. 87), who also notes that such jobs are normally low paid (1987, p. 87), a criticism made by Farver of employment in tourism in Gambia (1984) and, in fact, by numerous other critics of tourism in LDCs.

In calculating tourism's contribution to employment, it is also necessary to consider the stage reached by a specific tourist destination (cf. Butler, 1980). The number of jobs, their nature, and who does them will vary throughout the growth, decline or rejuvenation of tourist resorts. In addition, the role of international tourism in creating employment has to be weighed against its contribution to other sectors. In considering tourism development in Bali, for example, Rodenburg argues that whilst large, international hotels create more jobs than smaller local hotels and guest houses, paying higher wages and bringing in more foreign exchange, they also import more, have fewer linkages with the local infrastructure, and provide few entrepreneurial opportunities for the local population (1980). By contrast, it is reported that, in the Cook Islands, small, locally-owned establishments are more successful than larger, internationally-owned hotels in creating income, employment and government revenue (Milne, 1987), and similar conclusions have been reached for Thailand (Meyer, 1988, p. 478).

Tourist multipliers

Several techniques have been used by economists in measuring the economic impact of tourism and predicting the effects of investment in the industry. (cf. Sutcliffe, 1985). The most common (and controversial) is some version of the Keynesian multiplier (Archer, 1977 and 1989), which assesses the cumulative effect of a change in tourist expenditure on, for example, income, government revenue, employment, sales, output or level of imports. The effect of changes in tourist expenditure on income, especially, has figured prominently in the literature. Tourist multipliers have been calculated in different ways but, putting the issue somewhat crudely, a relatively high income multiplier of 1.5, for example, means that an increase in tourist expenditure of $1.00 would generate a further $1.50 in the economy of a given region as expenditure worked its way through the economy in the form of income, with a further fraction leaving the economy (as 'leakages') to pay for imports, thus providing income for people living outside the region.

Although the theory of multipliers sounds fairly straightforward, the difficulties in arriving at multiplier coefficients are well documented, both for LDCs (Bryden, 1973, pp. 71–82; Mathieson and Wall, 1982, pp. 64–71) and for developed societies (Gartner and Holecek, 1983; Archer, 1984). However, the more an economy can supply the required tourist goods and services, the greater the proportion of the initial expenditure will remain as income (Archer, 1989, p. 130). By contrast, regions heavily dependent on imports will have lower coefficients and greater leakages. In such circumstances, small societies, particularly islands, are especially vulnerable. Indeed, Wilkinson estimates that ten Pacific and twelve Caribbean 'microstates' can be regarded as 'tourist economies'. (1989, p. 156). Such territories tend to have low multipliers.

Table 1.10 Tourist income multipliers for selected countries, ranked according to area and population size

Country	Tourism income multiplier	Rank	Rank in terms of:	
			Area	Population size
Turkey	1.96	1	2	2
United Kingdom	1.73	2	3	1
Republic of Ireland	1.72	3	5	6
Egypt	1.23	4	1	3
Jamaica	1.23	4	9	7
Dominican Republic	1.20	6	6	4
Cyprus	1.14	7	10	10
Bermuda	1.09	8	18	16
Hong Kong	1.02	9	13	5
Mauritius	0.96	10	12	8
Antigua	0.88	11	15	15
Bahamas	0.79	12	8	12
Fiji	0.72	13	7	9
Cayman Islands	0.65	14	16	17
Iceland	0.64	15	4	11
British Virgin Islands	0.58	16	17	18
Republic of Palau, Micronesia	0.50	17	14	14
Western Samoa, Polynesia	0.39	18	11	13

Source: Fletcher, 1989, p. 527

Using evidence presented by Fletcher (1989), who compiled tourist income multipliers from a variety of sources, and comparing multiplier coefficients with data on area and population, there is considerable correlation, as indicated in Table 1.10. With the necessary caveats that methods of calculation have varied and were carried out at different times (not indicated by Fletcher), the pattern is clear enough. Bermuda, with its strong government controls (Wilkinson, 1989, p. 159) and Hong Kong (both somewhat peculiar colonial territories) are exceptions, as is Iceland, which has a small population over a relatively wide area. Generally, the large and more populated countries tend to have the highest tourist income multipliers. Small island economies, lacking natural resources, are at the other end of the spectrum.

Critics have argued that tourism receipts must be balanced against the 'leakage' any increased tourism expenditure incurs, either directly or indirectly. Indeed, it has been estimated that, at different times, and excluding induced effects, Hong Kong and Singapore have experienced import leakages of 41 per cent and 29 per cent respectively (Khan, Chou and Wong, 1990, pp. 416–7). In the Caribbean, with its many island economies, the debate has been intense (Bryden, 1973, chapters 5 and 9; Perez, 1973–4;). In recent years, some Caribbean islands, for example, Jamaica, St Lucia and Montserrat, may have increased the linkages of tourism with agriculture, thus reducing their food import bill (Momsen, 1986). However, such changes have not necessarily occurred throughout the Caribbean: 'It seems linkages between tourism and domestic agriculture do not always improve with time but continue to reflect the particular characteristics of individual islands' (Momsen, 1986, p. 22). Other commentators on Caribbean tourism note the continued inability of the agricultural sector to meet the requirements of the tourist industry (Bélisle, 1983; Alleyne, 1984). Similar arguments over the role of tourism and its relationship to other economic sectors have occurred in other regions.

More technically, there are often disagreements about which kind of multiplier should be used (Archer, 1984). However, multiplier analyses, and assumptions on which they are based, have been heavily criticised. They are alleged to ignore income accruing to non-nationals and to assume under-utilisation of labour and capital. Most importantly, they are said to take no account of opportunity cost, failing to measure what would have happened if investment placed in tourism had been directed elsewhere (Bryden, 1973, p. 77).

Although some may reject the idea that tourism brings economic benefits (Turner and Ash, 1975, pp. 113–126), it is unwise to generalise about the economic effects of international tourism in all LDCs. Clearly, it contributes to foreign exchange, government revenue and employment, but the extent of its contribution varies according to the area in question, any available alternative strategies, and the willingness and ability of government to create an environment for investment and encourage backward linkages with other sectors of the economy. It is also evident that tourism development may carry with it certain costs. Inflated prices for land, property and food are frequently reported (and are to be expected in any region following a successful development strategy) and inevitably there will be pressure on government to improve the infrastructure. As with any other product, tourist facilities need to be maintained, developed, and sometimes protected. Here, too, costs, including environmental costs (Romeril, 1989; Boo, 1990) are entailed.

Summary

In this chapter, I have indicated the growth of international tourism and shown how, despite the continuing dominance of Europe and North America, some LDCs, especially, have come to rely upon tourism's contribution to foreign exchange, employment, and the gross domestic product. Development strategies aimed at increasing the industry's role have not been formulated in a political and theoretical vacuum; rather, they have been based on different, sometimes competing, perspectives of what constitutes 'modernisation' and 'development'.

In all of these debates, it is noticeable that strictly 'objective' economic criteria are frequently replaced by social considerations. Whilst multipliers are probably rather poor predictors of future performance, the issue of differential opportunity costs tends to shift the debate to issues of policy and what would have happened if some other kind of policy had been followed in the past or were to be followed in future. Similarly, debates over economies of scale and the degree to which tourism development is able to meet prioritised economic objectives (cf. Jenkins, 1982) raise more general questions on the involvement of transnational corporations in tourism, their relationship to local entrepreneurs, and the role, willingness and ability of the state in LDCs to influence investment strategies and meet social objectives (cf. Jommo, 1987). Apparently 'objective' economic 'facts' prompt intense emotional debate. To take but one example, critics of tourist development, especially in LDCs, frequently assert that while the industry may create employment, the jobs it produces are of an inferior nature. Development, it is argued, does not come from a nation of waiters, bell hops and chambermaids, and far less from prostitutes and pimps. Although such assertions clearly go beyond economic criteria, they are at the heart of many criticisms of tourism development.

2 Tourism to less developed countries: the social consequences

David Harrison

Introduction

Numerous writers have tried to explain why people take holidays. For some, tourists are trying to escape, however unsuccessfully, the alienation of modern (or post-modern) society (MacCannell, 1976; Krippendorf, 1987; Urry, 1988 and 1990), seeking an 'authenticity' which, if found, will inevitably be destroyed. Tourism may be a form of pilgrimage, a 'sacred journey' (Graburn, 1989, first published 1978), a move from structured *societas* to unstructured *communitas*, perhaps echoing rites of transition practised in some pre-industrial tribal societies (Turner and Turner, 1978, p. 34–9). At a more general (and reified) level, underdevelopment theorists argue that paid vacations provide recreation for workers to enable them to continue their tasks in the productive system (Schiller, 1976, p. 14; Britton, 1987b, p. 172).

Whereas, in these accounts, tourism performs functions for Western society as a whole, others have examined the socio-psychological motivations of tourists (Crompton, 1979; Dann, 1981; Dunn Ross and Iso-Ahola, 1991) and the roles of marketing agencies and the mass media (Britton, 1979; Thurot and Thurot, 1983; Moeran, 1983; Uzzell, 1984; van Raaij and Francken, 1984; Cohen, 1989a). However, for whatever reason, millions of tourist trips are made every year. In this chapter, the focus is on the consequences of such a vast temporary migration for tourist-receiving societies, especially those categorised as less developed.

Consequences and problems

Domestic tourism is not unproblematic and, because of differences in class, status and ethnicity, its consequences may be similar to those of international tourism (Monk and Alexander, 1986). Domestic visitors can seem foreign, as did urban visitors to a *mestizo* village in Mexico (Nunez, 1963, p. 349), and it was Indonesian and not Western tourists who desecrated an ancient burial site on the Indonesian island of Sulawesi (Crystal, 1989, first published 1978, p. 150). In such circumstances, perceived 'foreignness' may bear little relationship to political boundaries.

However, in international tourism, where the 'modern' and 'traditional' stand in stark contrast to one another, the effects of 'modernisation', of which tourism is but one element, are most evident. While its economic consequences are not universally welcomed, the cultural and social effects of international tourism rouse the most passion, and the focus of this chapter is on these areas.

At the outset, a crucial distinction has to be drawn between social *consequences* and social *problems*. The former, arising from a well established pattern of modernisation, include alterations in the physical environment to accommodate and entertain tourists, deep and possibly traumatic changes in the social structure, and alterations in the value system, either throughout society or in some part of it. Such changes can be described, demonstrated and, in principle, explained. By contrast, social problems are defined according to perceptions of 'development'. Like beauty, they are in the eye of the beholder and lists of social costs and benefits provide a spurious objectivity to a highly evaluative selection process. Such remarks are not intended to trivialise the issue, for tourism development strategies raise serious moral dilemmas. Indeed, how these are dealt with, and by whom, becomes part of the social consequences, and may lead to the perception of other problems. Clearly, consequences and problems are linked – but they are not identical.

The physical landscape

Perhaps the most obvious effect of tourism is on the physical landscape. Initially, existing properties may be adapted to accommodate visitors, but increasing numbers soon prompt the construction of new buildings, perhaps in tourist 'enclaves'. The distinction between physical and social impact soon becomes blurred. There are debates on style ('traditional' or 'modern'?) and appropriateness, and government may legislate against alleged excesses. Where old buildings become hotels, links with the past may be retained, albeit ironically, as where abandoned sugar mills in the Caribbean are given a new lease of life, adding weight to the idea that tourism is 'a new kind of sugar' (Finney and Watson, 1975; Harrison, 1975). Hotels may come to symbolise 'modernity' (Wood, 1984, p. 368) and, as centres of entertainment, they are attractive, especially to the young, even from rural areas, and their use as conference centres often performs a similar function for older and wealthier local patrons (Meyer, 1988, p. 124). In such circumstances, 'unsuitable' local people may seek entry, not only to hotels and similar establishments, but also to 'public' beaches and other facilities, and questions of access, and its restriction, often arise. One answer, frequently implemented, is to charge high prices, both to increase revenue and to keep out the undesirable poor.

Increased commoditisation

Welcomed as necessary by advocates of modernisation (cf. Parsons, 1964, pp. 349–350), the continuing spread of market relationships has been greeted more ambivalently by proponents of underdevelopment theory, who have nevertheless charted the continued incorporation of 'underdeveloped' regions into the capitalist world system. Undoubtedly, tourism contributes to this process, extending the formal, 'modern' sector by increasing wage employment or cash payments for items valued by tourists deep into the rural 'hinterland'.

Tourism clearly affects the production and nature (and more arguably the quality) of local art forms. It is easy to scoff at tourist taste and its effect on indigenous arts and crafts (Turner and Ash, 1975, pp. 141–8) and most people are aware of the derogatory connotation of 'airport art'. According to Graburn, indigenous art production has moved from 'functional traditional art', rooted in religious ritual, towards commercial production for the tourist market, ultimately in the form of souvenirs and novelties. Whilst accepting that even 'functional traditional arts' may be the result of earlier diffusion (1984, pp. 400–1), he considers art forms developed for tourists to be divorced from local culture and less satisfying for the producer. They thus constitute a 'symbolically incomplete' experience (1984, p. 406) and result in the 'museumification' of traditional art forms and marginalisation and alienation of the minorities who produce them (Graburn, 1984, p. 414).

A similar process is described by Nason (1984) in his study of the Truk district of the Caroline Islands of the Pacific, which were subjected to successive colonial and cultural influences from Spain, Germany, Japan and the United States. By the 1970s handicraft production was increasing, especially among women, but there was a reduction in the production of *meettooch* goods, objects considered worthy of 'special aesthetic consideration' (1984, p. 427). Nevertheless, they continued to be made for local consumption. Somewhat grudgingly, Nason credited tourism with promoting handicraft production and increasing local awareness and estimation of material and cultural products (Nason, 1984, p. 446). Such issues have been more positively emphasised by others (Boissevain and Inglott, 1979, pp. 281–2; Cohen, 1988a; Richter, 1989, p. 45).

Although tourism sometimes seems to have a cheapening effect, as in the near-obscene transformation of pieces of the Berlin Wall into ear-rings, production for tourists is not necessarily less 'authentic' as a consequence. The African producers of popular art studied by Jules-Rosette, although constrained by the need to standardise and simplify their products, nevertheless searched 'for new designs, innovative combinations of styles, and bolder artistic messages' (1984, p. 236). What is deemed 'authentic', in fact, depends on the perspective of producer and buyer, both nodes in a highly complex network of continually negotiated meanings, rather than on allegedly 'objective' social scientists (cf. Cohen, 1988a), whose implicit assessments of good taste may be highly questionable, albeit evident from what they themselves have purchased on their travels, quite possibly at rates lower than market valuations (cf. May, 1975, p. 129).

That tourism need not lead to a diminution of standards can be seen from the Amish of Pennsylvania, islands of 'tradition' in an ocean of modernity. Traditionally, Amish women designed and produced quilts for local consumption. However, by the mid-1980s, 90 per cent of all quilts produced were being sold to tourists. As a consequence, new designs and materials were obtained from outside and 'traded among Amish quilters' (Boynton, 1986, p. 460), apparently without any deterioration in quality.

The effects of tourism on ritual, the heart of 'tradition', have been much discussed. Viewing the tourist industry 'as a vast school for the modernization of a people's values' (1972, p. 90), Greenwood alleged that the Alarde, a major ritual in Fuenterrabia, northern Spain, had degenerated into a mere tourist show. By being commoditised, it was no longer regarded as significant by the town's inhabitants. Later, however, he retracted this position as an expression of 'anger and concern', conceding that the ritual held considerable political significance for the townspeople of Fuenterrabia (1989, first published 1972, p. 181).

The example of Fuenterrabia, which has been widely quoted in the literature on tourism, is instructive. That the ritual became a tourist attraction, and was used as a source of income, undergoing changes in the process, is not at issue; that it lost meaning for the local people is highly debatable.

A similar argument has centred on the effects of tourism in Bali. Countering the view that tourism degrades culture, McKean and Noronha assert that it led to a strengthening of Balinese arts, crafts and tradition, and a similar position has been taken, somewhat more guardedly, by Crystal on Indonesia (1989, first published 1978, p. 165). According to McKean, 'economic interactions between Balinese and tourists bind the two in a common field' (1989, first published 1978, p. 98), whereas Noronha suggests that 'the Balinese want tourism; they also want to be involved in it' (1979, p. 201). For him, Balinese traditions are only marginally affected by tourism. Indeed, through profits made in tourism, they are strengthened:

Tourism has thus affirmed these most important ties which link the past with the present and the future and which form the boundaries through which no outsider can penetrate, not even Balinese who are not members of the same bandjar [village section] (Noronha, 1979, p. 202).

The story may not be so simple. Dances traditionally performed in temples may become forms of entertainment, but the opposite also occurs (Picard, 1990, pp. 52 and 61), thus blurring the distinction between 'sacred' and 'profane', as when dancers continue to wear consecrated masks and obtain religious benefit when dancing specifically for tourist audiences. 'In short, while the regional authorities endeavor to "disenchant" parts of the world, the dancers continue to move in a totally "enchanted" world (Picard, 1990, p. 70). The entire situation is made even more confusing because the Balinese authorities, faced with the continued threat of Indonesianisation of their culture, use tourism to assert their national identity:

In other words, their culture has become, for the Balinese, on the one hand what characterizes them as a specific society, and on the other hand what provides their tourist product with its distinguishing feature (Picard, 1990, p. 74).

As part of a wider modernisation process, international tourism contributes to the spread of market relationships and tourist receiving societies must inevitably adapt. How such changes are interpreted by those they most affect cannot be postulated in advance, however disadvantageous they may appear to outside observers. Furthermore, perceptions change over time, as in the Catalan coastal town where, having replaced fishing as the main source of income, tourism came to be seen as the *traditional* industry, to be defended against the ravages of a later invasion of fishermen (Pi-Sunyer, 1989, first published 1978, pp. 196–7).

Changes in social structure

Along with other forms of modernisation, tourism creates new opportunities in the formal and informal sectors of the economy, new criteria of social status, and contributes to changes in such basic social institutions as the family, reinforcing the role of established political and economic institutions and leading to new structures, often associated with increased state involvement. Finally, it facilitates the spread of western norms and values, sometimes in direct contrast to 'tradition'.

Owners and entrepreneurs

As Butler suggests (1980), tourist regions tend to develop in stages. Where tourist development has been most intense, the more extensive and expensive facilities have often been taken over by transnational companies, perhaps in partnership with the state, leaving the smaller and less profitable part of the market to local entrepreneurs. Although there have been exceptions to this pattern, as in centrally-planned economies where the state has dominated (Allcock and Przeclawski, 1990; Hall, 1991), or where previously non-utilised areas have been developed for tourism, the internationalisation of tourism in LDCs, as elsewhere, is clearly the (statistical) norm. This is indicated (to cite but a small selection) in empirical studies of the Pacific (Britton, 1982 and 1987a), Malta (Oglethorpe, 1984), the Bahamas (Debbage, 1990), India (Chandrakala, 1989), Kenya (Jommo, 1987; Bachmann, 1988), the Gambia (Wagner, 1982; Farver, 1984), the Caribbean (Bryden, 1973; Perez, 1975; Poon, 1987), southern Africa (Crush and Wellings, 1987; Harrison, 1989) and Thailand (Meyer, 1988). The pattern is confirmed by more general studies of the involvement of transnational companies (UNCTC, 1982; Dunning and McQueen, 1982), and in several chapters of this volume.

Where indigenous entrepreneurs do emerge, they often come from those with existing links to the wider business community. Indeed, a few entrepreneurs can wield considerable influence, as among cushion producers in parts of Thailand (Parnwell, 1992). Some entrepreneurs may be 'marginal', for example, ethnic Chinese in Malaysia (Din, 1982, p. 458; Bird, 1989, pp. 31–2) or returning migrants (or their descendants), whose experience elsewhere has increased their expertise and access to funds. Examples can be found in the gemstone and jewellery industry of Thailand (Parnwell and Khamanarong, 1990, pp. 14–17), in Negril, Jamaica (McKay, 1987, pp. 143–4), and Brittany, France (Shurma-Smith, 1988). Retiree tourists, too, have been found to occupy important entrepreneurial roles, acting as 'change agents' in such diverse places as the Caribbean (Lowenthal, 1976) and the Scottish Inner Hebrides (Kohn, 1988). However, not all returning migrants are impressed by tourism and its effects. Temporarily leaving Vermont, USA to revisit the island of Antigua, Kincaid saw tourism as the successor to colonialism and bitterly defined every tourist as an 'ugly, empty thing, a stupid thing, a piece of rubbish pausing here and there to gaze at this and that' (1988, p. 17).

Structures inherited from the colonial period may prevent individuals or groups from developing entrepreneurial talents, or restrict them to specific market sectors. In Kenya, only local owners of up-country hotels catering for domestic tourists were successful and Jommo noted '[the] collapse of almost every venture undertaken by indigenous large-scale investors in hotels' (1987, p. 89). Among tour operators, where there was substantial 'local' involvement, it was largely white or Asian (1987, pp. 97–8). In Nairobi, too, souvenir shops were owned and run mainly by Asians, and restaurants and places of entertainment catering for international tourists were also owned primarily by non-Africans (Jommo, 1987, p. 117). By contrast, in Fiji, although expatriates again held the top admininstrative positions, Indians reportedly occupied low-status labouring jobs, whilst indigenous Fijians held more prestigious positions as waiters, barmen, receptionists and security guards (Samy, 1975, pp. 113–7).

In addition to competition among ethnic groups, the business community in tourist-receiving societies may be riven by divisions between local (small-scale) and metropolitan (large-scale) interests, with the latter perhaps held responsible for importing 'alien' foodstuffs and values. 'To Hell with Paradise', enunciated by a Caribbean politician (also involved in running a small hotel) then becomes a nationalistic rallying cry, aimed at discouraging large-scale tourism, exaggerated advertising and metropolitan 'hype' (Mitchell, 1972). Indeed, residents of Bequia, from which he comes, are reported to be divided on the benefits of tourism of any kind. Those with land to sub-divide (including former planters), housing to rent, hotels to run, and labour, goods or services to sell, legally or otherwise, favour the industry's expansion, even with foreign involvement. The landless and many of the poor are less impressed (cf. Price, 1988, pp. 206–244). In such circumstances, tourism may simply reinforce the pre-existing social structure.

Frequently, élites in LDCs become partners of overseas capital. Meyer, for instance, emphasises a 'triple alliance' of Thai élites, including the royal family and the Chinese commercial class, the Thai government and transnational companies, which together dominate Thailand's tourism (1988, pp. 113–95). The UDT perspective is neatly summarised by Britton, who considers international tourism to be constituted by a three-tiered hierarchy, with metropolitan capital, based in developed societies, at the top, followed by local, comprador capitalists and, at the bottom, small-scale enterprises, whose success depends on that of the two higher categories, which cream off most of the profits (1982, p. 346). Power allegedly remains in the metropole – for Nash, another advocate of UDT, a sufficient definition of 'imperialism' (1989, first published 1978, p. 38) – and LDCs themselves are left with '. . . a largely passive and dependent role' (Britton, 1982, p. 347).

As with UDT in general (cf. Harrison, 1988, Chapter 4), there are problems with this kind of analysis. First, it is not clear whether the objections are to capitalism as such, or to the dominance of international capital (cf. Phillips, 1977, p. 19). Both positions have their problems. Referring approvingly to Tonga's 'monarchic structure', which 'sheltered the country from outside forces' and controlled the expansion of the tourist industry (1982, p. 349), Britton elsewhere suggests the country's tourism industry suffered because it 'was not exploited as a fully-fledged colony' (1987a, p. 131). Secondly, hostility to tourism development often centres on the (alleged) increase in inequality across classes in LDCs. Indeed, successful entrepreneurship may even be regarded as inherently undesirable, as by Wagner, whose analysis ignores a woman entrepreneur whose dominance in handicraft production was achieved through good timing, use of her social network, and advertising (1982, pp. 9, 13, 57–8).

If all participants in tourism obtain some benefit (Britton, 1982, p. 346), increased inequality is not necessarily problematic. However, tourism development can increase social inequality and lead to other consequences commonly regarded as unacceptable. Thai villagers, for example, have been evicted for outsiders to develop tourist resorts (Ekachai, 1990, pp. 89–99, 114–8 and 141–5) and elsewhere in Thailand other development projects have increased rural poverty, sometimes increasing migration to urban centres and the less acceptable regions of the informal economy. In such circumstances, the extent of the disruption is conditioned by the response, at local, national and international levels, of the people, the state (Boissevain, 1977) or of other agencies.

Job opportunities in tourism

Elites in many LDCs actively promote tourism and the benefits accruing to LDCs through tourism (or, indeed, any development strategy) are rarely distributed equally. As with other labour-intensive industries, few jobs in tourism are well paid, as numerous critics have noted. Seen in the context of a colonial history, work in tourism may be a sensitive issue. When tourists are white and hotel employees are black, as in the Caribbean, 'service' may be interpreted as a continuation of servility (Perez, 1973–4, p. 476). In such circumstances, calls for 'flexibility, segmentation and diagonal integration', a 'new' tourism (Poon, 1989, p. 91; also Poon, 1990), however understandable at the industry level, may be difficult to implement when lower-level participants in the industry are reluctant to 'serve'.

Whether or not jobs in other industries are (or could be) available at higher rates of pay is a moot point (Lin and Sung, 1984), but in most countries they probably pay more than agriculture. However, numerous studies draw attention to the 'inferior' nature of employment in tourism and the tendency for administrative and other senior positions to be held by outsiders (for example, Kent, 1975, pp. 182–90; Price, 1988, p. 209; Bird, 1989, pp. 29–33). Indeed, in the 'informal' sector, a mass of 'unofficial' and unwaged entrepreneurial activity is revealed. Unlicensed guides, pavement sellers, beach hawkers, and male and female prostitutes, adult and child, are all in this category which, as the following pages indicate, is highly comprehensive.

Women, especially, carry out many of the lower-status jobs in the tourist hierarchy (Enloe, 1989, pp. 33–41), not merely because they are cheaper than men but because, in many respects, 'travel for pleasure and adventure has been profoundly gendered' (Enloe, 1989, pp. 40–41). Nowhere is this more evident than in sex tourism, and international tourism has undoubtedly contributed, directly or indirectly, to prostitution of all kinds.

But tourism has not caused prostitution. In Thailand, which 'enjoys' one of the sleaziest reputations in such matters, (cf. Meyer, 1988, pp. 289–374), it was once confined mainly to Chinese women, increasing in the 1950s with rural-urban migration, developing further during the Vietnam war, and receiving added impetus as Thailand attracted foreign tourists. According to one 'guesstimate', up to one million women in Thailand are involved in prostitution, more than in any other occupation except for farming and housework. However, only about seven per cent are alleged to depend on overseas tourists for their livelihood (Meyer, 1988, p. 371). If this is anywhere near the case, blaming international tourism for Thai prostitution is to indulge in scapegoating; the *roots* of prostitution may lie, instead, in 'traditional culture and Thai consciousness' (Meyer, 1988, p. 301). A similar perspective is offered by Truong (1990), who links Buddhist ideas on sexuality to the development of the Thai state and the increased commoditisation of sexual reproductive services. After the Vietnam war, when Thailand was used as a Rest and Recreation centre, these combined with international tourism, with its focus on hospitality and its advertisement of the 'otherness' of the East (Truong, 1990, p. 200), to produce a different kind of 'packaged' holiday.

By contrast, Graburn argues that in Korea, Taiwan, Indonesia, the Philippines, Vietnam and Japan, prostitution is closely linked with war and tourism (1983, p. 441), thus implying that, morally, all three are equally dubious. Indeed, following many proponents of UDT, he regards tourism itself as analogous to prostitution, where poor countries with few development alternatives must sell their beauty for foreign currency, being psychologically 'penetrated' by tourists from developed nations (1983, pp. 441–2).

Sex tourism is undoubtedly significant to some tourist destination regions, and in tourism advertising – as in advertising generally – images of women play an important role. Nevertheless, tourism may bring women some benefits. In Bequia, a Caribbean island adminstratively associated with St Vincent, they gained increased independence from their menfolk as a result of part-time and seasonal work in tourism (Price, 1988, pp. 225–6), a feature also noted by Chant, later in this volume, for women in Mexico. For such women, and for many men, tourism represents another set of opportunities, however limited, in a social world where options are few.

As well as prostitution, which is technically illegal in many tourist-receiving societies, including Thailand, other occupations in the informal sector operate on the borders of the law. Unlicensed guides, hustlers, beach boys, pavement sellers, and many others live on the margin, eking out a precarious existence and often receiving the opprobrium of middle class society for their pains. On the illegal side of the margin, too, it is often alleged that tourism increases crime rates. Given the relative wealth and obvious presence of tourists, it would be surprising if it did not do so, and crimes against property, for example, bag-snatching, theft and burglary, generally increase where there are heavy concentrations of tourists (Mathieson and Wall, 1982, pp. 150–2; Chesney-Lind and Lind, 1986). As 'outsiders', involved only in transitory contact with local people, tourists may be considered fair game (as in some Sri Lankan shops, for example, as Crick later indicates) and they are less likely to be able to rely on local support when in difficulties. In such respects, as in many others, LDCs are no different from developed countries, especially large cities, where crowds also attract a sizeable criminal element.

Tourism may specifically attract some criminal activities. Politically-motivated crime is more likely to gain publicity when directed against tourist-populated areas, as by opposition groups, for example, in the Philippines during the 1980 conference of the American Society of TravelAgents (Richter, 1989, pp. 63–4) or by Basque separatists in Spain. At a different level, illegal currency dealings may be advantageous to all but the government concerned (Lehmann, 1980). They may even be a tourist attraction; according to one travel writer, in Burma, '. . . changing money on the black market is temporary liberation from the economic madhouse' (Fielder, 1991, p. 27) and local dealers are drawn to foreign tourists, who possess valued currency but little knowledge of the 'going' rate. Drug dealers or pimps, too, recognise that tourists may engage in forms of behaviour regarded as socially unacceptable, perhaps criminal, in their own countries. Inevitably, such forms of behaviour may necessitate extra policing.

Finally, tourism may sometimes create categories of crime which previously did not exist, or were considered unimportant, again creating the need for more police. Before the Mexican village of Cajititlán was developed for (largely domestic) tourism in the 1960s, for instance, male villagers regularly expressed their machismo by racing horses and firing pistols in the streets. With tourism came three rural policemen and such activities were forbidden. In addition, 'unsuitable' clothing was discouraged, as was urinating in public, and stray dogs and livestock were cleared from the streets (Nunez, 1963). Elsewhere in some LDCs, for example, Tunisia, police are posted on beaches allegedly to protect tourists from over-zealous salesmen, but perhaps also to prevent local people becoming too agitated, in one way or another, at the sight of so much public near-nakedness – itself offensive to many members of the host population.

Changes in family structure

According to Peake (1989), before the development of tourism in Malindi, on the Kenyan coast, the Old Town was dominant. Economic and political power was held by the elders, who occupied important positions in mosques and headed extended family households. With tourism, the Old Town became marginalised and the authority of the elders declined as other family members, especially young men, gained independent sources of income. Some, the 'clerks', obtained office jobs in tourist establishments, using their income to form nuclear families and purchase consumer goods. Others, 'beach boys', disregarded the elders, turned their backs on their families, refused to attend the mosques, and entered the informal sector, perhaps as male prostitutes. They thus rejected their Swahili identity in favour of the tourist 'scene', where they publicly displayed their dubiously-acquired wealth. In response, the elders withdrew into ecstatic Islamic fundamentalism, romanticising the Swahili past and worrying about the effects of tourism on the values of the young. However, the separation of beach boys was not necessarily permanent. Those who profited from tourism could later redeem themselves by taking an active role in the community, even to the extent of becoming elders themselves.

Although a similar pattern may have emerged with the introduction of another source of income, Peake's example shows how new job opportunities in tourism had ramifications for family organisation, removed power from the traditional elders and influenced the political structure and status system of the community.

Similar changes have been reported elsewhere. After reviewing the evidence, Kousis (1989) notes that, in Drethia, rural Crete, the alienation of land to outsiders led to a loss of control by older male household heads, which was exacerbated by increased government assistance to young people in the form of business loans and grants. Land was no longer given as dowry, being replaced by property, furnishings and fittings, and village endogamy declined, with some local men marrying foreign tourists (Kousis, 1989, p. 327–8). Women played an important role in owning and running tourist businesses, but continued to be more restricted in their sexual activities than their male counterparts. However, as Kousis points out, extended family members continue to assist kin in tourist enterprises, for example, by looking after children, dish washing and cleaning, or advertising the establishment to visitors (1989, p. 324).

The effects of tourism on family structure vary according to the extent and type of tourism and the 'traditional' base. In Thailand, tourism development has been implicated in the breakdown of family life and mental health problems, especially among women in the age group 'most over-represented in tourism-related activities' (Meyer, 1988, p. 495). However, the causal connections are not demonstrated, and in Thailand (as elsewhere) agricultural decline and rural–urban migration occur independently of tourism. That many young female migrants enter tourist-related prostitution, often with the assistance of their families (Ekachai, 1990, pp. 168–180; Srisang, 1991, p. 41), neither makes the practice morally acceptable nor shows that tourism is the cause of family breakdown.

New social institutions

As tourism expands, existing institutions are transformed and new ones created. In Bali, members of the old élites became influential in the hotel business and established dance academies. There, as elsewhere, a Tourism Development Board was created, along with numerous voluntary associations (Noronha, 1979, pp. 193, 197–9). Typically, the government sets up the Board, either within a government department responsible for tourism or as a para-statal, to which organisations and groups with a direct interest in tourism are then affiliated. The breadth of representation, and whether or not it includes groups and individuals opposed to tourism, indicates the extent to which government is prepared to tolerate internal dissent.

Hoteliers, too, set up their own business associations, which then act as pressure groups to further their perceived interest, sometimes differentially defined by indigenous and foreign owners. Other official or quasi-official organisations are also formed to promote or protect cultural and physical assets. The role of National Trusts, or their local equivalents, will be enhanced, to advertise, protect (and possibly even define) the nation's archaeological and natural heritage. Where relevant, organisations to promote national parks and wild life reserves are formed or expanded, often with tourism as their major justification (and indignous resentment as a major preoccupation). Arts Councils, perhaps aided or opposed by religious interests, may perform similar functions for the nation's culture.

If sufficiently organised, professional and worker organisations gear themselves to promote their members' interests – or protect them from 'exploitation'. They may be community-based, for example, village councils, or occupationally-based, as with guides, dancers' and craft associations. Broadly speaking, their aims will be similar: to promote, oppose or modify tourism when it is in their perceived interest to do so.

Indeed, one result of tourism is the development of pressure groups specifically to oppose tourism, or aspects of it. Issues are then politicised, with local parties adopting an anti-tourist, nationalistic stance, as occurred in parts of the Caribbean during the 1970s, in the Philippines under Marcos and, more recently, in Goa with the Vigilant Goans' Army (JGF). At other times, overtly 'non-political' national organisations may be formed, with or without significant international support. In Thailand, for example, the Thai Development Support Committee, established in 1962, exists to raise awareness of the human costs of 'development', including tourism (Ekachai, 1990), whereas the Ecumenical Commission on Third World Tourism (ECTWT), based in Bangkok, is an international organisation, regularly publishing accounts of the perceived excesses of tourism, in Thailand and elsewhere, and providing details of other pressure groups with similar aims (Holden, Horlemann and Pfäfflin, 1985; O'Grady, 1990; Srisang, 1991).

In Nepal, the international context of such concern is evident in the work of the Annapurna Conservation Area Project (ACAP). Formed in 1986 by the King Mahendra Trust, it attempts to counter detrimental effects of trekking tourism, for example, deforestation, pollution and degradation of the natural habitat, as well as increased crime, and to further the interests of local people. Publicised in Europe (Tüting, 1989), the programme promotes reforestation, improvements in the tourist infrastructure, and education in environmental awareness. With a national director, it involves numerous newly-formed local organisations and receives assistance from several international bodies, including the German Volunteer Service (GVS), the German Alpine Association and an ecological institute in the USA (Tüting, 1989, pp. 15–18). Furthermore, it has been commended by at least one travel programme on British television for promoting environmentally-sympathetic tourism – which may well increase the number of tourists visiting the country. The scheme, and the international support it receives, indicates how environmental and other problems raised by international tourism are increasingly met through international co-operation.

Despite the internationalisation of tourism, the role of the state is crucial. Although not detailed in this book, the impact of tourism on the environment may often be considerable (cf. Romeril, 1989). If it is to be protected, a thorough assessment of the possible consequences of tourism must be made (Boo, 1990, Vol. 1, Chapter 4). More generally, development plans, taxation, training, joint ventures, policies for agriculture and other sectors, education (of local people and tourists) and law enforcement all involve the state, as do controls on aspects of tourism development considered to be unsavoury.

Unfortunately, it is not that simple. As Wood notes for South-east Asia (1984), the state may plan and market tourism, arbitrate when conflicts arise, and provide a venue for new forms of political action. Depending on the class and religious structure of any LDC, these roles may conflict with or contradict other functions of the state. Religion is a particularly delicate issue. In Muslim Indonesia, for example, Islam is absent in the marketing of tourism, which emphasises the Hinduism of Bali (Wood, 1984, p. 365), and Malaysia reportedly operates a double standard, allowing tourists a moral laxity denied to the indigenous population (Din, 1989, p. 558). The position taken by other Islamic societies ranges from discouragement, through to isolation, accommodation and *laissez faire* (Din, 1989).

In fact, some of the most virulent debates in development theory have centred on the role of the state (Harrison, 1988, pp. 138–145 and 168–9) and numerous tourism studies (for example, Jommo, 1987, pp. 137–145) suggest that in this sector, too, the state is frequently ineffective and inefficient. The absolute power and ability of a monarch to control tourism, as in Bhutan (Richter, 1989, pp. 176–9), is rarely found elsewhere. Even if there were a consensus on the most appropriate policies to be followed in tourism 'development', the state in most LDCs simply lacks the power, ability or will to formulate and enforce them. And yet, as de Kadt notes (1990, pp. 27–32), state intervention in tourism is frequently essential. It is a crucial dilemma.

Interaction, values and dependency

The degree to which locals take on the values of tourists varies. Much depends on the extent of interaction between tourist and local, which is not always encouraged (Hall, 1984; Richter, 1989, p. 46) and one has to ask, which tourist? Which local? Younger and less 'organised' back-packers, certainly, live among (some would say off) indigenous people and may bring economic benefit to rural areas (Meijer, 1989). However, they may not be welcomed by the authorities and, in any case, their closest links are often with other back-packers (Riley, 1988). Other visitors, including such excursionists as cruise ship tourists and residents of more expensive hotels, especially in enclaves, meet locals only fleetingly, and then on well-established tourist circuits. And almost by definition, tourists primarily interested in a country's history or its flora and fauna spend little time interacting with its residents. That said, however, in exceptional circumstances 'tourist-host' interaction may be transformed. In 1987, for example, independent Western tourists in Tibet witnessed the violent repression of demonstrations against Chinese rule. Although 'hippies' dissociated themselves from political involvement, other tourists were outraged and set up an informal network to provide medical assistance for the injured and actively collect and disseminate information on the events to outside Western news agencies. Further disturbances in 1988 and 1989 evoked a similar response (cf. Schwartz, 1991). In these circumstances, at least, tourists identified themselves with members of the 'host' society and became political activists.

Interaction is greater in sex tourism and home-stay tourism. Although the former is morally suspect, it actually covers a wide variety of relationships, not all of which are instrumental and affectively-neutral (Cohen, 1982b; Meyer, 1988, pp. 344 and 355). Indeed, sex plays a role in many kinds of tourism and, for some hosts, interaction with tourists brings the possibility of increased status and the chance to leave home for more affluent and (allegedly) congenial surroundings (Cohen, 1971; Wagner and Yamba, 1986; Price, 1988, pp. 228–234). By contrast, home-stay tourism, although sometimes a supplement to hotel tourism, especially in Eastern Europe (Böröcz, 1990, p. 22), has a more acceptable image of 'paying visitor'

(Stringer, 1981; Frater, 1982; Cohen, 1989b, p. 136). However, among visitors from 'developed' countries, this kind of tourism is not highly favoured and it will probably remain a minority interest – as it must, if it is to survive as an 'alternative' to more organised forms of travel.

As Peake shows in his study of Malindi Old Town (1989), behavioural responses to tourism within a society may vary considerably. North American Indians make jokes at tourists' expense (Evans-Pritchard, 1989; Sweet, 1989), a reaction probably more common than imagined, whereas others may (quite literally) greet them with open arms or overt hostility. Tourist responses, too, are varied. Many holiday-makers make repeat visits – such business is crucial in most tourist-receiving societies – and some retire to the 'host' society, with considerable economic and social ramifications. However, although patterns of interaction may change over time (Machlis and Burch, 1983) and according to the purpose of the visit, the relationship between tourist and host is usually one of market symbiosis.

However, as an aspect of modernisation, international tourism undoubtedly reinforces the transference of Western values and patterns of behaviour to members of 'host' societies, a form of acculturation often subsumed under the term 'demonstration effects'. The issue was raised in early studies of tourism (UNESCO, 1976, pp. 93–94) and has been noted more recently. In Kenya, for example, tourism has reinforced the influence of the westernised elite, with young people 'imitating not only Western clothing but also the behaviour and life-style of Europeans and American visitors, including their ethical and moral codes' (Bachmann, 1988, p. 191). Similar patterns are reported elsewhere, including India (Chandrakala, 1989, pp. 15–8) and Malaysia (Bird, 1989, pp. 51–2), where even young back-packers attract envy and unwanted attention through their possession of valued goods (Bird, 1989, p. 52). However, as Bird also points out, new norms and values are frequently introduced by domestic tourists, who communicate easily and interact more closely with local people.

Demonstration effects are the cultural equivalent of the spread of market relationships and commoditisation, an association leading some critics to refer to such acculturation as 'cultural imperialism', a term more judgemental than descriptive. As LDCs have been subjected to economic domination, so the argument goes, their cultures have been undermined.

At the economic level, this argument has some merit: power differentials are a feature of the world system and some countries clearly depend on tourists from a few developed societies, often former metropolitan colonial powers (Hoivik and Heiberg, 1980, p. 75), as indicated by concentration ratios detailed in the previous chapter. However, at a political level, the argument is problematic. There is no direct evidence, for instance, that such 'dependence' leads to political compliance, or that those who rely on tourists from the USA obtain a disproportionate share of grants or other forms of aid from that country (Francisco, 1983). Furthermore, as Erisman remarks for the Caribbean (1983), élite members are not equally influenced by Western culture (which, in any case, contains within itself the seeds of opposition), and nationalism, religion and other social movements, among élites and lower down the social hierarchy, may frequently counter the effects of westernisation.

Given the role of hotels and other tourist establishments as centres of entertainment, their attraction for the young is not surprising. Indeed, acculturation is undoubtedly occurring. However, there is more than a hint of hypocrisy, for example, when members of developed societies bewail the desire for consumer durables among residents in LDCs, or when the middle classes of those societies criticise lower-class ambition. There is no *inherent* virtue, for example, in the extended family, which may as often be a source of repression and autocratic (and patriarchal) control as one of security and freedom. Similarly, the superiority of palm wine over Western beers, or of traditional dress over blue jeans, may be affirmed but, ultimately, is a matter of taste.

Indeed, there is something quite patronising in the view that the culture of many LDCs is weak and in dire need of protection from outside. In fact, the cultures of tourist-receiving societies, for example, the Pacific Islands, may possess some kind of 'deep structure' which allows them to adapt to new influences and yet retain – even reinforce – their vitality and coherence (cf. Ritchie, 1975). As MacNaught argues, for the same region, the 'fatal impact' thesis 'assigns Pacific Islanders a helplessly passive role in the conflict of cultures, ignoring a mass of evidence that it was often a two-way process' (1982, p. 363). He later remarks that changes so deplored by Western outsiders were enthusiastically welcomed by many islanders (1982, p. 364), a finding certainly echoed elsewhere. Once again, the direction of socio-cultural change is not at issue. Instead, the debate is centred on how desirable such changes are. We are once more in the realm of development.

Some continuing themes

International tourism in LDCs has been a key element in modernisation, and economic change has had ramifications at social and cultural levels. With new physical landscapes have come new centres of growth and entertainment. Market relationships have spread, and traditional crafts and cultures have been increasingly commoditised.

New patterns of ownership – and sometimes landlessness – have been associated with increases in tourism (as with other forms of economic growth). 'Traditional' classes have frequently joined forces with metropolitan capital, at other times competing for slices of the tourist cake. New employment prospects have arisen, in the formal, waged sector and in the informal sector, often of dubious legality. Clearly, some tourism-related activities have led to understandable moral outrage, as with child prostitution in Asia (Srisang, 1991), which demands effective state and international intervention, but the *causes* of such behaviour go deeper than the tourist trade.

As an aspect of modernisation, tourism has influenced social institutions. With new sources of income, some groups have gained in status and others have lost ground. On occasions, a decline in the extended family and the influence of male elders has been noted. Pre-existing social and political institutions have been given new roles, old trading relationships have been confirmed and new ones established.

All of these themes, and many others, are raised in the following pages. The chapters by Richter and by Sinclair and her co-authors focus on the international political and economic contexts within which tourism operates. Richter demonstrates the importance of security – or rather tourists' perception of it – and the effects on tourism of publicised unrest, be it internal or regional. Television news can ruin a tourism industry in minutes. As a consequence, far from (unintentionally) promoting international peace and stability, hapless tourists may become pawns in political struggles and the industry (or aspects of it) the object of political opposition. In such circumstances, local participation and a careful use of indigenous resources become politically and economically expedient as well as morally preferable.

Moving to the economic sphere, Sinclair, Alizadeh and Onunga detail the immense role played by transnational companies at all levels of international tourism, through direct foreign investment, joint ventures and other kinds of agreement. They then focus on Kenya which, with its own national and charter airlines, has a relatively developed tourism sector. Despite the dominance of transnational capital, the state has a key role as hotel investor, legislator, negotiator and owner of the national airline. Discussing types of contractual relationships, they acknowledge that country needs vary over time and according to circumstance, and note how groups within a 'host' society may be differentially affected by existing arrangements.

A different kind of 'host' is the focus of Michael Hall's chapter on sex tourism, a highly commoditised and, for many, a highly unsavoury element of international tourism. Prostitution in South-east Asia, notably Korea, the Philippines, Taiwan and Thailand, is tourism-related but not tourism-specific. Constructed on an indigenous base, and developed during periods of colonialism, military activity and rapid economic change, images of 'exotic oriental women' attracted tourists from the West and massive increases in tourism from Japan, the regional 'centre', encouraged further expansion. The trade knows no borders: Filipino and Thai women work in Europe and elsewhere, and Australia, while providing clients and operators of brothels and similar establishments, especially in the Philippines, now also plays host to Japanese sex tours.

Sex tourism does not occur in a vacuum. Indeed, Taiwan and Korea are already NICs and Thailand, one of the fastest-growing economies in the world, is *en route* to NIC status. Much of the region's growth, which is largely export-led, is the result of foreign direct investment (FDI). By 1988, for example, Thailand was second only to the USA as a recipient of Japanese FDI and the Japanese were also major providers of FDI to Malaysia (Ishigami, 1991, p. 24). The Japanese government, too, has provided loans at favourable rates of interest to its neighbours in East and South-east Asia (Lewis and Kapur, 1990, p. 1365). Where investment has led, tourists have often followed. Although sex tourism is discussed in Mackie's chapter, her main concern is the growth of Japan as an important source of international tourists, especially for the countries of South-east Asia. Noting the pivotal role of the state in Japan in promoting domestic tourism, she shows how such policies have been extended quite deliberately beyond national boundaries. Aid, technical assistance and capital from Japan have become increasingly influential to tourism-related projects. As a consequence, Japan's trade imbalance has been reduced but the Japanese leisure industry, especially golf, has been extended, along with a wide range of associated effects, to less developed countries in the region.

Tourism of a different kind features in Chant's chapter, which deals with Latin America, especially Mexico and Costa Rica. In both countries the state actively promotes tourism but Costa Rica, with a relatively narrow range of attractions and a less developed infrastructure, tends to specialise in environmental tourism which, while not without problems, has apparently benefited some local residents. Mexico, with a wider range of tourist attractions, relies more on visitors from the neighbouring United States. Interestingly, Mexican women interviewed by Chant, although in low-paid, labour-intensive jobs, and still burdened by the double day, compared their life-style with that of women visitors and valued the financial and other freedoms provided by their employment in tourism. For them, modernisation was a positive process.

Few countries illustrate more graphically the changing international political and economic environment than Cuba, which is part of Latin America and the Caribbean. As Derek Hall indicates, before Castro's revolution it was a major

Caribbean destination for tourists from the USA. Afterwards, its (now declining) association with the former USSR failed to reduce dependency, and tourist arrivals from other socialist countries could neither offset the trade embargo of the USA nor produce the 'hard' foreign currency so desperately needed. In recent years, tourism from capitalist societies has again been encouraged but, despite formal approval of joint ventures, conflicting messages have emanated from the political environment. How Cubans feel about such changes is unclear but the 'demonstration effects' of North American culture have long been apparent, albeit coupled with a pride in the country's resistance to its powerful neighbour. Forbidden to hold convertible currency themselves, Cubans reportedly resent tourists being given preferential access to restaurants, hotels and scarce consumer goods. In such circumstances, 'demonstration effects' are likely to be negative if the means of indigenous 'improvement' are denied.

At a more 'micro' level, Bowman and Crick shift the emphasis to the role of tourist guides, who figure much in tourism literature (cf. Cohen, 1985). For Bowman, who examines 'Holy Land tourism', official Israeli guides in the formal sector quite consciously interpret selected sights for tourists according to the dominant ideology, thus performing a vital political function on behalf of the state (Matthews and Richter, 1991, p. 126). In this, they are aided by tourists themselves who, 'full of partialities and prejudices . . . entered the country with their verdicts already prepared' (Twain, 1896, quoted in Katz, 1985, p. 53). Palestinian guides employed by the state (a declining category) must not step out of line. Other Palestinian guides are relegated to the informal sector. In such circumstances, official guides reinforce rather than mediate culture, purveying existential experience to willing subjects (Cohen, 1979, p. 197). How far they actually *alter* tourist perceptions, in Israel or elsewhere, is a moot point and a matter that requires further research.

In Sri Lanka, estimated by that country's *Sunday Times* (8th December, 1991) to contain some 10,000 child prostitutes, mainly young boys, guiding is often a highly fluid category. Unlike Palestinian guides, the unlicensed guides of Sri Lanka described by Crick are not part of a politically disenfranchised ethnic group. However, they live on the margin of 'respectable' society. Operating in the street and the café, they employ their 'cultural capital', like others elsewhere (Wagner, 1982, pp. 33, 39 and 53), to 'catch' 'non-institutionalised' tourists (Cohen, 1972, p. 174), hoping, again like other workers in tourism (Cohen, 1971; Wagner and Yamba, 1986; Price, 1988, pp. 228–35), for that one special tourist to facilitate emigration and their escape from poverty and insecurity. Trapped in the informal sector, they were distrusted yet needed by guest-house proprietors and retailers, thus bridging the (often arbitary) gap between the formal and informal sectors of the tourist economy.

In the final chapter, I suggest that 'tradition' and 'modernity' are blurred in Swaziland, where the formal sector is small but important. Tourism is dominated by Sun International and the monarchy, which is both 'traditional' ruler and the basis of 'modern' government. The monarch is the acknowledged (and ardent) guardian of the very tradition which legitimates his position. Contradictions arise because tourism, in which the royal family has invested heavily, allegedly undermines the control exercised by traditional authorities over the young, especially women, who are 'corrupted' by Western fashions and life-styles, thus indulging in unacceptable 'immoral' behaviour. Furthermore, by using 'tradition' to market Swaziland to whites in the Republic of South Africa, the tourism industry runs the risk of reinforcing existing, unfavourable racial stereotypes.

In their different ways, all these chapters illustrate the role performed by international tourism in the modernisation of LDCs. How far they indicate 'development' is for the reader to decide. It is hoped that they will prompt debate and sustained empirical research into the effects of international tourism, funding for which has hitherto been sadly lacking. However, the role of international tourism in modernisation, however unpalatable, is a fact. What is *not* agreed is, first, whether or not such changes are good for the LDCs involved and, secondly, how far the state and other organisations, in or outside LDCs, can influence the pattern of future events. Here, the issue is less one of moral evaluation and more a matter of formulating priorities and assessing how far existing states have the will and the ability to carry them out. In view of present trends, one thing is certain: international tourism, with an estimated 638 million international arrivals by the year 2000 (WTO, 1991a, p. 7), will continue its growth worldwide, increasingly involving more LDCs. The social consequences – and the problems – will not go away.

3 Political instability and tourism in the Third World

Linda K. Richter

Introduction

Political instability is endemic in much of the Third World. Scarcity, deprivation, inequality, remnants of colonialism and the proxy wars of the superpowers set the stage for random violence, ethnic conflict, revolution and even hostage-taking. At the same time, the antiquities, culture, flora and fauna associated with the less industrialized societies make tourism a seemingly attractive option in nations with all too few alternatives. The very underdevelopment that exacerbates the resolution of political demands and frustrates economic aspirations is a potential asset in attracting tourism. Thus we have a paradox: nations which are veritable hellholes for most of their citizens are sold as 'unspoiled paradises' to outsiders. Societies teeming with squalor, conflict and insecurity set out to attract those seeking serenity, beauty, simplicity and oneness with nature. That this 'odd coupling' of goals often fails should be less surprising than the fact that it sometimes succeeds, and thereby keeps the hope of progress through tourism alive. In Part I of this chapter, the magnitude of tourism is contrasted with its seasonality, the boom-bust cycles, the fickleness of its clientele and its vulnerability to decline and/or destruction by political discord. Though such pitfalls are in no way unique to tourism in developing countries, overall conditions in Third World nations make political conditions generally more erratic, and resilience less likely and more difficult to predict. Moreover, absolute levels of instability and rates of violence are less important than perceptions of insecurity by potential travellers.

In part II, political instability that impacts on tourism is examined and four specific types of political discord are considered. First, instability in the region may negatively affect neighbour nations because of interruption of air, sea or overland routes or because publicity about instability makes the whole region sound volatile. Secondly, internal upheaval within a country may be far from tourist areas or close enough to spill over into areas frequented by tourists. In either case, tourists are dissuaded from coming or staying because of the conflict. Thirdly, the tourist may sometimes be deliberately targeted by anti-government forces to embarrass the government, weaken it economically, and draw attention abroad to the political conditions the opposition finds salient. Finally, tourism development may itself be a factor in political instability. These four types of problems are discussed in depth and, in Part III, ways of predicting, minimising or coping with political instability are examined.

Part I   Tourism: the fragile heavyweight

It is almost a press agent cliché to describe international tourism as the world's biggest and fastest growing industry (Waters, 1989). Sometimes the price of oil eclipses tourism's number one status, and some still grumble that tourism is a service sector industry and thus its employment numbers may mean relatively low-paying positions compared to manufacturing – but caveats aside, estimates suggest one in sixteen people in the world works in tourism. (Edgell, 1990).

Moreover, most of the demographic and future trends augur well for tourism generally. People are better educated globally speaking, live longer, have more discretionary income, have longer vacations, and increasingly see leisure and travel as necessities rather than luxuries. Germany, for example, has a national average of five to six weeks vacation annually. The Japanese, once restricted to Japan by balance of payments concerns, are now encouraged by their government to travel abroad to ease trade imbalances (Yacoumis, 1989: 18). Moreover, the scope for increased travel is also evident in the elasticity for individual travel. Only 50 per cent of all Americans take an annual vacation – a figure much lower than in Europe. The political events of 1989 in Eastern and Central Europe also suggest that a pent-up demand to travel will result in much greater international tourism.

Most such tourism will probably continue to be domestic, as 93 per cent of American tourism has been or will be within North America and Europe, but tourism to developing nations will increasingly expand. Moreover, given the level of existing infrastructure, low levels of personal wealth, levels of unemployment, and general lack of economic diversification, tourism in developing nations will have a profound effect far disproportionate to the numbers that actually arrive.

Despite the strength of the tourist demand and the constant desire for new and more exotic experiences., individual tourism destinations must compete as never before for the fickle, usually seasonal interest of the travelling public. Developing nations, especially of Africa, the Pacific and Asia, are quite distant from major tourist-generating markets. Their unique cultures may be little understood or appreciated by travellers. Establishing a comparative advantage over alternative destinations or agreeing upon a regional strategy may be very difficult.

Sun, sand, sea and sex, the four 's's', are often seen as the core of a developing nation's appeal (Crick, 1989, 308). A fifth 's' is even more critical: security. Tourism as a discretionary activity is incredibly vulnerable to political instability. Even such natural disasters as earthquakes or hurricanes do not have the lasting and devastating impact of political unrest.

The issue is not whether tourism as a phenomenon can be killed, but whether it will survive in particular places in the face of civil strife and with what costs to the societies that depend on it.

Any political instability can cause tourism arrivals and receipts to plummet, but in developed, well-diversified economies, the tourism sector is buttressed by domestic markets that may persist even if international arrivals decline. Moreover, business travel is likely to be more resilient than discretionary travel. The developed nation is likely to see in-bound tourism as a desirable component in the balance of trade but, even if a leading revenue source, it may contribute less than 20 per cent of the GDP. Depending on the source of political instability, a developed nation may be able to exercise effective damage control or contain the political upheaval so that tourists are out of harm's way and relatively unaware of problems. This is particularly true of conflicts among linguistic groups, as in Belgium or Canada.

Developed nations own and control air, train and sea links and can redirect tourism traffic.

The developing nation has far fewer resources with which to cope. First, it may be far more dependent on tourism. After all, was it not alleged that tourism would make money from (and for) pristine, undeveloped, non-industrial societies? Was it not supposed to employ the unemployed, bring in hard currency and support beautification? The litany goes on.

Secondly, developed nations are less diversified. Tourism is not one among many industries, but often the chief or leading industry. Because it was not built amidst a developed economy, tourism revenues are less likely to stay in the society. Capital for tourism development often comes from outside and thus tourism itself is less diversified. It is more likely to be built on a generic international model – Hilton, Marriott, McDonalds's or Kentucky Fried Chicken. Thus on-going supply for the industry is also external. Thirdly, developed nations rarely have a domestic base for tourism to cushion seasonality or to absorb some tourism capacity when international tourism falters. Exceptions are found in South Asia, especially India, Pakistan, Sri Lanka, and Bangladesh, where there is a widespread practice of religious pilgrimage, be it to Hindu, Muslim, Buddhist or Sikh shrines or to other holy places. Domestic tourism in these countries is extremely important for employment, though it does not bring in the foreign exchange, the chief economic lure of international tourism (Richter, 1989: 104–106).

Fourthly, if or when political instability occurs, the developing nation's ability to cope is far less. International loans for industry become impossible to finance. There is usually no alternative use for luxury cottages or resorts. Having opted for luxury tourism, for example, China, Sri Lanka and Fiji found conversion of deserted tourist facilities all but impossible (*Beijing Review*, July 3–9, 1989: 43; Yacoumis, 1989). Most were too remote, too lavish, too energy dependent, and too costly to maintain or for alteration to be feasible.

Furthermore, the developing nation may have much less ability to control, modify or re-direct transportation than a developed nation. In fact, the tourism of developing nations is often dependent on the timetables and routes of other nations' airlines or cruise ships. If those re-route, cut flights or skip their ports, it is academic what the real political conditions are, for it will be months to years before the bookings and tourist traffic regain their former momentum. Developing nations are also often unable to control events, to contain mobs, quash guerrilla activity, or insulate tourists from the political strife that might be manageable for more developed nations.

The actual political conditions prevailing in a country are almost incidental to the perception of security that governs tourism decisions. Under President Marcos, the Philippines represented the most bizarre linkage of tourism and political instability. In 1972, the President declared martial law, ostensibly because of Muslim separatists, urban violence, and the New People's Army (a rural guerrilla group). He then proceeded to pursue an aggressive course of promoting tourism based on martial law discipline and a building spree focused on luxury hotels (Richter, 1980, 1982, 1989). Because the public relations were unusually lavish and adroit, and the actual unrest at the time rather minimal, over the period 1972 to 1980 Marcos managed to dramatically increase tourism from its pre-martial law levels. His downfall would come later.

In 1989, Hong Kong represented an almost totally different scenario. Tourism had always thrived in democratic, stable Hong Kong, with its superb location, excellent facilities and diversified economy. But in 1989, the Crown colony suffered from triple jeopardy. First, after the June 4th crackdown on pro-democracy supporters in Beijing's Tiananmen Square, tourism to China plummetted. As the gateway to the mainland for hundreds of thousands of tourists, Hong Kong was badly hit (Greenberg, 1989; *Asiaweek* September 22, 1989: 74). Secondly, tourism and trade between Chinese and Hong Kong Chinese, which was substantial (Chow, 1988: 206–207), was badly damaged. Finally, scenes of citizens in Hong Kong protesting about events in China left an impression with Western television viewers that Hong Kong, too, was volatile and dangerous. Perception then, not objective political events, governs travel decisions. Countries without well-defined images among the travelling public are often even more damaged by well-publicized strife in nearby countries.

Another factor affecting perceptions is how violence is labelled. For example, Americans tend to associate going abroad with a certain level of increased risk which, for most Americans in most vacation spots abroad, is simply not the case (GAO Reports, 1989: 21–22). Americans live in an unusually violent nation, with some of the world's highest rates of murder, rape, and armed robbery, where drug use is epidemic and security businesses enjoy boom times. Nearly twice as many Americans died from handgun injuries in the United States from 1965–1975 as died in Vietnam over the same period. In 1989, more were killed by firearms in Los Angeles than in Beirut. It may make little difference to the victims whether they die at the hand of a drug-crazed person or as a result of an urban guerrilla's bomb, but it does to the travelling public, particularly Americans.

Americans assume political stability. Acts of terrorism, civil strife, or political conflict strike irrational fear (Woodward, 1990). In 1986, for example, an estimated 1.8 million Americans changed their travel plans from Europe to other destinations as a result of several isolated acts of politically-inspired terrorism (Richter and Waugh, 1986). Statistics showing that one is more likely to die from lightning or in a bathtub than from political violence do not dispel the concern that deflects travel decisions away from controversial destinations and towards more serenity. This may partially explain how the tiny city state of Singapore managed to attract more foreign tourists in 1989 (4.1 million) than Pakistan, India and the Philippines combined (Waters, 1989: 116). Their immense territories, variety of mountain, seashore, and cultural complexity and a combined population of nearly one billion people was no match for the strategically located, homogeneous, clean and politically placid nation (Matthews, 1990).

To Japan, or to other nations generating significant tourism to the Third World, the issue of physical security is even more salient. The US is clearly a high risk adventure: ordinary crime, especially robbery, is so common in the US that many Japanese are reluctant to visit. It is even more likely, therefore, that travel to the Third World be premised on political serenity. The Japanese government is also unusual in the degree to which it monitors and advises travellers as to the relative safety of certain destinations. The Ministry of Foreign Affairs even edits a book entitled *Handbook for Safety Overseas*, which includes a 122-point checklist for tourists (O'Grady, 1990: 26).

The United States also monitors threats to its travelling citizens from political or criminal activity. In 1990, the US State Department, through its Citizens Emergency Centre, recommended against travel to over twenty nations and proffered advice on avoiding problems in another thirty (Trick, 1989; Edgell, 1990: 22). Almost all these nations are developing countries.

Part II   Variations on instability and tourism collapse

Because of scarcity and the perceived need to import heavily for tourism, developing nations generally tend to become involved fairly early in the tourism development process. However, this is less true in such colonial regimes as India, Kenya, and the Philippines, which already had substantial tourist infrastructure in place at the time of independence. Nevertheless, most developing nations need the ability to build into the tourism planning process an awareness of, and preparation for, possible challenges to tourism from instability. What follows is a discussion of some of those threats to tourism. The perspective taken will be that of the government affected. That in no way implies sympathy for any particular regime, simply an assessment of factors to consider in terms of each type of instability.

The impact of regional conflict

Depending on the type of political system, tourism development in developing countries may be found in a wide variety of formats – centralized or decentralized, publicly owned, privately owned, or mixed, enclave or integrated, luxury, budget or mixed (Richter and Richter, 1985). In general, the pattern tends to follow other forms of industrial development in the country.

What is usually not carried out, however, is a clear and realistic assessment of the internal political situation or the regional political and economic climate. How likely is political turmoil in neighbouring countries? Will it be ethnic-based? Are ethnic groups in country A likely to become involved as a result? How will transportation links be affected if regional instability occurs? How clearly defined is country A's image? Will travellers be able to distinguish it from nearby countries? Does country A have the drawing power and places of interest to be a destination on its own, or is it part of a larger round-the-world or regional curcuit? Should country A develop its tourism on the basis of a regional circuit? Should country A develop its tourism on the basis of a regional strategy or on the basis of its own autonomy? These are just a few of the political questions that seem to be important in tourism planning in order to anticipate the impact of regional instability on national tourism development. This may appear obvious, but in looking at tourism plans and commentaries in over nineteen developing nations, I have never seen any discussion of these issues before problems have arisen.

This appears to be because tourism is usually selected by governing élites as much for political prestige as economic viability. Before development occurs, there are few if any organised groups – academic, business, labour, or community-based – to intervene for or against public or private tourism initiatives. Outside tourism industry consultants, if involved, tend to be preoccupied with infrastructure needs, an inventory of potential tourist sites, and with tax or government concessions to assist the necessary capital formation.

That the regional political environment needs to be considered can be shown from a few examples. Nepal, itself torn, at the time of writing, by political conflict based on populist demands for democratic rule, was for years dependent on perceptions of political stability in South Asia, especially India. Disasters, political or otherwise, in India, Bangladesh, or Pakistan – of which there is no shortage – could be traced immediately in the arrival figures for Nepal (*Asia Travel Trade*, 1980).

Even though it had air links with stable Thailand, Nepal's proximity and identification with its more turbulent neighbours had a dramatic effect. Religious and ethnic roots to the political dispute over Kashmir have not only divided a region of enormous tourism potential between India and Pakistan, but have also poisoned opportunities generally over the years for these two huge and fascinating nations to collaborate on tourism or on much of anything else.

Political turmoil, however, is not always possible to anticipate. On the eve of a major tourism initiative in 1977, Pakistan found its overland arrivals from the Middle East and Europe abruptly terminated by the Iran-Iraq war and the sudden December, 1979 Soviet invasion of Afghanistan (Richter, 1989). Similarly, the assassination of Prime Minister Indira Gandhi of India in 1984 depressed arrivals in both neighbouring Pakistan and Nepal (*U.S. News and World Report*, 1984: 45).

In Central America, despite its political stability, attractions and democratic institutions, Costa Rica has had a very difficult time building tourism. Although Costa Rica does not even have an army, it suffers from the publicity of the violence and warfare that have raged through neighbouring Nicaragua, El Salvador, Guatemala and Honduras. Only recently has it been able to project an image distinct from the other nations of Central America. Tourism should flourish if the general political situation in the region can stabilise (Waters, 1989: 83).

Violence in Peru by the guerilla group, Shining Path, has crippled travel to the famed ruins of Machu Picchu but this may ease pressure on the Galapagos Islands, which are often a part of tour packages to the region. Ecological reasons for restraint in tourist numbers usually do not prevail in developing areas, but the Shining Path of Peru may be able to influence island numbers indirectly beyond the most earnest attempts of conservation groups. Unfortunately, this lesson is being learned by other ecological and opposition groups, who may see sabotage as more politically effective than dialogue.

No better example of the impact of turmoil, specific or regional, exists than Africa. Despite countries of historical, cultural, scenic and biological richness, Africa receives only 2.6 per cent of global tourism receipts and only 2.8 per cent of all arrivals. Nor has that percentage changed markedly in 20 years (Waters, 1989: 6–7).

While distance from major tourist-generating markets and lack of investment capital explain part of that lacklustre record, 'of equal, or sometimes greater, significance are political factors which inhibit the expansion of tourism in Africa' (Teye, 1988a, p. 330). Of these political factors, political instability appears the most salient.

Zambia, Zimbabwe, Angola, Mozambique and Namibia represent those nations involving wars of national liberation. Coups d'état and attempted coups are even more common. Teye notes that over the period 1956–1985 'there were 60 successful and 71 attempted coups in Africa. There were 120 additional reported plots in which segments of African military policy or security forces played a major role' (Teye, 1988a, p. 333). In fact, only four small nations of sub-saharan Africa (Botswana, Cape Verde, Dibouti, and Mauritius) did not have military intervention (Teye, 1988a, p. 335). Thus even these four nations are scarcely well-placed to develop tourism, let alone the rest of the continent. Similarly, well-meaning efforts to control the political situation exacerbate the functioning tourism: airport and border closures, curfews, the absence of all evening entertainment and transportation services are but a few of the problems the intrepid tourist faces (Teye, 1988a: 349–350). Not only are tourists not coming, but investment for tourism infrastructure is also scarce in such a political climate. Like the rather forlorn Bangladesh poster urging 'Come to Bangladesh before the tourists come', there is still time in most of Africa.

Nations sometimes benefit in increased tourism because of regional instability. Barbados, the Cayman islands, Aruba and Bermuda have prospered over the last thirty years as first Cuba, the Dominican Republic, Haiti, Jamaica, and then Grenada suffered from political instability. The Caribbean is different from other regions in that the islands are close to the tourist-generating areas of North America and yet physically separate from one other (except for Haiti and the Dominican Republic). Such geographical factors mean that tourists are likely to make individual countries a destination rather than a 'stop' on a regional tour. In addition, the countries themselves are better known than those of Africa and Asia to most North Americans.

Thailand is an exception for another reason. Being a relatively stable oasis in a turbulent South-east Asia was obviously an advantage for Thailand. First, as Rest and Recreation Centre for American GIs during the Vietnam War and then as a major tourist destination in its own right, Thailand has made tourism its main industry. During this period it has had several military coups, but most have been bloodless and the continuity provided by the monarchy has meant that the international media have paid very little attention to the jockeying for power at the top. As the former head of the Tourism Authority of Thailand put it: 'Most tourists are quite familiar with Thailand's unique ability to solve its internal problems without any serious incidents' (Elliott, 1983: 381).

An area of turmoil

One of the most common problems of political instability and tourism is that episodic violence or conflict far removed from tourist areas receive so much media attention that it appears the entire nation is engulfed in violence. This is particularly true for developing nations, unfortunately often ignored by Western media unless disaster, war, coups d'état, or revolution force them into the headlines. Geographical ignorance then compounds the problem, because few viewers or potential travellers can discern conflict areas from non-conflict areas.

Jamaica, Sri Lanka, Fiji and the Philippines are four nations where localised violence and, in Fiji's case, two coups have shattered economies heavily dependent on tourism. In Jamaica's case, the US government's opposition to the nationalist leadership of the Manley regime meant that American travel advisers neither minimised the rather mild political unrest nor noted that it was far removed from tourist centres. When the Manley government was defeated, there was a decided upsurge in favourable articles about Jamaica. The Jamaican government's advertising in US print media mirrored the political philosphies of the regimes. Under Manley, the advertising proclaimed 'Jamaica's More Than a Beach, It's a Country.' Under Manley's successor, the slogan was: 'Jamaica's Jamaica Again', with much emphasis on the close ties between the US and Jamaica and the pampering North American visitors could expect:

It starts with a country house or a beach cottage . . . that comes equipped with gentle people named Ivy or Maude or Malcolm who will cook, tend, mend, diaper or launder for you. . . . (Erisman, 1983: 338)

Sri Lanka built an elaborate and costly tourism infrastructure, based almost entirely in Sinhalese areas and in Sinhalese hands. Whereas, in 1967, 19,000 tourists arrived, by 1982, 407,230 tourists came to Sri Lanka. 'Serendib', from which the term 'serendipity' is derived, appeared to have it all (*Pacific Travel News*, 1984). Beautiful mountains, an exotic Buddhist culture, and sun, sand, sea and sex. The latter was a concern to many citizens in this traditional society, but sex tourism was largely confined to such beach communities as Hikkaduwa (*Asia Travel Trade*, 1977: Supplement 2; *Pacific Travel News*, 1984: 42–48, 12–25).

Despite being largely the monopoly of the dominant Sinhalese, tourism does not seem to have been significantly involved in the savage ethnic conflict between the Tamil minority and the Sinhalese. Few tourists have been affected by the conflict, which has dragged on for more than six years, but the costs to the tourism industry have been devastating. Following the first eight days of violence, the industry estimated a loss of $7 million a month, one fifth of the employed and supporting service and supply sector (*Asia Travel Trade*, 1984: 17–22).

Only Sri Lanka's ethnic conflict makes the news. Because the major tourism infrastructure was designed for luxury-seeking Westerners at remote locales, conversion is impractical. Now the government's tourism policy is itself a political issue. The irony of creating accommodation for foreigners who will not come, and at one hundred times the cost of housing citizens who need accommodation immediately, is broadly apparent in a way only a few pessimists could forecast ten years ago (Goonatilake, 1978: 15).

In Fiji, ethnic conflict was ostensibly a major cause of the 1987 coups. In the context of protests against French nuclear testing in the Pacific, and the departure of New Zealand from the ANZUS Pact following its refusal to accept US nuclear ships in port, some sources hinted that the US was not displeased to see the first coup. It had replaced a government that was beginning to flirt with a nuclear-free zone in the Pacific. In any case, in Fiji there is tension between the Indian majority, which dominates the tourism industry, and the native Fijian minority, progressively reduced in numbers and power but struggling to recover political control.

Tourists were never in any apparent danger, but the industry clearly was. Despite being, by South Pacific standards, a major power, Fiji's air links and cruise stops, which are absolutely critical to the nation's tourist economy, are by no means guaranteed. And although Fiji is now apparently calm, there have been drastic cutbacks in international flights, making future marketing and the viability of Fiji's resorts problematic (Waters, 1989: 113).

China, however, is the nation that currently epitomises the links between political unrest and tourism. After building international tourism for over ten years into a three billion dollar-a-year business, the government forfeited its image abroad in a savage crackdown on pro-democracy supporters (Day, 1989: 6–8). And it did so on world-wide television in the largest public square on the globe (MacFarquhar, 1989: 35). It was not a subtle move and it has cost the government dearly in tourism and investments. It also meant that the Chinese government has, for the long term, lost its image of innocence. The euphoria that had been associated with Western views of China since the death of Mao Tse Tung will not be easily recaptured.

Despite price-slashing of fares on Air China, and China's announced willingness to provide political risk insurance to investors (*U.S. News and World Report*, September 18th, 1989, p. 18; Tyson, 1989, p. 4) analysts expect a 2-billion dollar tourism loss in 1989 and continued slowdown in travel revenues for two to five years. Although the attention span of the travelling public is short, it is likely that, with the approach of 1997, when Hong Kong is transferred from British to Chinese hands, there will be continued reminders of the Chinese crackdown. Even without new human rights abuses, these may serve to keep terror and tourism linked in the minds of travellers.

The tourist as political pawn

Under Aquino, the Philippines continues to see its tourism industry jerked to and fro by political forces jockeying for power at the centre. The political exploitation of tourism by President Marcos was unparalleled in its complexity and excesses but that has been detailed elsewhere (Richter, 1980, 1982, 1989). President Aquino has not been preoccupied with tourism, but she inherited a legacy of bankrupt hotels and resort properties that she expected to become the core of a renewed but balanced tourism industry. Yet, despite the size and beauty of the Philippines and its undisputed attractions, the momentum for tourism development keeps being derailed by coup attempts against her government; at the time of writing, there have been more than six. The last and most serious, in December 1989, not only caught the government off guard at the height of the Philippine tourist season, but also resulted in over 800 tourists being held hostage by rebels in four luxury hotels (Blanco, 1990: 9). The rebels knew there was no safer place from which to harass the government in a prolonged stalemate than in a hotel filled with tourists that neither the government or the US ally would jeopardize. In 1987, another coup attempt against Aquino was launched in yet another luxury hotel, though in that instance no hostages were taken.

Using tourists as political pawns goes back nearly two decades in the Philippines. At that time, the Moro National Liberation Front, a secessionist Muslim organization in the Southern Philippines, kidnapped several Japanese tourists for sustained periods. The Japanese government reacted with its customary watchfulness, strongly advising all Japanese to avoid the Southern Philippines. Almost all did . . . for the next fourteen years!

Currently, it is expected that as the US and the Philippines negotiate the future of key US naval and airforce installations, random attacks on American service personnel may be extended to attacks or threats against US tourists. In such a scenario, it is likely that the New People's Army, a quasi-Marxist guerrilla group, will claim responsibility. It seeks to escalate the cost of American military and business investment in the Philippines.

In such a political environment, tourism is clearly vulnerable. The opposition, left or right, is unlikely to topple Aquino or US investment in a head-to-head clash, but random violence can discourage tourism or other types of business investment. Already conventions and group travellers are dissuaded by US advisors. Those that go anyway find an ambience that is scarcely reassuring. Searches and the checking of firearms is routine in major hotels. At some point, the security apparatus, for example the armed guards at McDonald's, itself serves as a deterrent, quite apart from any political violence.

The tourist is also a pawn in a political struggle in Kenya between the government and the poachers of wildlife. Ironically, it was big game hunting that once lured tourists to Kenya; now it may be illegal big game hunting that destroys it. There is a two-pronged problem for Kenya's national government: how to protect the game tourists come to see and how to protect the tourists. In both instances the stakes are high: a World Conservation Union study estimated that in Kenya one lion is worth $7,000 and an elephant herd $610,000 annually in tourism income. Yet poachers seeking quick profits are killing not only the wildlife, but also tourists. Increasingly, tours report that some portions of game parks have been made off-limits and that armed guards have been assigned to tourist jeeps. Tourists preferring not to become the target of big game hunters may well go elsewhere, and with them will go Kenya's largest source of foreign exchange. Indeed, U.S. Travel advisories in 1989 and 1991 followed waves of attacks on game park visitors (Waters, 1991: 126).

Tourism as rationale for political unrest

In some countries, tourism, or a type of tourism, is itself a source of political strife. Five examples taken from the Third World illustrate some of the problems that have made tourism development a destabilising force. The classic case of using tourism development politically, that of the Philippines under Marcos, is also the classic case of tourism undoing a regime. In fostering tourism development, no effort was too great. At one time, in Manila alone, twelve luxury hotels were being built on money borrowed from the nation's social security system and with ownership titles in the names of Marcos family members and their cronies (Richter, 1980). Other tourism infrastructure was constructed during round-the-clock building frenzies, even while social services and quality of life plummetted for most Filipinos.

Though tourism did increase, by 1981 the excesses of the Marcos-controlled tourist industry generated an enormous backlash against the industry. Without legal recourse during the nine years of martial law (1972–1981), the political opposition found, in attacks on Marcos-owned luxury hotels, a successful way of destroying the very tourism industry he had created to enhance his legitimacy and his international image. By selecting a sector of the economy that was largely foreign-managed and foreign in clientele, domestic reaction was muted and publicity beyond the reach of Marcos was assured. One by one, the 'light-a-fire' movement burned luxury hotels throughout the country. At the start of this ambitious project, the American Society of Travel Agents held its long-scheduled convention in Manila. The President opened the gala affair, decrying the hysterical Western press for proclaiming unrest in the Philippines, and forty feet away the bomb exploded! The most influential travel industry marketeers thus experienced an forgettable introduction to Philippine politics (Richter and Waugh, 1986).

In Thailand as well as in Sri Lanka, the Philippines and Kenya, the massive prostitution associated, especially, with Third World tourism has made the industry a concern to church, youth, women's and health groups. While prostitution is not unknown in most societies, sex tours, paedophilia tours, and the transient nature of tourism prostitution generally, make its links with tourism especially dangerous to all the parties involved. The advent of AIDS has further aggravated the fears of many that a generation of young men and women is being sacrificed for tourist dollars. So dependent have such nations as Thailand become on selling sex to tourists that government authorities are loath to discourage prostitution. At the same time, they fear that AIDS and gonorrhea may be lasting souvenirs for many Thais and tourists alike, ultimately killing (also) the country's main industry. In several countries, tourists are now required to prove that their HIV tests have been negative before they are admitted, a policy which may be followed by other nations as the epidemic spreads.

Political opposition to prostitution has not yet become political instability, but it has focused attention of the selling of children for sex and on the health crises surrounding prostitution. Such countries as Japan, notorious for sex tours to the

Third World, have tightened restrictions on travel agents. In addition, on several occasions Japanese public officials have travelled abroad, only to be met by demonstrations against Japanese tourists' exploitation of Third World children and women (O'Grady, 1990: 22). But no nation has a monopoly on procuring or purchasing sexual favours.

The Ecumenical Coalition on Third World Tourism, based in Bangkok, has monitored social problems associated with tourism in developing nations, but it and affiliated organisations around the globe see the problems growing (O'Grady, 1990: 79). However, de-sleazing destinations is difficult. Efforts to regulate some of the seamier aspects of Pattaya, Thailand's tourist trade, for example, resulted in an angry demonstration of 50,000 against regulation (Richter, 1989b).

More effective have been the demonstrations against tourism and tourist facilities in Goa, India. Evictions to facilitate the construction of hotels, and other government acts that appeared to favour hoteliers over local people, have led to numerous and well-publicised anti-tourism demonstrations. Through the efforts of non-profit groups and churches, enough pressure has been generated to reverse, halt, or modify earlier government schemes (O'Grady, 1990: 55).

These incidents represent only a few of the cases where tourism itself has become politically de-stabilising. In general, the political effects were localised. However, the Philippine example should serve as a cautionary tale for any who assume tourism can be developed without heed to who gains and who loses. International tourism is not very subtle; it is often associated with a level of luxury especially incongruous with the general poverty of Third World societies. Barely tolerated under conditions where overall well-being is increasing, it can be extraordinarily vulnerable to sabotage if disaffected interests should so choose.

Part III Anticipating, coping, and preventing threats to tourism from political instability

This chapter has demonstrated that political instability can have a devastating effect on Third World tourism, either through political unrest within nations or the region, or because tourists or tourism itself have created opportunities that political opponents of the regime or the industry can exploit.

There are no easy answers as to how the advantages of tourism revenues can be garnered without significant risks to the society or the industry. One thing seems clear: for all the rhetoric that surrounds tourism as an agent of peace and goodwill, this study found no evidence at all that the prospects of tourism income contributed to political stability, to a willingness to compromise, internally or within the region, or that the tourism industry became less controversial over time. In fact, one might argue just the opposite: the presence of tourists may embolden dissidents, as in Tibet, Beijing or Mecca, to make long-repressed demands. Unfortunately for the protesters, tourists who witness such displays cannot ensure any insulation from the often harsh reprisals that many follow (Moynihan, 1989: 10–11). The regime may pay for the ensuing crackdown in tourism losses, but the protesters remain vulnerable (Trick, November 14, 1989).

If there is any security associated with Third World tourism, it is in planning a level, pace, and type of tourism congruent with indigenous resources. A tourism transportation system that supplements local needs, or which can be used by tourist and citizen, may be viable with or without tourists and bridges the lifestyles of both. Resorts and hotels designed to keep a low profile and to be modest users of electricity and water are also more likely to survive disruptions of both services and are less likely to be perceived as competing with local needs. In addition, pre-arrival information on culture and customs may make tourism less controversial.

If national planners were to consider a political audit of possible internal and external sources of political disruption, alternative sources of transportation, security and supplies, and some contingency or risk analysis, it would be time well spent. Too often, potential attractions are listed and sources of investment capital wooed before the necessary political evaluation takes place. Even such corrupt and repressive regimes as those in the Philippines and Haiti caused suffering which was unnecessary and unrelated to the regimes' advantage.

Finally, governments would do well to recognise that long-term wealth and political security is based not only on understanding who gets what, when and how, but also on 'who already has what' (Parenti, 1977). Diffusing opportunities in and gains from tourism modestly, be it on ethnic, linguistic, or regional grounds, may protect élite investments more surely than favouritism or monopolies.

This study has no vested bias for political stability, particularly in unrepresentative or repressive political systems. However, it should be recognised that in developing nations, resources are scarce. Committing precious resources to tourism in a political atmosphere ripe for revolt or violence may only increase hardship and accelerate impoverishment without even the solace of political freedom for the population or political control or censensus for the government.

4 The structure of international tourism and tourism development in Kenya

M. Thea Sinclair, Parvin Alizadeh and
Elizabeth Atieno Adero Onunga

Much of the past literature on tourism and developing countries has discussed the recent growth in the demand for and supply of tourism, tourism's contribution to income, employment and foreign exchange earnings, and the economic and social costs associated with tourism. However, there has been a general lack of attention to the ways in which such effects are influenced by the interrelationships between tourism enterprises in developing countries and other major intermediaries in the tourism industry, for example, foreign airlines, tour operators and travel agents. Tourism takes place in an international context dominated by the actions of large foreign firms, whose headquarters are usually in industrialised countries. The benefits and costs associated with tourism development are therefore greatly influenced by the nature of the interrelationships between foreign firms and those based in the host countries.

One form of interrelationship which has received particular attention, and been the source of some controversy, within the literature on manufacturing development in developing countries is direct foreign investment by multinational corporations. Emphasis on ownership by multinationals can, however, have the effect of concealing other forms of contractual relationship between domestic and foreign firms whose effects are of equal or greater importance to the destination country. If foreign firms possess a high level of bargaining power, they may not need to engage in direct investment to obtain advantageous relationships with the host country. Study of the tourism sector shows that total ownership by multinationals of tourism enterprises located within developing countries is one end of a spectrum of relationships; other major forms are joint ventures involving joint ownership by domestic and foreign residents, industrial co-operation agreements such as management contracts or technical agreements, franchising, long-term contracts and short-term contracts. The alternative types of contractual arrangement are associated with different costs and benefits to the developing country, and may be more or less appropriate to the needs of countries with different degrees of 'development' of the local tourism industry, different social and political contexts and different policy objectives.

Awareness of the potential advantages and disadvantages associated with alternative contractual arrangements is an important precondition for developing countries' attempts to increase their benefits from international tourism. This chapter focuses on the structure of international tourism and the relationships between developing countries and foreign firms within this structure. First, it provides the context by discussing tourism's potential as a means of economic development, pointing out the general neglect of tourism in economic development literature and the inappropriateness of some well-known development and trade models for analysing it. Since developing countries' potential comparative advantage in tourism is greatly influenced by the actions of large foreign firms, industrial organisation and integration theory is likely to provide a useful framework for analysing the sector. The next section examines the structure of the international tourism industry and the range of contractual relationships which exist between different firms within it. Empirical evidence concerning prevalent forms of contractual relationships, together with their advantages and disadvantages, are provided, based on information from interviews with major participants in the tourism sector. Particular attention is paid to the Kenyan tourism industry. The final section examines the implications of the theoretical and empirical findings and discusses the extent to which governments of developing countries can mediate between local and foreign firms, thereby tilting the balance of advantages and disadvantages in favour of the host country.

Tourism and economic development

Economic development and growth is often impeded by a foreign exchange constraint (Thirlwall, 1983, p. 296). This constraint has not, in general, been alleviated by the growth of the service sector in developing countries, which is dominated by firms from industrialised countries (Schott and Mazza 1986; Nayyar 1988). However, the contribution to foreign exchange earnings made by tourism is an important exception (Lee 1987, Sinclair and Tsegaye 1990). Furthermore, tourism is not only a sector of current economic importance, but is also expanding, as many developing countries have a revealed comparative advantage in tourism. This is reflected in Table 4.1, which provides a brief summary of the current account balance of developing countries by region in 1986.

It is clear from Table 4.1 that developing countries as a whole are a net importer of services but a net recipient of foreign exchange from travel, which constitutes the generally accepted proxy for tourism earnings. With the exception of the developing countries of West Asia, which include the OPEC countries, tourism makes a considerable net contribution to foreign exchange earnings. In developing

Table 4.1   Current account balance of developing countries, 1986 (in billions of dollars)

Balance	West Asia	Other Asia	Latin America	Africa	Total developing countries
Merchandise	9.0	16.9	18.2	5.3	49.4
Interest	23.0	−8.7	−31.3	−8.0	−25.0
Property	−0.4	−3.1	−3.7	−2.2	−9.4
Labour	−9.0	9.0	2.1	3.0	5.1
Transport	−6.9	−6.1	−5.2	−3.5	−21.7
Travel	−1.6	2.6	2.6	0.7	4.3
Other Services	−6.6	−1.2	−0.7	−3.2	−11.7

Source: From Annex Table 11, *Trade and Development Report 1988*, (UNCTAD 1988)

countries in the rest of Asia, Latin America and Africa, in 1986, net foreign exchange receipts from tourism contributed 2.6, 2.6 and 0.7 billion dollars respectively to the balance of payments.

Given the importance of tourism, it is surprising that the sector's contribution to economic development, whether in terms of its contribution to foreign exchange earnings or income and employment generation, has been largely ignored in economic development literature which, with its emphasis on the significance of manufacturing industry and the agricultural sector, has paid little attention to the role of services. In the 1950s and 1960s, the literature was primarily concerned with the structural transformation of developing countries through state-induced industrialisation. Explicit or implicit in the literature is the notion of the two sector economy, consisting of agriculture and industry. Lewis' two-sector model (1954, 1958) is a particularly well known example of such models. The economy is posited to consist of two sectors: a traditional, subsistence, overpopulated agricultural sector, in which the marginal productivity of labour is zero so that 'surplus labour' can be withdrawn from the sector without any loss of output, and a modern urban industrial sector, characterised by high labour productivity and a high rate of capital accumulation. In this model, the process of economic growth is based on the reallocation of cheap labour from the agricultural to the industrial sector.

Since the late 1960s, there has been a shift of emphasis in development literature from industry to agriculture. It is now widely accepted that the emphasis placed in the 1950s and 1960s on the modern industrial sector was excessive, given that it failed to absorb the 'surplus' rural population. Concern with the social and political implications of open urban unemployment shifted the focus towards 'rural development' and ways of keeping the population on the land (Todaro, 1985). The effect of the early emphasis on the two sector model, followed by the more recent emphasis on rural development, was to obscure the developmental significance of tourism as well as a wide range of other activities which come under the heading of services in the national accounts. The importance of the service sector to employment generation in developing countries only received general recognition in the late 1980s (UNCTAD 1988).

The neglect of tourism is not confined to development literature but extends to international trade theory, which is mainly concerned with the exchange of goods rather than services. Can 'exports' and 'imports' of tourism be understood in the context of international trade theories? An obvious candidate for consideration is the Heckscher-Ohlin theorem, which proposes that differences in factor endowments among countries influence the direction of trade; countries export commodities whose production requires intensive use of those productive factors which are available locally in relative abundance. Developing countries, for instance, are argued to have a comparative advantage in manufactured goods which require little physical and human capital relative to unskilled labour (Caves and Jones, 1981: 159).

It appears that a similar analogy can be drawn with respect to 'exports' of tourism, so that a country which possesses natural or historical attributes such as beautiful beaches or monuments has a potential comparative advantage in tourism. However, the analogy between the export of goods and of tourism requires some modification. Unlike the export of goods, the movement of people, as consumers, is essential for the 'export' of tourism. Furthermore, beaches or monuments are not productive factors and may be public goods. The property of a public good is that its consumption by one person does not exclude its consumption by others. Thus public goods are sometimes priced through taxes and similar devices to prevent those who do not pay from consuming them (Stiglitz, 1988).

When applied to tourism, the main weakness of the Heckscher-Ohlin and comparative cost theorems is their failure to capture the composite nature of tourism, which involves a variety of services, ranging from travel to accommodation and insurance. Thus tourism depends not only on the availability of a specific physical or natural attribute in a country, but also on the production of a range of services which are consumed in a sequential fashion. Tourism therefore exhibits the characteristics of an industry in which the production of a composite product entails the provision of a range of services, frequently supplied by firms from both developing and industrialised countries. Firms from industrialised countries play an important role, for example, in determining the effective demand for tourism by means of marketing and influencing the accessibility of destinations in developing countries. In this respect, the theory of industrial organisation and integration can provide a useful framework for analysing international tourism, as will be seen during the following sections which examine the structure of the tourism industry and the different forms of interrelationship of the major agents within it.

The structure of the international tourism industry

The international tourism industry is dominated by firms from industrialised countries. The world's largest airlines are from industrialised countries and, although airlines from India, the Republic of Korea and Singapore have been among the top twenty scheduled airlines (United Nations Centre on Transnational Corporations, 1982), no developing country appears to have had an independent charter airline of note. The international tour operator sector has been almost completely dominated by tour operators from industrialised countries (UNCTC, 1988). Of the top twenty-six hotel chains in 1978, only one (the Indian Oberoi Hotels) was from a developing country and no chain from a developing country operated a hotel in an industrialised country (Dunning and McQueen, 1982). By 1988–90, of 273 hotel properties belonging to major hotel groups, only twenty-four belonged to companies based in non-industrialised countries (Go, 1988). The participation of the developing country is usually confined to the hotel sector, local agents, local transportation and part of the international transportation sector. This can be clarified by reference to Figure 4.1, which shows the linkages between the major agents in the international tourism industry: travel agents, tour operators, consolidators, airlines, hotels and local agents. For simplicity, forms of travel other than airlines, and such small-scale enterprises as restaurants and souvenir shops are not considered. The following discussion briefly considers the role of the tourism agents shown in the figure, and then discusses the range of contractual relationships which exist between them.

The marketing of tourism is generally carried out by firms located in and owned by residents of industrialised countries. A particularly important type of agent within the travel retailing sector is the travel agent, who sells air tickets and inclusive tour holiday packages, as well as other forms of travel and insurance. Travel agents purchase air tickets from the airlines of both industrialised and developing nations, obtaining commission of the order of 9 per cent for sales of economy seats and 24 per cent for sales of first class seats to individual, non-inclusive tour travellers. They may also purchase airline tickets from consolidators, obtaining similar rates of commission. Consolidators are intermediaries who are generally located in industrialised countries but a number originate in developing countries, for example, East African Asians now based in London. Although consolidators

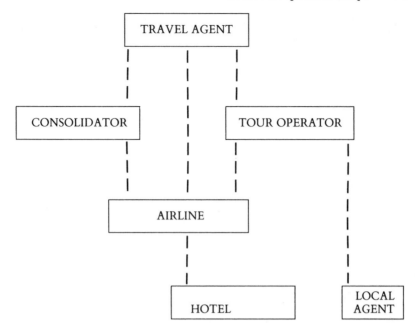

Figure 4.1   The linkages between major agents in the tourism industry

purchase at standard rates of commission from all airlines, their main interest lies in purchasing blocks of seats for specific routes flown by airlines from industrialised and developing countries. They obtain block allocations of seats by means of annual contracts with the airlines, and pay the airline a discounted price when the seats are sold; additional seats can sometimes be obtained at a discount approximately five weeks before the flight. It is in the airline's interest to provide different consolidators with block allocations of seats for different routes in order to spread its risks; for example, a large airline may provide block seat allocations to three consolidators per route and may deal with twenty consolidators. Consolidators perform a marketing function for airlines, selling small numbers of tickets to the public but making most of their sales to travel agents on the basis of such techniques as mail shots.

Inclusive tour holiday packages, also sold by travel agents, are supplied by tour operators, most of which are located in and owned by residents of industrialised countries. Tour operators usually sell only in one country but some large tour operators, for example, Kuoni and Jetset, sell holidays in a range of industrialised countries. The airline seat component of the packages that major tour operators supply is obtained as a block allocation from scheduled airlines at discounted prices or by chartering planes. Although developing countries usually have their own 'flagship' airline, this does not always provide long-distance international flights and its route allocation between countries is usually limited. Few developing countries have a charter airline. Thus the majority of tourists, having purchased their tickets from travel agents or tour operators based in industrialised countries, use an airline owned by residents of industrial countries when travelling to their destination. While individual, 'wanderlust' tourists often stay in small, locally-owned hotels, the rooms purchased by tour operators, at discounted prices, and through block allocation, tend to be in relatively large hotels, which are more likely to involve foreign ownership or some other form of contractual relationship with firms in industrialised countries. However, local agents are paid by tour operators to meet tourists on arrival and transport them to their hotel, and such agents may often book rooms for small tour operators and sometimes provide excursions.

A variety of relationships link foreign and developing country enterprises involved in tourism, but those occurring most frequently are complete foreign ownership, joint ventures with local participants, industrial co-operation agreements, franchising agreements, long-term contracts and short-term contracts. Although the degree of foreign ownership decreases from the former to the latter, the extent of bargaining power and influence that foreign firms can exert over developing country enterprises does not decrease proportionately. This will become apparent during the subsequent discussion of the contractual relationships that exist between Kenyan and foreign firms. However, first, it will be useful to examine the economic characteristics of the main types of linkage.

Contractual relationships within the tourism industry

At one end of the spectrum of possible relationships between local and foreign firms in the tourism industry lies the multinational corporation, where there may be up to 100 per cent foreign ownership of locally-based firms. This type of relationship has tended to attract most attention in the development literature, particularly in relation to the manufacturing sector (for example, Balasubramanyam, 1980; Dunning, 1979; Lall, 1974). Multinational linkages between firms based in developing and industrialised countries may occur in a vertically integrated form, whereby an enterprise owns up to 100 per cent of the firms supplying its inputs and/or the firms selling its output. Within tourism, examples of vertical ownership are Scandinavian Airlines System's ownership of the Inter-Continental hotel chain, and the International Thomson Organisation's ownership of Thomson Holidays, Portland Holidays and Skytours tour operators, Britannia Airways, Orion Airways and the Lunn Poly chain of travel agencies. Horizontal ownership is the form of integration in which there is common ownership of enterprises producing the same type of product, for example, the Hilton hotel chain. There is also conglomerate ownership, in which an enterprise not specialising in the production of a particular product acquires the ownership of a firm producing that product, for example, the Lonrho Corporation's investment in hotels in Africa.

Where a multinational enterprise includes a completely vertically-organised structure, tourists can book holidays through a travel agency which is part of the same ownership group as that of the tour operator which organised the holiday, the airline by which they travel to their destination and the hotel in which they stay. Within economic literature, an important explanation of the multinational enterprise is the theory of internalization (Casson, 1987; Coase, 1937). It is argued that if firms buy and sell from other firms, costs are involved in negotiating and agreeing contracts for the different exchanges that take place. The integration of such firms means that transactions can be co-ordinated (i.e. 'internalized') within one firm, thus decreasing costs and facilitating checks on quality. Integration may also occur when the firm wishes to retain a monopolistic or monopsonistic advantage (Hymer, 1976), for example, a particularly efficient form of production or management.

Theories of vertical integration can be included in three main categories:

contractual problems, market power and technical factors, and are discussed in more detail by Casson (1987) and Bote et al. (1989). Contracts are drawn up in a context of uncertainty and, in the first case, it is argued that integration can assure a market for the firm's output (Carlton, 1979) or decrease uncertainty about the prices and availability of the firm's inputs (Arrow 1975; Oi and Hurter, 1965). Integration can decrease uncertainty in a context of considerable innovation, and precludes the possibility of contract-breaking. The second explanation of vertical integration is that it enables the firm to increase its market power and profits by such means as the imposition of barriers to entry against potential competitors, the monopolisation of the supply of inputs or transfer pricing. Finally, the existence of such technical factors as continuous flow technology, the need for efficient synchronisation of the different activities within a production process, or economies of scale in the use of such indivisible assets as aeroplanes constitutes the third explanation.

Complete ownership by one firm of activities at different stages of the production process can be considered a limiting case among the range of linkages that occur between firms. The joint venture, where ownership of firms – for example, hotels – is shared by industrialised and developing country participants, is an alternative form of relationship which is often more acceptable to developing countries. The varying structures of ownership and control under complete foreign ownership and joint ventures involve significant differences in the allocation of risk and managerial responsibility. Under conditions of complete foreign ownership, the control of production and marketing is the responsibility of the parent company, which is usually located in an industrialised country. Joint ventures differ in that control as well as ownership is usually shared by both parties, although there are variations in the distribution of each.

Joint ventures may enable the firm to acquire or retain monopoly or monopsony power concerning, for example, production technology or management, and to maintain or improve product quality. Under joint ventures, not only is there joint access to knowledge, experience and managerial expertise, but also to joint distribution channels, thereby increasing output sales and profitability. Governments of developing countries may view the substitution of complete foreign ownership by joint ventures as a means of decreasing their degree of economic dependence on industrialised countries. However, joint ventures may, in fact, provide the foreign company with the advantage of easier access to capital and operating licences in the host country, while switching the distribution of risk towards the latter.

The third type of linkage between firms is a co-operation agreement, for example, a management contract in which a hotel in a developing country is managed by an international hotel chain. In this case, the ownership of the firm and the investment-associated risk lie with the host country. The control of production and marketing may be the responsibility of the foreign enterprise, or it may be shared with the local firm. Co-operation agreements are one way of permitting the transfer of such knowledge as production methods from an associated foreign company to the host country. Management contracts can involve project planning, development, design, construction and the day-to-day operation of the business. The foreign company is usually responsible for supplying the managerial techniques and for controlling the quality of the output, and may market the product. It is a common assumption that management contracts involve a lower level of dependence on foreigners by developing countries than is involved in complete foreign ownership of joint ventures. However, a foreign company involved in a management contract often has direct control over the finances of the local business and, since it does not have an equity stake in the firm, it avoids the risk of expropriation.

The fourth type of linkage, the franchising agreement, has many of the features of the management contract but a greater degree of risk is often borne by the host country. An example of a franchising agreement is the use by local hotels of the Hilton or Holiday Inns trade names. The associated company provides the local company with knowledge of production and marketing and exerts indirect control over the quality of output by a process of monitoring, for example, regular inspections or the presence of resident representatives. The extent of knowledge transfer from the foreign company to the host country is lower than in the case of the management contract and may be more concerned with the transfer of marketing expertise. Direct responsibility for management and production lies with the destination country enterprise.

The fifth type of contractual relationship is the long-term contract, such as the seven to ten-year contracts which some UK tour operators made with Spanish hoteliers during the late 1960s, a period of excess demand for accommodation along the Mediterranean coastline (Wright, 1975). The characteristics alleged to be conducive to long-term contracts are a stable economic environment, considerable use of illiquid capital assets, fairly large numbers of participants in the market and knowledge readily available to all (Williamson, 1975). Long-term contracts have the potential advantage to the firm of decreasing the costs involved in the formulation of more numerous short-term contracts and assuring a long demand for its output or supply of inputs. However, the specification of complete contracts, covering all possible eventualities, is usually impossible, particularly in a sector such as tourism, which is characterised by fluctuating demand. As a consequence, long-term contracts also involve the potential problem of 'moral hazard', where one of the parties to a contract reneges on the agreement.

Short-term contracts are a common alternative to long-term contracts, particularly in situations of uncertainty (although integration is a possible alternative outcome). Within international tourism, uncertainty can stem from such factors as political instability and changes in exchange and relative inflation rates; for example, some developing countries have experienced extremely high rates of inflation and currency depreciation. Changes in the relative costs of different destinations encourage the substitution of cheaper for more expensive destinations and constitute a disincentive to contractual arrangements which impede such substitution. Short-term contracts are particularly appropriate when there is a ready availability of knowledge, a large number of participants in the market and a low likelihood of 'moral hazard'. They are often preferred to long-term contracts when the costs of contract-making are low, when only short-run forecasts are required, and when a firm which acquires an original contract does not obtain a monopoly or monopsony advantage. Consequently, short-term contracts are conducive to the interests of tour operators, which generally wish to avoid large-scale investment in hotels in destination countries.

Short-term contracts enable subsequent contracts to incorporate new information in a relatively short period, decreasing the probability that contracts will be broken. Thus, for example, if tour operators forecast a deterioration of conditions in a particular destination, they can decrease their demand for hotel rooms and airline seats during the subsequent contractual period without breaking their current contracts with the destination country's suppliers. Short-run contracts also permit hoteliers and airlines to alter, within a short period, the sizes of the block room or seat bookings allocated to particular tour operators if the effective demand for rooms or seats has exceeded or fallen short of the block bookings previously contracted. Short-term contracts between firms in developing and in. countries have not usually attracted the concern about developin. dependence which has been associated with investment by multination ever, as will become evident in the subsequent section, the terms of the may cause firms in developing countries to shoulder a considerable amou risk associated with the tourism industry.

The Kenyan and international tourism industries

The benefits and costs which developing countries derive from international tourism arrivals are related to the contractual relationships that exist between tourism enterprises in developing and industrialised countries. The general lack of past discussion of this issue stems mainly from the absence of published information concerning the nature of the contractual relationships that prevail within the international tourism industry. The authors therefore carried out over twenty in-depth interviews with members of major firms and organisations within the international tourism industry. They took place in 1989–90, with representatives of airlines, tour operators, consolidators, hotels and government officials. Particular attention was paid to international tourism in Kenya, since tourism is that country's foremost source of export earnings, in 1988 contributing over one third of total export receipts. Through its history of 'capitalist' development and well established tourism industry, Kenya has experienced many of the advantages and disadvantages associated with different types of contractual relationships between locally-based and foreign firms.

The increasing importance of tourism to Kenya is indicated by data on tourism departures which, in only five years, rose from 306,300 in 1983 to 676,900 in 1988, an increase of 121 per cent (Central Bureau of Statistics, 1984, 1989). German tourism is the largest non-domestic source of demand, constituting 18 per cent of the total, followed by the UK with 13 per cent, Switzerland with 8 per cent and France with 5 per cent (Central Bureau of Statistics, 1989). Many of the tourists who spend holidays in Kenya purchase inclusive tour holidays organised by such international operators as Kuoni, Hayes and Jarvis, Jetset, British Airways' Speedbird, TUI, Polmans, Universal Safari Tours, I Grandi Viaggi and Franco Rosso. Kenya's real foreign exchange earnings from tourism increased from £45.4 million in 1983 to £55.7 million in 1989 in 1972 prices (calculated using data from the Central Bank of Kenya, 1989). Whereas in 1973 tourism contributed 13 per cent of the country's export earnings, compared with 20 per cent for coffee and 9 per cent for tea, by 1988 tourism provided 37 per cent of total earnings relative to 26 per cent for coffee and 20 per cent for tea (Central Bank of Kenya, 1989). The country has thus become increasingly dependent on tourism as a source of foreign exchange.

Tourism in Kenya consists mainly of safari and beach holidays, and cheaper beach-only holidays, and tends to be concentrated in a few game reserves – for example, the Masai Mara National Reserve and Amboseli National Park, and in the Mombasa, south coast and Malindi coastal areas. The country has scheduled and charter airlines providing international and domestic flights, a supply of good quality hotels, including a nationally-owned hotel chain, and local agents which provide such services as road-based transportation within the country. What, then, is the nature of the interrelationships between tourism enterprises located in Kenya and those which are based in foreign countries? The following discussion concentrates on the linkages among the major actors in the tourism industry: airlines, tour operators and hotels. The role of travel agents located in industrialised countries is not considered, as there are rarely direct linkages between them and tourism enterprises in Kenya or other developing countries.

Kenya Airways and international tour operators

Most developing countries have a 'flagship' airline which provides flights on a domestic and/or international basis, although such airlines may be managed or partly owned by airlines from industrialised countries. Governments of developing countries are keen to increase the number of passengers and the share of transit traffic using their 'flagship' airline. Most airlines operate in a context in which route allocation, the frequency and capacity of flights, intermediate landing and take-off rights are determined by one of two types of arrangements. The first is commonly known as a Bermuda-type agreement, whereby the airlines of two countries formulate an agreement on commercial grounds; pooling agreements in which they pool and share the revenue from all flights are common. In the second type of arrangement, the government of the destination country regulates the distribution between domestic and overseas airlines of the landing points and routes flown within the country, as well as the associated numbers of flights by foreign airlines.

In the case of Kenya, the route allocation between Kenya Airways, the scheduled airline, and foreign airlines is determined in bilateral negotiations between the Kenyan government and foreign governments, at which representatives of both Kenya Airways and the foreign airline are present. Kenya's policy is to limit the access of foreign airlines to routes with a high level of traffic, for example, Nairobi/Harare, and offers by foreign airlines to allow Kenya Airways to fly lower-volume routes in exchange for permission to fly high-volume routes have been rejected. Kenya has introduced direct as well as stop-over flights between cities such as London and Nairobi in order to compete with foreign airlines for the higher income segment of the market. However, Kenya Airways frequently fails to obtain its desired arrival and departure times at overseas airports because the most favourable landing and take-off 'slots' are generally allocated to the overseas country's national carrier.

In the context of a rapid growth in demand for 'long haul' tourism, from which airlines from some developing countries have been able to extract increasing revenue, one response by overseas tour operators has been to increase the use of charter flights. Requests for foreign charter flights to Kenya are considered by the Kenyan Civil Aviation Board, which meets three times a year. When responding to such requests, the Board has attempted to discriminate, initially refusing permission for charter flights to Kenya from such countries as the UK, but permitting charters from Germany and Italy. The aim was to allow Kenya Airways to maintain its share of the traffic on those routes characterised by more inelastic demand but to permit foreign charter airlines to supply lower-priced fares to beach destinations from origins in which high volume, mass tourism demand could be tapped.

UK tour operators responded to the Kenyan government's refusal to grant them permission to use charter flights by side-stepping the regulations. For example, short-term contracts were made with airlines to supply flights from the UK to Italy, where UK tourists would board a charter flight to Kenya, thus switching some tourism demand from scheduled flights provided by Kenya Airways to charter flights provided by foreign airlines. However, additional demand arising from the provision of the cheaper charter flights was also generated. Given the context of ineffective regulation but increasing total earnings from tourism, during the 1980s and Civil Aviation Board greatly increased the number of licences allocated to foreign charter airlines and permitted charter flights from the UK to Mombasa.

The actions of foreign tour operators thus have important effects on the demand for travel on destination countries' airlines and the associated revenue which the countries receive. Relative to the airlines of many other developing countries, Kenya Airways is considered to be well-established, so the contractual arrangements it negotiates with foreign tour operators are likely to be equivalent or superior to those which other developing countries' airlines are able to negotiate. Initially, Kenya Airways reserves, for its own sales, most of its first and business class seats – approximately 25 per cent of the seats in, for example, an Airbus. Blocks of economy class seats are then allocated to major tour operators and consolidators. For the London/Nairobi route in 1989, for example, these were British Airways' Speedbird, Hayes and Jarvis, Kuoni, Jetset, International Leisure Group's Select Holidays, Thomson Holidays, and the consolidators ABC, Allison Brothers and Holiday Planners. Contracts are made approximately six months prior to the flight, although other airlines make seat allocation contracts between six and twelve months prior to the flight. The allocation of seats between the tour operators and consolidators depends upon the number of seats sold during previous contractual periods. Seat prices are determined by bargaining between the airline, the tour operators and the consolidators and are lower for those operators or consolidators who have previously purchased and are likely to continue to purchase high numbers of seats. Prices also vary by season, higher prices being charged during periods of peak demand.

Short-term contracts provide all parties with the advantage of flexibility. Kenya Airways monitors the monthly seat sales by each tour operator and consolidator and can sometimes 'persuade' a tour operator or consolidator to return part of the allocation if seats are not selling well. Tour operators may request additional seats, but do not always obtain them. Five weeks before the flight, they inform Kenya Airways if they will fill their remaining seat allocation – the 'release-back' date being between four and six weeks for most airlines, but occasionally being as late as seven days before the flight. If they are unlikely to fill their allocation, they return seats to the airline, which then allocates them to consolidators to fill. Kenya Airways receives no compensation for unfilled seats. However, the airline can decide to alter the allocation of seats during the next round of contract negotiations, and has sometimes ceased dealing with a tour operator if it has sold few seats during the preceding period. In this case, the tour operator has to pay additional commission in order to obtain seats from other agents. The tour operators who won the original contracts did not, therefore, obtain a monopoly advantage. Information – for example, about changing levels of demand – is generally available and can be acted on during a contract period by returning seats to the airline if demand is lower than anticipated, as well as during the next round of contracts. This practice avoids the problem of moral hazard in the form of broken contracts; Kenya Airways and all six of the tour operators and consolidators dealing with the London–Nairobi route who were interviewed stated that, once made, contracts are not broken. The airline retains the expertise and control over the 'production' aspects of tourist transpotation, but short term contracts with tour operators and consolidators mean that foreign firms control most of the marketing of the transportation provided by Kenya Airways.

Contractual arrangements between tour operators and charter airlines differ from those between tour operators and scheduled airlines in that charter planes are leased approximately twelve months prior to departure, some 10–15 per cent of the seat price being paid as a deposit, with the remainder paid between two months and two weeks prior to the flight. The advantages to the tour operator include the availability of a direct flight to the destination and a seat price which may be half the price of a seat on a scheduled airline such as Kenya Airways. Kenya's response to the changing structure of air transport has been to attempt to compete in the charter market by providing charter flights on Kenya Flamingo Airways, a subsidiary of Kenya Airways.

Kenya is unusual as an African developing country in having its own charter airline, thus benefiting from tour operators' practice of chartering an entire plane and providing pre-flight payment in foreign currency. A degree of protection has been important in enabling Kenya Flamingo Airways to compete in the charter market, since foreign charter airlines have the advantage of attaining high load factors by meeting the seasonal demand for short haul flights to European destinations and meeting the demand for holidays in countries with warmer climates during the off-peak period for European tourism. Like Kenya Airways, Kenya Flamingo Airways must also overcome international tourists' general preference for travelling on their national airline or that of another industrialised nation. Furthermore, the demand for charter flights is subject to considerable instability of demand, which charter companies in developing countries may be less able to withstand. Kenya Flamingo Airways attempts to overcome this problem by prioritising the provision of flights to markets with relatively stable demand over time, and by making short-term contracts to charter planes from other airlines, with which it shares the revenue, thereby avoiding the high cost and risk of investment in additional capital equipment.

Hoteliers and international tour operators

Some of the problems resulting from the contractual relationships between Kenya's airline and major foreign tour operators are similar to those that arise from short term contracts made by tour operators with hoteliers. Foreign tour operators block-book rooms in a range of hotels by means of annual contracts. Because of the considerable bargaining power major tour operators are able to exert vis-a-vis the more fragmented hotel sector, they can obtain extremely low prices for accommodation. These may be up to 30 per cent less than the price, in Kenya shillings, charged by hoteliers to individual clients in mid-season and up to 50 per cent less in the low season, although discounts given by larger hotels may average 20 per cent during the year. The depreciation of the Kenya shilling has sometimes resulted in a real decrease in the foreign currency price paid by overseas tour operators.

The contractual relationships between tour operators and hoteliers are such that large tour operators, for example, Hayes and Jarvis or Kuoni, are not required to pay hoteliers a deposit on booking rooms and small tour operators pay only a small deposit. Payment for rooms occupied is usually made when the tour operators receive an invoice from the Kenyan hotelier, approximately one month after the departure of the tourists. Tour operators who do not wish to use their full room allocation make use of a 'release back' system, notifying hoteliers that they will not require the rooms. The release back date which applies to major tour operators is as late as seven to twenty-eight days before the arrival of tourists, although that for tour operators based in Kenya is of the order of thirty-five days. Kenyan hoteliers receive no compensation for unused rooms.

The response of hoteliers (and airlines) to the risk of unused capacity is to allocate more rooms (or seats) then they actually possess. Tour operators interviewed stated that this practice has resulted in over-booking problems when effective demand for rooms (or seats) has exceeded the supply, but that they tend to continue to make contracts with hotels which have a good location and provide good quality service. For their part, Kenyan hoteliers stated that contracts with foreign tour operators are a vital means of increasing their occupancy rates and did not appear to resent the contractual terms negotiated. Many hoteliers are highly dependent on bookings from overseas tour operators; for example, coastal hoteliers may fill 60–80 per cent of their rooms with tour operators' clients.

Foreign investment and management contracts

Short-term contracts constitute a particularly important form of contractual arrangement between tour operators and hoteliers. However, tour operators, as well as other foreign individuals and institutions, have also invested in hotels. Investment in hotels in developing countries can take the form of total ownership by foreigners or joint ventures between foreigners and locals, and developing countries have traditionally held widely differing attitudes towards direct foreign investment, particularly by multinational corporations. In Kenya, although foreign investment was welcomed for many years, majority ownership was supposed to remain in Kenyan hands, and the official policy is now one of Kenyanisation. By contrast, neighbouring Tanzania, with very similar climatic and geographical characteristics and natural tourism attractions, has traditionally been hostile to foreign investment. However, by the end of the 1980s, with the debt crisis and changes in political leadership, foreign investment was being encouraged.

Most large hotels in Kenya have a component of direct foreign investment, which has come from a variety of sources, particularly countries with traditional ties in East Africa – for example, the UK and Germany. There has been investment by such Swiss, UK, French, German and Italian tour operators as Kuoni, African Safari Club, Hayes and Jarvis, Universal Safari Tours, Polmans, TUI, Franco Rosso and I Grandi Viaggi, and airlines, including BA and Lufthansa, have had equity holdings in hotels such as the Serena chain. There has also been investment by such conglomerates as the UK Lonrho Corporation, with interests in the Norfolk Hotel, Mount Kenya Safari Club, the Ark, Aberdare Country Club, Ol Pejata Ranch, Mara Safari Club and Sweetwaters Tented Camp. The United Touring Company (UTC), of which the BET Traction Company is the parent, owns the large Block Hotel chain, has hotel management, touring, travel and 'sell-drive' divisions, and acts as local agent for major overseas tour operators.

Available evidence indicates that approximately 78 per cent of the major hotels in coastal areas, 67 per cent of hotels in Nairobi and 66 per cent of lodges in National Parks and Game Reserves have some foreign investment. The percentages of coastal and city hotels and wildlife lodges which are entirely foreign-owned are approximately 16, 17 and 11 per cent respectively. A detailed study of international hotels in the coastal areas of Malindi, Watamu and Lamu showed foreign ownership to be 60, 55 and 53 per cent of total ownership (Bachmann, 1988: 229–231). Joint ventures, involving investment by both overseas and Kenya investors, such as the examples cited above, have a range of advantages relative to complete foreign ownership of assets in a destination country. For example, joint ventures provide overseas investors with access to local capital, local knowledge of regulations and a benign attitude on the part of the Kenyan government. Partial or total ownership of a tourism enterprise by residents of the destination country may or may not be accompanied by control over its operation. The degree of local control varies both between different destination countries and between enterprises within a given country.

Direct foreign investment is not the only means by which Kenya has acquired specialist knowledge concerning the establishment and operation of hotels. Other forms of contractual arrangements include management contracts, in which a firm such as Inter-Continental takes over the management and operation of hotels, including such foreign-owned hotels as the Nairobi Safari Club. Management contracts have enabled Kenya to take advantage of international computer reservation systems and increase its knowledge of hotel management and marketing, which are particularly necessary for hotels located in the capital city, catering for business as well as holiday tourism. Of particular interest is the fact that the large domestic hotel chain, African Tours and Hotels, provides management services to other Kenyan hotels.

Examination of the hotel sector of the tourism industry thus demonstrates the complexity of the range of contractual arrangements that exist between local and foreign enterprises. Although foreign investment has been opposed by many developing countries on the grounds that it creates dependency, it has the advantages of facilitating the provision of scarce capital, increasing the supply of tourism accommodation and ensuring the maintenance of good quality facilities and services, thereby contributing to the maintenance of a high level of demand for tourism in the destination. It could be argued that Kenya's 'open door' policy towards foreign investment in tourism, combined with a policy favouring the employment of locals, has enabled the country to obtain a large supply of good quality hotels and has helped local residents to gain sufficient specialist knowledge to manage hotels efficiently. However, despite the transfer of such knowledge and the Kenyanisation policy, the majority of middle and upper category hotels are still joint ventures with foreigners. Countries such as Tanzania, which traditionally favoured domestic ownership and a limited number of management contracts rather than direct foreign investment, have been able to retain a considerable percentage of the profits of hotel operation within the country. Nevertheless, limitations on foreign participation in the tourism industry may have prevented such countries from acquiring the quantity and quality of hotels necessary for the attainment of a high level of tourism revenue which could, in turn, have contributed towards the goal of decreasing international indebtedness with its own specific form of foreign dependence.

Conclusions

Given the well known problems that developing countries face in establishing internationally competitive manufacturing sectors, some are attempting to use tourism as a means of economic development. At first sight, such a strategy would seem advantageous, since many appear to have a comparative advantage in tourism, possessing attractive environments, sunny climates and diverse cultures. However, tourism is a complex product of which developing countries only supply a part – primarily accommodation and some transportation, as well as goods and services supplied by such small-scale establishments as local shops and restaurants. Tourism retailing and much of the transportation used by tourists is supplied by firms based in industrialised countries. The costs and benefits that developing countries obtain from international tourism thus largely depend on the contractual relationships between firms located in destination countries and those in the industrialised countries, from which most tourists originate.

Contractual relationships between local and foreign tourism enterprises vary across different sectors of the industry. The predominant form of relationship between the airline sector and foreign tour operators, for example, is the short-term contract, whereas contractual arrangements involving the hotel sector, tour operators and other foreign firms include short-term contracts and other types of arrangements. The latter include management contractors, franchising agreements and common ownership of hotels, tour operators and, in some cases, airlines, mainly through joint ventures between local and overseas investors. In addition, different types of arrangement may overlap, so that a hotel located in a developing country may be owned by one foreign firm and managed by another.

The roles played by governments of developing countries in the tourism industry are important, and vary across different sectors of the industry. Within the hotel sector, the government may directly own a hotel chain and usually legislates with respect to foreign investment in that sector, thereby influencing the growth of accommodation supply and the terms on which it occurs. In addition, the government sometimes attempts to influence the terms of contracts made by locally based hoteliers and foreign firms, for example, by attempting to impose minimum prices for accommodation. However, such attempts are usually frustrated. Local hoteliers, faced with competition within the country and from other developing country destinations, are dependent on foreign tour operators, who control the overseas marketing of the accommodation.

The government usually plays a central role in the airline sector. Airlines based in developing countries are often owned and/or subsidised by the government which, with representatives of the airlines, negotiates route allocations, flight frequencies and related conditions with foreign airlines. Thus the commercial and negotiating ability of government and airline representatives is crucial to the maximisation of revenue for the national airline, and there may be a trade-off between protection of the national airline and its revenue and the growth of total tourism demand and the associated revenue accruing to the country. Even when countries do not supply international flights to and from the major tourist origin countries, the government's ability to negotiate favourable terms for access to the country by foreign airlines is a prerequisite for maintaining or increasing the destination country's returns from international tourism.

The operation of a scheduled air service is costly and the provision by developing countries of a charter airline may entail further investment involving a high level of risk. Competition between scheduled airlines of developing countries and foreign charter companies causes some tourists to switch from scheduled flights to charter services. In this context, a developing country may attempt to increase the load factor for its aircraft by negotiating pooling agreements with other developing nations, possibly giving some protection to the national airline. However, such pooling agreements are rare; political differences between developing nations are common, and countries whose airlines have already attained a competitive advantage do not participate. The provision of such ground facilities as aircraft maintenance or training of airline employees by one developing country for others in the region is more usual.

The different types of contractual arrangements between agents within the tourism industry have advantages and disadvantages. Short-term contracts between tour operators, airlines and hotels can be changed annually, in response to the constantly changing conditions which are a feature of international tourism. In practice, there is often flexibility concerning contract terms if demand is lower than anticipated within the contract period. However, airlines and hotels of developing countries bear the risk of unused seats and hotel rooms. They receive very little notice from tour operators of a lack of demand for airline seats or hotel rooms which have been block-booked and usually receive no compensation for unused capacity. Given the competition among different tourism destinations, a significant improvement in contractual terms is likely to require the co-operation of developing countries, at least at regional level.

Direct foreign investment in tourism enterprises in developing countries occurs in the form of complete ownership or joint ventures and, for the countries involved, can have several advantages. These include the provision of scarce capital, mobilisation of domestic savings and an increase in the supply of tourism establishments, and provide an incentive to foreign countries to maintain a higher level of demand, resulting in an increase in foreign exchange for the destination country. In addition, foreign investment may enable local firms to acquire specialist knowledge and provides the government with an additional source of tax revenue. However, the disadvantages of foreign investment may also be considerable, and include the cost of supplying expensive, often locally-financed infrastructure, expenditure on imported inputs, costly subsidies for investment, tax concessions, transfer pricing and the evasion of foreign exchange controls and tax payments. Dualism, dependence and other social and political costs can be of equal or more importance. Joint ventures, involving part ownership by residents of developing countries, may decrease social and political costs and have often been a more acceptable form of foreign involvement than complete foreign ownership. However, joint ventures require greater provision of capital by developing countries, and the transfer of the associated risk to them.

Management contracts and franchising agreements allow specialist knowledge to be transferred to the host country in the context of varying degrees of local ownership. Whereas management contracts with overseas companies involve foreign control of production, franchising agreements leave control mainly in local hands. In both cases, marketing is usually undertaken by foreign firms. Some potential disadvantages of direct foreign investment, such as expenditure on costly infrastructure and imported inputs, may also apply to management contracts and franchising arrangements. As Dunning and McQueen argue in their report for the United Nations Centre on Transnational Corporations (UNCTC, 1982), such contracts and agreements take a variety of forms, and the terms are sometimes unfavourable to developing country interests. Consequently, although contractual arrangements do not involve direct foreign investment and leave ownership with developing country residents, the latter may bear a higher level of risk while control is retained in foreign hands. This change in the distribution of risk is likely to be more of a problem for countries with infant tourism industries than for countries with well established tourism industries and stable or increasing levels of demand.

Different types of contractual relationships are therefore likely to be appropriate for countries whose tourism industries have been established for varying lengths of time, are subject to different demand conditions and have different objectives in terms of the desired combinations of local and foreign ownership, control, risk and returns. Further knowledge of the types of contractual relationship likely to be most appropriate in different contexts may be obtained from comparative studies of the interrelationships between foreign and national tourism industries for a range of developing countries. Such research could shed light on the extent to which existing contractual relationships are advantageous or disadvantageous to developing countries and the needs of the different groups within them, and the problems they would face in negotiating more beneficial arrangements. A particularly important item for the agenda is whether those developing country residents responsible for negotiating contracts with overseas enterprises are able or willing to alter prevailing contractual relationships.

5 Sex tourism in South-east Asia

C. Michael Hall

Introduction

There are undoubtedly few issues in the study of international tourism more emotive and prone to sensationalism than that of sex tourism. Sex tourism may be defined as tourism where the main purpose of motivation is to consummate commercial sexual relations (Graburn, 1983). Sex tourism is an overt component of the touristic attractiveness of several countries of South-east Asia, with the tourism flow from tourist generating regions being partially motivated by prostitution (O'Grady, 1981; Jurgensen, 1987). According to Gay (1985, p. 34), 'Between 70 and 80 per cent of male tourists who travel from Japan, the United States, Australia, and Western Europe to Asia do so solely for the purpose of sexual entertainment'. In many countries of the region, sex tourism is 'becoming one of the most pressing social issues . . . tourism prostitution in South-east Asia . . . has become a multinational sex industry' (Matsui, 1987a, p. 29).

Sex tourism emerged as a legitimate area of Third World tourism studies as academic perspectives shifted 'from a generally supportive and technocratic approach to tourism's role in development to some questioning of its overall efficacy and the prevalence of its negative social impacts' (Lea, 1981, p. 19). The study of sex tourism potentially unites many of the major research concerns of students of Third World tourism. According to Richter:

the most prominent tourist-related issues tend to be associated with the exploitation of women, the advantages and disadvantages of tourism as a means of economic development, and the problems poor nations have in retaining control over their own tourism destiny' (1989, p. 2).

Nevertheless, as the following discussion demonstrates, substantial methodological barriers remain in any study of this controversial area.

The study of sex tourism also has practical significance. The spread of disease, race relations issues, the connection of sex tourism to international crime, and the cultural impacts of tourism are all emerging as areas of concern for both government and industry. The appearance of new forms of sexually transmitted diseases, particularly AIDS (Acquired Immune Deficiency Syndrome), creates substantial problems for the tourism industry and for tourism generating and receiving countries, especially at those destinations where sexual attractions are a major determinant of tourism flow (Cockburn, 1988a, 1988b). Similarly, negative responses to international tourists by residents because of sex tourism may discourage international visitation to particular destinations and harm international relations.

Methodological issues

Prostitution may be defined as

a business transaction understood as such by the parties involved and in the nature of a short-term contract in which one or more people pay an agreed price to one or more other people for helping them attain sexual gratification by various methods (Perkins and Bennet, 1985, p. 4).

Given the often informal and illegal nature of the activity, and the general unwillingness of authorities even to acknowledge its existence, it is extremely difficult actually to measure the scale of prostitution, sex tourism and the accuracy of sex workers' claims. Correspondingly, there is a general lack of systematic research on men and women employed in such marginal occupations as prostitutes, sauna bath attendants and hospitality girls. Furthermore, 'the widespread disdain for prostitutes has undoubtedly hindered the ability of many to see or inquire about them, or to receive accurate accounts from informants' (Burnley and Symanski, 1981, p. 239).

There are several major forms of prostitution. The first involves the casual prostitute or freelancer, who moves in and out of prostitution according to financial need. In this situation, prostitution may be regarded as incompletely commercialised and 'ridden with ambiguities' (Cohen, 1982b, p. 411). The second, and more formalised, form of prostitution involves call girls and boys who operate through intermediaries, brothel workers, and sex workers who operate out of clubs. Since prostitution is generally illegal, prostitutes are often forced to use such entertainment establishments as bars in order to ply their trade with the blessing of authorities. Similarly, brothels are often regarded as a mechanism for the containment of prostitution. The third form of prostitution is that of bonded prostitutes, who have often been sold in order to pay debts or reduce loans. In many cases, this type of prostitution is a form of slavery; unlike the previous two forms, it has not been entered into through an act of will. Prostitution is usually spatially and economically differentiated between locals and tourists, a point often forgotten by many researchers who tend to blame all prostitution on tourism. Sex tourism also occurs in two different forms, a casual type in which travellers arrange for their own sexual services, and a packaged form, in which services have been pre-booked with hotels and agencies.

Discussions on the relationship between tourism and prostitution are frequently speculative (Mathieson and Wall, 1982). Studies of sex tourism often become acts of moralising or sensationalising and frequently suffer from the cultural blindness and sexual taboos that affect attitudes towards prostitution (Ericsson, 1980). Leaving aside ethical questions, it should be recognised that prostitution may potentially have positive economic effects. For instance, in the case of Fiji in the early 1970s, Naibavu and Schutz (1974, p. 6) argued:

Prostitution is a fully localised industry which gives employment to unskilled female workers for most of whom no other jobs are available. It requires no investment of foreign capital, yet it brings in large amounts of foreign exchange with a minimum of leakage back overseas.

However, an oversimplified utilitarian justification for prostitution may obscure the gender and class interests associated with prostitution (Rosen, 1982). While Hawkesworth (1984), pp. 88, 85, 89) went so far as to argue that when the

facile legitimations of functionalist arguments . . . raise the spectre of social benefit, they stimulate a justificatory response which tends to minimise the costs of prostitution [and] 'consists of the betrayal of human dignity'.

According to such feminist researchers as Hawkesworth (1984) and Rogers (1989), prostitution is a direct result of the patriarchal structure of society. Barry (in ISIS, 1984, p. 4) argued that:

acceptance of prostitution as an inevitable social institution is lodged in the assumption that sex is a male right. . . . Viewing prostitution as woman's choice is a way to *reduce all women to the lowest and most contemptible status of women* in any male dominated society.

Therefore, from a feminist perspective, the study of sex tourism encapsulates many of the problems which are fundamental to women and development:

Prostitution is both an indication of an unjust social order and an institution that economically exploits women. But when economic power is defined as the causal variable, the sex dimensions of power usually remain unidentified and unchallenged' (Barry, 1984, p. 9).

The economic and social problems of Asian women tend to be viewed by Western feminists as stemming from the patriachal nature of local cultures. However, Ong (1985, p. 2) argued that 'the new commerce in the labor-power and bodies of Asian women, is more rooted in corporate strategies of profit-maximisation than in the persistence of indigenous values'. From the perspective of political economy, sex tourism may be regarded as a result of shifts in the international division of labour and the spread of consumerism to the Third World. Several commentators have emphasised the need to examine the nature of capital and tourism movements between the core and periphery of the tourism system and the resultant impacts on the host society (Turner, 1976; Hoivik and Heiberg, 1980; Britton, 1982; Richter and Richter, 1985).

Tourism is not, as is often claimed, a spontaneous phenomenon. It does not occur in a disorderly way, as a result of uncontrollable demand. It is a product of will. It unfolds under the impetus of a powerful tourist promotion mechanism, supported at the highest level (Lanfant, 1980, p. 15).

Therefore, it is the movement of capital and tourists that will determine the economic, social and environmental impacts of tourism on the host region.

Third World sex tourism

The relationship between tourism and prostitution has come to be regarded as particularly strong in the Third World (de Kadt, 1979; O'Grady, 1981). A primary attraction is the important cost differential that exists in the provision of both tourist and sexual services in the Third World and in the industrialised world. This differential, with the attraction of the exotic, provides a drawcard to sex tourists in a large number of Third World destinations and has been reported in Africa

(Harrell-Bond, 1978; Crush and Wellings, 1983), Latin America (Roebuck and McNamara, 1973), and the Caribbean (Matthews, 1978; Bélisle and Hoy, 1980; Ennew, 1986). In the case of South-east Asia, the differential has also served to act as an incentive for the use of South-east Asian women in Japanese and European brothels. According to Matsui (1987a), '100,000 women per year are arriving from the Philippines, Thailand, South Korea and Taiwan to support the Japanese sex industry'.

In Asia, despite strict Islamic laws forbidding prostitution, such countries as Bangladesh and Pakistan have major red light districts. Trafficking in women has become a serious social problem in Nepal where, because of the extreme marginality of much of the country, large numbers of women are being sent to India. Matsui (1987a) states that approximately 50,000 Nepali women are being exploited in Bombay's Falkland Avenue and other brothel districts. However, while tourists and visiting businessmen do frequent these districts, the indigenous form of prostitution has long been established. As in the case of Sri Lanka, there is perhaps some evidence that the demonstration effect of tourism may lead some men and women into prostitution (Ahmed, 1986). Similarly, research by D. Jones (1986) illustrates that the customers of Balinese brothels were mainly Balinese and other Indonesians. Prostitution for overseas tourists generally occurred on the beach or was provided by call-girls on a charter basis (similar to Thailand). Brothel prostitution and chartering employed very few local girls. Outdoor soliciting employed few local girls on a full-time basis, but did attract local part-timers, often of school age. Therefore, in the case of Bali, prostitution was not caused by tourism, but had changed 'its form in some senses in response to tourist demand' (Jones, D., 1986, p. 247).

Despite Islamic laws prohibiting prostitution, tourism prostitution also exists in Malaysia, particularly Penang and Kuala Lumpur. Hong (1985) argued that sex tourism to Malaysia would grow in relation to the demands of the increasing number of Japanese tourists. However, she went on to note that the rate of STD infections was also increasing, with the tourist destination of Penang having the highest rate of infection. The growth of prostitution in Malaysia is perhaps associated with the perception among many Westerners that subservient females and free sex are more readily available in South-east Asia and the Pacific than other regions (Thitsa, 1980). Indeed, advertising for many of the Asian and Pacific nations openly plays on the notion of the 'exotic orient', South Sea romanticism and the image of a 'lost paradise' which has existed since the seventeenth and eighteenth centuries (Lea, 1988). For instance, Davidson (1985, p. 18) reported a Frankfurt advertisement that stated, 'Asian women are without desire for emancipation, but full of warm sensuality and the softness of velvet'.

In South-east Asia, prostitution clearly existed before the arrival of tourists. One of the ironies of the current Japanese involvement in sex tourism is that the Japanese used to export their own prostitutes, *Kara-Yuki San*, to their colonies. These bonded Japanese women were sent abroad to serve as prostitutes in ports frequented by Japanese merchants and soldiers. However, in the 1920s the Japanese Government issued the Overseas Prostitution Prohibition Order and, in 1958, legal prostitution in Japan was prohibited. As a consequence, women from the former colonies 'are now imported into Japan as prostitutes' (Graburn, 1983, p. 440). The fast-developing Japanese tourist industry has allowed the Japanese Mafia, the Yakusa, to become well established in Bangkok, Seoul, Hong Kong and Hawaii, with the result that 'almost the whole of Japan's current sex scene is Yakusa controlled, if not directly, then by minor linkage' (Lamont-Brown, 1982, p. 335).

The post-war development of the new international division of labour has meant radical restructuring of the traditional economies of the South-east Asian region. The influx of rural women to urban centres to support village families has led to the marginalisation of female participation in the labour market. In the light manufacturing industries of the electronics revolution and in the sex industries, women have been integrated into the global economy. Indeed, Ong (1985) argued that women who have lost jobs in the industrialised sector have been forced to seek work in hotels and brothels. Nevertheless, while the earning power of a prostitute may be relatively high for a short period of time and economically lucrative 'compared to other types of occupation in the industrial or services sector' (Truong, 1983, p. 543), the costs are also extremely high. In general, health services are of a poor standard and there is a lack of protective legislation for sex workers. Therefore, the prostitute's economic gains need to be weighed 'against the psychological and social damage which their work and life style inflict upon them'(Cohen, 1983, p. 424).

Sex tourism might be regarded as a series of linkages involving a 'legally marginalized form of commoditization (sexual services) within a national industry (entertainment), essentially dependent on, but with a dynamic function in, an international industry (travel)' (Truong, 1983, p. 544). In South-east Asia, the institutionalisation of sex tourism commenced with the prostitution associated with American military bases and Japanese colonialism and has now become transformed through the internationalisation of the regional economies into a major item of systematised foreign trade. Technically, prostitution is illegal in many South-east Asian countries, but the law is poorly enforced. The prevailing sentiment appears to be, 'that what a tourist does in the hotel room, is none of the authorities business' (Senftleben, 1986, p. 22), particularly when it results in economic returns.

The evolution of sex tourism in South-east Asia

As the following case studies of Korea, Philippines, Taiwan and Thailand indicate, sex tourism in South-east Asian demonstrates several characteristics. The evolution of sex tourism in the region has gone through four distinct stages. The first stage is that of indigenous prostitution, in which women have been subjected to concubinage and bonded prostitution within the patriachal nature of the majority of Asian societies.

The second stage is that of economic colonialism and militarisation, where prostitution is a formalised mechanism of dominance and a means of meeting the sexual needs of occupation forces (primarily American and Japanese). In this stage, the occupied culture's general acceptance of various forms of prostitution has been used as a justification for economic or military enforced prostitution. In addition, this stage commences the economic dependency of host societies on the selling of sexual services as a means of economic development.

The third stage is marked by the substitution of international tourists for occupation forces. Following periods of occupation and the restructuring of traditional economies within the post-war international economic order, sex tourism becomes a formalised mechanism for obtaining foreign exchange and furthering national development. A common element in this stage is the authoritarian nature of governments during periods in which sex tourism has been promoted. It is possible that the denial of individual rights by authoritarian regimes may encourage the perspective that individuals are sexual commodities to be utilised for advancing the national economic good.

The fourth, and current, stage for most of the nations of the region is that of rapid economic development. In this stage, many of the primary goals of economic development have been attained or are at least within sight. However, it is as yet unknown whether increased standards of living will reduce dependency on sex tourism or whether the growth of consumerism will become a new factor in the maintenance of the sex tourism industry. In addition, the powerful forces that created the economic, political and ideological framework within which sex tourism operates may take many years to dismantle.

Korea: Kisaeng tourism

Kisaeng originally referred to women who were hired as companions and served a similar social function to the geisha in Japan. However, the word is now synonymous with prostitution. A survey of *kisaeng* girls by Korea Church Women United estimated that 'no less than 100,000' tourist service girls were operating in 1978 (1983, p. 2). However, this figure excluded a large number of unregistered sex workers. For instance, Gay (1985) estimated that some 260,000 prostitutes were operating in South Korea.

From September, 1973, after the severing of diplomatic ties with Taiwan, there was a massive increase in Japanese tourism to South Korea. A major reason for Japanese men to visit South Korea was the *kisaeng* party (ISIS, 1979). In 1983, some twenty-seven *kisaeng* houses existed in South Korea, with fourteen operating in Seoul, seven in Pusan, two in Cheju and the four in Kyongju. A survey of the four cities indicated that many *kisaeng* workers came from economically marginal rural areas (Korea Church Women United, 1983). South Korean women have also assumed the role of field wives, forming steady relationships with either a few men or with one patron. The field wife function is often associated with Japanese companies with branches in Korea and, as in the case of the pre-war *Kara-Yuki San*, is regarded as an integral component of Japanese business overseas. Similarly, the interrelationship of the Korean and Japanese economies is reflected in the export of *kisaeng* to Japan (Korea Church Women United, 1983).

Through the 1970s and 1980s, the authoritarian nature of successive South Korean governments and the limitation of individual freedoms played a major role in the commoditisation of people through *kisaeng* tourism. Prospective *kisaeng* endured lectures by male university professors on the crucial role of tourism in the South Korean economy before obtaining their prostitution licences. Even more telling is the attitude of the South Korean Minister for Education, who stated that 'the sincerity of girls who have contributed with their cunts to their fatherland's economic development is indeed praiseworthy' (Witness 2, 1976 International Tribunal on Crimes against Women, 1976, p. 178 in Symanski 1981, p. 99). *Kisaeng* girls were required to obtain identification cards from authorities in order to enter hotels. The orientation programme was regarded as similar to that given by the Japanese to the 100,000 Korean women who were forced to serve in the 'women's volunteer corps' as prostitutes to the Japanese troops during the Second World War (Yoyori, 1977, Matsui, 1987b). According to Korea Church Women United (1983, p. 27), 'The only difference we can find . . . is the circumstances under which they are conducted – the one during the Japanese invasion days was in a war effort; the other, currently in a sovereign state'.

As South Korea has modernised and become a substantial economic force in the Pacific Rim region, the Korean Government has increasingly promoted cultural and natural attractions to visitors. In particular, the 1988 Seoul Olympic Games witnessed the imposition of a facade of respectability on the face of Korean tourism. However, the extent to which the facade will become a reality remains unknown.

The Philippines

Hundreds of thousands of women have collectively become the third largest source of foreign exchange for the Philippines (Philippine Women's Research Collective, 1985, p. 8). The scale of sex tourism in the Philippines is enormous. In the early 1980s, it was estimated that between 70,000 and 100,000 hospitality girls were working in Manila (Wihtol, 1982), with approximately 200,000–300,000 over the country as a whole (Gay, 1985). In addition, child prostitution has become strongly linked with the Philippines and is associated with areas that have both a strong tourism and military presence (Rogers, 1989). The Philippine Women's Research Collective (1985), estimated that there were 3,000 child prostitutes in Metro Manila alone.

Militarisation continues to play a major role in the sex industry. The 12,000 registered and 8,000 unregistered hostesses in Olongapo City provide the major source of sexual entertainment for United States military personnel based at Subic Naval Base and Clark Air Force Base. The city has become economically dependent on the military presence and a number of city ordinances have ensured that prostitution has become legitimised, regulated and protected by the state. The city government, for example, maintains and operates a social hygiene clinic which certifies that hospitality workers are free from communicable diseases. In addition, the city enforces an anti-street walking ordinance which ensures that the soliciting of customers can only occur inside clubs, thereby assuring club owners of fees derived by the provision of sexual services (Claire and Cottingham, 1982, p. 209).

Wihtol's (1982) study of the socio–economic circumstances and working conditions of girls in the ago-go bars in the tourist nightlife belt of Ermita, Manila, illustrated the relationship of the sex industry to rural poverty. Manila hospitality girls, mainly from relatively low-income rural families in the Eastern Visayas, Central Luzon and Bicol regions, migrated for economic, educational and employment-related reasons. Their income is derived from working at the bar and direct payment from customers for sexual relations, with many girls using almost a quarter of their income to support family members in Manila or sending remittances to their home province (Philippine Women's Research Collective, 1985). However, unless appropriate mechanisms of economic development can be promoted in the rural provinces, typhoons, militarisation and the government's neglect of basic rural services will ensure that rural families continue to lead a marginal existence.

The Marcos years left the Philippines economically dependent on foreign capital and foreign markets. Under martial law, imposed by Marcos in 1972, sex tourism became a form of export for much-needed foreign exchange, and many hotels at which prostitution occurred were owned by the ruling élite. For instance, a tourism poster was distributed featuring the Filipina Miss Universe and the slogan 'There's more where she comes from' (Philippine Women's Research Collective 1985, p. 1). However, the transition from 'smiling martial law' under Marcos to 'smiling people power' under Aquino has not substantially affected the state of the Filipino sex industry (Center for Solidarity Tourism, 1989). As in Korea, Filipino women are trafficked overseas as entertainers or are encouraged to become mail-order brides for foreigners. The trafficking of Filipino women to Japan is highly organised with the Japanese Mafia, the Yakusa syndicate, reportedly being heavily involved with Filipino prostitution in Japan (Philippine Women's Research Collective, 1985).

Women's groups have played an important role in highlighting the impact of institutionalised prostitution on the Philippines and have assisted in legislative action on child and mail-bride prostitution. However, unless laws can be implemented, they will make little difference to the day-to-day reality of sex workers. For instance, while Filipino law limits foreign ownership of bars, many bars are foreign-owned through a Filipino wife or girl friend. Moreover, the urgent need for foreign exchange by the Filipino government means that tourism development will continue to be encouraged, regardless of who holds power. Therefore, as Wihtol (1982, p. 39) commented:

Any major change in the role at present played by the hospitality industry will depend on national policies to reduce the inequality of income distribution in general, and to promote more equitable development between rural and urban areas, and particularly on policies to increase employment opportunities in rural areas and in urban areas other than Metropolitan Manila.

Taiwan

As in other South-east Asian nations, prostitutes were accepted within traditional Chinese society provided they were discreet in their activities. From the Korean War until the end of the Vietnam War, the American presence in Taiwan provided a major stimulus for visitor-oriented prostitution, which was centred on Shuang Cheng Street in Taipai. However, the normalisation of United States' relations with mainland China and the American defeat in Vietnam led to a decline in Taipai's nightlife, with American servicemen replaced by Japanese male visitors. Similarly, the Japanese recognition of mainland China in 1973 created a shift in sex tourism from Taiwan to South Korea.

The growth in Japanese sex tourism to Taiwan has been associated with attempts to control prostitution in Japan. However, as Senftleben (1986) has reported, Japan has been involved in Taiwanese prostitution since the early eighteenth century. Hot spring resorts first developed over the period 1895 to 1945, the Japanese colonial era. After the Second World War, the resort of Peitou achieved rapid development, and prostitution was legal until 1979. During this time, Peitou was a favoured rest and recreation area for American forces and the Taiwanese élite. However, although prostitution continues 'underground', the resort is returning to the potential health benefits of its hot springs as the mainstay of its attractiveness (Senftleben 1986).

As in the Philippines, there is an interrelationship between hotels and call girls, with the hotel management often profiting from sexual services. The borderline nature of prostitution is seen in *kan ching* activity, where the relationship is considered to be of a higher level than that of prostitute and client because the customer will provide expensive gifts and/or pay living expenses for the bar girl (Senftleben, 1986). The majority of prostitutes are not Han Chinese; they come from the island's aboriginal population, which is Polynesian–Malayan in origin and live in the marginal rural areas. Nevertheless, although Taiwan is increasingly prosperous and industrialised, Matsui (1987a, p. 32) argues that prostitution will continue, less for sheer economic necessity than for more materialistic reasons, as Taiwan becomes increasingly incorporated into the international capitalist economic order.

Thailand

Prostitution and concubinage have long been accepted elements of Thai society. Nevertheless, considerable controversy has surrounded the status of women in Thailand (Truong, 1983; Davidson, 1985). Patriachal Buddhist culture has allowed concubinage and polygamy to be legitimised and has cast a ready-made framework within which sex tourism can occur. 'The result was an erotic industry promoted by a government hungry for foreign exchange and built upon the solid base of a hundred years of institutionalized prostitution' (O'Malley, 1988, p. 107). In 1957, there were 20,000 prostitutes, by 1964 there were 400,000, and by the early 1980s there were between 500,000 and a million (Phongpaichit, 1982; Taylor, 1984; Hong, 1985). However, while the numbers are large, not all prostitutes cater to sex tourists. Nevertheless, Rogers (1989, p. 21) argued that tourism 'induces the demand for prostitutes, creates the available supply and hence makes a vicious cycle'.

The north-east and northern provinces of Thailand are sources of many prostitutes. Their economic marginality forces many rural households to depend on remittances provided by migrant girls (Phongpaichit, 1981, 1982). However, the northern provinces remain structurally disadvantaged within the Thai economy (O'Malley, 1988) and, given the lack of economic development in the north, the supply of workers for the sex industry in the nation's urban and industrial centres seems assured. 'The rapid and very uneven development of Thailand has closely integrated militarization, tourism, and industrialization as institutionalized systems of female exploitation' (Ong, 1985).

The number of Thai women involved in sex industry activities outside of Thailand is substantial, although exact numbers are difficult to ascertain. Tourists visiting Thailand may obtain 'rented wives' (*mia chao*) who often return to tourist-generating regions, where they may suffer linguistic and social isolation while often being forced to perform sexual services. From a series of case studies of Thai women working as prostitutes in Europe, Sereewat (1983) concluded that the majority had already been working in the sex industry in Thailand, motivated mainly by the need to provide family support, and with a background of failed marriages and a lack of self-esteem. However, their reasons for travelling to Europe need to be seen within the social and structural context of sex tourism and prostitution in Thailand rather than as a form of escapism.

The Thai Government places great emphasis on the promotion of tourism to Thailand and has done little to jeopardise the country's sex trade (Mingmongkol, 1981; Barang, 1988). For instance, Thailand's Vice Premier informed provincial governors that sexual entertainment of tourists was necessary for the creation of jobs (Gay, 1985). The 1960 Prostitution Act makes prostitution illegal, but the registration of brothels and massage parlours as eating houses and the payment of protection money to government officials and the police mean that the law is rarely enforced. Nevertheless, AIDS has become a major source of concern to the Thai government. Early in 1988, government screening revealed that 194 people were HIV positive. One year later, the figure had grown to 3,138 people (*Bangkok Post*, 10 February, 1989). Although the spread of AIDS in Thailand has been essentially drug-related, the sex tourism industry has been recognised as a potential channel of transmission from the drug and homosexual population to the wider heterosexual community (Cohen, 1988b). A study by the United Nations Fund for Population Activities found that of a sample of 1,000 prostitutes, a quarter were regular drug users (Gay, 1985). Indeed, despite attempts by the Thai health authorities to encourage safe sex practices, a survey published in November, 1988, found that '77 per cent of addicts shared needles, only six per cent of prostitute's customers were using condoms, and 70 per cent of homosexuals still engaged in anal and oral sex, more than half of them with foreigners' (*Bangkok Post*, 10 February, 1989).

Sex tourism represents a major dilemma for the Thai authorities. Although it continues to be a major attraction, and hence a source of foreign currency, they are increasingly worried by Thailand's reputation as the sex capital of Asia. Nevertheless, as long as the gap between city and rural areas continues to widen and real living standards in the country remain low, Thailand's sex industry will thrive. As Richter (1989, p. 101) observed, 'The tragedy of Thai tourism is that one tawdry segment has been allowed to eclipse so much that is elegant, refined, and exquisite about Thailand'.

Australia and sex tourism[1]

Australia has been a sex tourist-generating region to South-east Asia since the time of the Vietnam war and Australians have become heavily involved in the ownership of brothels and nightclubs and in the organisation of sex tours, particularly to the Philippines. Probably the most conspicuous aspect of Australian sex tourism is the bar names, such as Ned Kelly and Waltzing Matilda. Although only Filipinos can hold the permit for a bar and there must be at least 60 per cent Filipino ownership, Australian criminal elements appear to have made substantial investments in the sex industry, with Angeles City being a major area of interest. Bacon (1987, p. 21) reported that 'Australians now have a financial interest in more than 60 per cent of the 500 bars and 7,000 prostitutes around the base, although not one Australian name appears in the local register'.

In the early 1980s, Australia became one of the main destinations for Filipino mail-order brides. In 1976, 1,596 Filipino women were married to Australians, a figure that rose to 4,470 in 1981. Promoted as 'meek, docile, submissive, home oriented and hav[ing] tremendous capacities in bed', Filipino women have been sought by many Australian males through pen-pal clubs and mail order bride businesses (Philippine Women's Research Collective, 1985, p. 19). The increase in mail order brides and Filipino marriages has led to considerable controversy over the motivations and status of Filipino women going to Australia, and the subsequent stability of their marriage (Chuah et al., 1987). Opposition to marriages occurred because they were arranged and because of the stereotyped view of Asian women as subservient that developed through the debate: 'many wanted Asian wives because they were fed up with the demands Australian women make and their unfaithfulness' (Brown, 1980, p. 10). Undoubtedly, the perception of Filipino women as subservient has substantially contributed to the demand for Filipino brides from Australian males (Shoesmith, 1981). However, while the economic and cultural position of women in Filipino society is an import 'supply' factor, other considerations, such as the availability of single Australian males, contributed to the conditions that prompted the growth in arranged marriages.

A further dimension of Australia's involvement in sex tourism has been provided by the rapid growth of inbound tourism to Australia in the 1980s, particularly from Japan. Such destinations as the Gold Coast have witnessed an increase in the amount of tourist-oriented prostitution and Asian girls have often been bought into the country to cater for both Australian and Japanese tourists. As M. Jones (1986, p. 111) contended:

Modern tourism requires a well-regulated supply of women and the pragmatic Queensland industry knows that these services must be provided, especially if the Coast is to compete with Asia'.

Jones' comments were somewhat prophetic and, in 1989, the Gold Coast Chamber of Commerce advocated the legislation and licensing of prostitution in order to attract tourists (Hall, forthcoming). Prostitution tourism is an integral part of the tourist product of Australian attractions and events (Hall, 1989a). As in South-east Asia, Australian governments are seeking the tourist dollar to promote economic development and overcome balance-of-payments problems. In this climate it would seem unlikely that the contributions of the sex industry to tourism will be disturbed.

Conclusion

Tourism-oriented prostitution has become an integral part of the economic base in several regions of South-east Asia. Sex tourism has resulted in people being regarded as commodities. The economic reliance of developing nations on tourism has led to dependence on source areas, incorporated them into the demand structures of the West and Japan, and has impeded the pursuit of autocentric development (Schürmann, 1981). The 'tourist first' attitude of many governments and their advisors has transformed the processes of development to place economic 'needs' well ahead of those social concerns, for example, rural–urban migration, which feed into tourism. As Awanohara (1975, p. 6) commented, 'Japanese travel agents have organised these trips to Asia and not to other countries only because Asian countries allow it. They need the foreign exchange'.

Fish (1984a, 1984b) has argued that a more effective mechanism of controlling sex sales to tourists would place a heavier proportion of the costs of law enforcement and sanctions on the hotels, operators and their customers. However, such an approach, built on assumptions of schedules of the elasticity of demand, fails to recognise the broader economic and socio-cultural context within which sex tourism occurs. Such short-term measures as counselling may be useful, but sex tourism demands long-term solutions (Fernand-Laurent, 1985). Banning prostitution may be counterproductive and only create even greater hardship for those who engage in it. 'Legislation to protect prostitutes, and to improve their working conditions and occupational health, is preferable to legislation that would deprive them of their livelihood' (Truong, 1983, p. 534).

The sexual relationship between prostitute and client is a mirror image of the dependency of South-east Asian nations on the developed world. The institutionalised exploitation of women within patriarchal societies of South-east Asia has been extended and systematised by the unequal power relationship that exists between genders and between host and advanced capitalist societies (Ong, 1985). Demonstrations and rallies against sex tourism are likely to lead to only superficial changes in the sex industry. Profound change can occur only with the removal of the US military presence, a transformation of gender relations, and an economic development strategy that places the host first and lessens the demand for foreign exchange.

Note

1.   When undertaking the research and writing of this chapter it was originally intended to focus largely on the interaction between Australia and South-east Asia. However, because of the nature of Australia's libel laws this section has had to be severely curtailed.

6 Japan and South-east Asia: the international division of labour and leisure

Vera Mackie

Introduction

Tourism is expected to grow rapidly in Asia in the 1990s. In addition to Japan's economic dominance in the region, such nations as Hong Kong, Taiwan, South Korea, Malaysia and Singapore have recently shown high figures of economic growth, relative to the more developed economies. Recent research in South-east Asia has also highlighted the growth of the middle classes, and they can be expected to join the ranks of travellers within the region.

Despite this overall growth, however, there are several reasons why the Japanese presence has come to dominate the tourist industry in South-east Asia. First, the Japanese are now the largest single nationality group of visitors in many countries, and are often the biggest spenders. Secondly, an increasing proportion of Japanese foreign investment is now directed at real estate and resort development rather than manufacturing and, finally, Japan is one of the largest donors of official development assistance (ODA), with an increasing amount of foreign aid being directed at tourism-related projects.

For many nations in South-east Asia, the tourist industry involves a series of unequal relationships: inequality between tourists and the workers who look after their needs, between investors and the targets of their investment, and between donors and recipients in ODA programmes. The relationship between Japan and selected South-east Asian nations can thus be seen as a case study in the social, economic and environmental effects of tourism development carried out in the context of such unequal relations.

The growth of tourism in Japan

In order to understand the recent growth in international travel by the Japanese, it is first necessary to survey recent developments within Japan. At first glance, the increase in both domestic and international tourism simply seems a matter of increasing affluence, but the role of government and private capital in promoting tourism and resort development must also be considered.

After the rise in the value of the yen in 1985, Japan was under increasing pressure to rectify its trade imbalance with the United States and other countries. Published in April, 1986, the Maekawa Report was the response of the Nakasone cabinet to international concern about Japan's economic dominance. It described measures aimed at improving Japan's trade balance by transforming its domestic industrial structure and stimulating domestic demand. The process included attempts to stimulate the construction of domestic infrastructure projects and consumer spending on imports (Fujiwara, 1991, p. 37).

In the industrial restructuring, several companies formerly involved in heavy industry turned their attention to leisure-related projects. This was a logical development of a shift from manufacturing to 'high tech' and service industries. The emphasis on leisure development was also welcomed by rural areas suffering from agricultural stagnation and a drain of population to urban centres. There was thus a coalescence of international and domestic concerns.

The government contributed to this process by passing the Comprehensive Resort Region Provision Law (Sōgō Hoyō Chiiki Seibi Hō), commonly abbreviated as the Resort Act, in 1987. The stated aims of the Act involved the promotion of effective use of leisure time, the stimulation of domestic demand, and relief for heavy industries suffering from recession. By the end of 1989, so many towns, prefectures and villages were competing for the designation of 'resort area' that 19.2 per cent of the land area of Japan was involved, with 646 projects under way and 205 more at the planning stage. A total of 17.25 million hectares of Japan's land were to be devoted to resort development, outstripping the 5.5 million hectares devoted to agriculture (McCormack, 1991a, p. 123). By early 1991, forty of Japan's forty-seven prefectures had submitted plans for resort developments and twenty-seven prefectural master plans had received approval to commence construction (Fujiwara, 1991, p. 39).

Because many of the designated resort areas have hitherto been undeveloped, the provision of facilities and infrastructure is expensive and private developers have been reluctant to become involved. However, according to the Act, both national and local government may provide preferential taxation measures and infrastructural support for private businesses embarking on construction projects in resort areas.

The major beneficiaries of the new emphasis on resort developments have been companies involved in the construction of hotels, resort facilities and golf courses. As such development favours large-scale projects carried out by major construction companies, real estate developers, trading companies, banks and other financial institutions, the benefits to local small- and medium-scale businesses may be questionable (Fujiwara, 1991, p. 38). Most proposed projects have required large capital investment and golf courses, marinas and ski resorts have been especially popular. Inoue cites examples of major shipbuilders turning to the construction of luxury liners and promoting marine resorts, and steel companies turning idle yards into amusement parks. The buzz phrase for such developments is 'third sector development', denoting collaboration between local government and private capital (Inoue, 1991, p. 7).

However, since the promulgation of the Resort Act there has been criticism from several fronts as the promised benefits of resort developments failed to materialise. Many proposals were ill-conceived and local communities and outside developers often conflicted over issues of control. There was dissent within local communities over whether or not projects should be implemented (Inoue, 1991, p. 8) and citizens' and residents' groups opposed them on environmental grounds. Many developments utilised areas previously set aside as National Parks and the environmental consequences of golf courses are frightening (*AMPO*, 1991).

While recognising criticisms of the implementation of the Resort Act, this is not to deny the need for improved leisure facilities in Japan. However, the real problem is less the lack of tourist infrastructure but more the poor employment conditions of

Japanese workers, who have limited opportunities to enjoy existing resort facilities. Despite official campaigns to increase the number of official holidays (OECD, 1989, p. 61), they still work longer hours than their counterparts in most OECD countries – around 2,100 hours a year, which is at least 200 hours more than in comparable nations (McCormack, 1991a, p. 122). Indeed, many prefer to keep their annual leave for such eventualities as sickness, and the question of paid annual leave is irrelevant to casual and temporary workers.

The Japanese as international tourists

The role of the State

As well as promoting tourism within Japan, the Ministry of Transport also encourages the Japanese to travel overseas as a way of alleviating trade friction with neighbouring countries. The increase in foreign travel is relatively recent, but over the last five years it has been spectacular. In post-war Japan, overseas travel was initially restricted, a situation eased only in 1964. In 1965, only 159,000 Japanese tourists travelled overseas, compared with 369,000 foreign visitors to Japan. However, after the introduction of jumbo jets in 1970, overseas travel from Japan increased and, by 1971, Japanese travelling overseas outnumbered visitors to Japan, reaching 2,289,000 in 1973. In 1985, after the rise in value of the yen, overseas travel again showed significant growth, reaching 5,516,000 in 1986 (Inoue, 1991, p. 4).

The focus of the Ministry of Transport's promotion of overseas travel, conceived as a way of improving the foreign trade imbalance, was the 'Ten Million Plan'. Launched in 1987, it aimed to send ten million Japanese tourists abroad every year by 1991. Estimates suggest that this target was reached by 1990 (Noda, 1991, p. 34).

Such growth has occurred in a general context of tourism expansion throughout the region. By 1990, Japanese tourists were the largest single nationality group of visitors in several Asian countries, as in Singapore, where 19 per cent of overseas visitors were Japanese, Hong Kong (22 per cent), South Korea and Taiwan. Japanese visitors were also the biggest spenders in Singapore and other regions (Goldstein, 1991, p. 44).

Measures to promote international tourism include publicity campaigns to encourage the Japanese to take longer holidays and to travel overseas. In addition, since 1987 the government has raised the tax exemption limit for souvenirs from 100,000 yen to 200,000 yen and extended companies' tax exemption for recreational travel from two to three nights (OECD, 1989, p. 61). Furthermore, the Overseas Economic Co-operation Fund (OECF) and the Japan International Co-operation Association (JICA) have been involved in projects aimed at the 'development of international resorts in developing countries' (Noda, 1991, p. 34). The JICA has participated in development research and technical co-operation programmes, while the OECF has given yen loans for the expansion of tourism-related infrastructures (Noda, 1991, p. 34).

Japan is now a major donor of official development assistance (ODA), a role in which, in recent years, it has overtaken the United States. Its official aid policies have been discussed elsewhere (in English, cf. Rix, 1990 and AMPO, 1990; in Japanese, cf. Asahi Shinbun, 1985; Iida, 1974; Suzuki, 1989 and Murai, 1989) and its aid to several South-east Asian countries has made it an important influence in their economic development (*AMPO*, 1990). Significantly, an increasing proportion of the ODA budget is being allocated to tourism-related projects, either directly or indirectly, as discussed below.

Up to 1988, although very few projects were directly categorised under the heading of tourism, aid provided to upgrade the infrastructure – for example, roads and other transport facilities – had implications for the tourism industry. However, from October to December, 1988, a Tourism Promotion Seminar was conducted by JICA and the Ministry of Transport in Tokyo. Twenty-two participants from twenty-two developing countries were invited to this group training course. A similar seminar was held in 1989 (Noda, 1991, p. 35). In 1987 and 1988, the Japanese government sent tourism experts to Thailand, Indonesia and other developing countries as part of its Technical Co-operation Programme. Furthermore, the ASEAN Centre for Trade, Investment and Tourism, established in Tokyo in 1981, and mainly funded by the Japanese government, held a series of seminars on tourism in 1988 (OECD, 1989, p. 61).

Other projects are based in specific countries. The Total Community Development Project in Malaysia, for example, aims to 'identify potential areas for development in the eastern region of the Malay Peninsula, and conduct feasibility studies for total community development programs using tourism as its main focus' (Noda, 1991, p. 35). Japan is now Malaysia's largest source of foreign aid and foreign investment (Tsuruoka, 1991, p. 50).

The OECF has participated in such schemes as the provisional Project for Basic Facilities for Resorts in Thailand. This regional development programme aims to encourage employment and the acquisition of foreign currency primarily through tourism. Basic infrastructure – for example, roads, communications and water – will be provided for resorts in eight regions, and loans are to be used to purchase equipment and to pay for consultants and other services (Noda, 1991, pp. 34–5).

The connection between ODA projects and tourism can also be seen in Bali, where the Bali International Airport Expansion Plan at Ngurah Rai has been carried out by the Taisei Construction Company with the assistance of a yen loan (Murai, 1991, p. 28). In nearby Benoa, Japanese ODA funds have been used to construct port facilities for the Indonesian fishing industry. Tuna caught in the Indian Ocean are washed and packed in Benoa and then air-freighted to Japan from Ngurah Rai International Airport. The same carriers taking Japanese tourists to Bali are responsible for transporting tuna to Japan (Murai, 1991, p. 31).

The role of private investment

In Japan, although resort developments and regional technology centres (known generically as 'technopolis') have been promoted as solutions to problems of regional development, critics have suggested that the former benefit Tokyo-based investors rather than local businesses, and that the latter rarely provide the promised transfer of skills to the regions.[1] Many South-east Asian nations also regard tourism as an attractive route to economic development and there, too, tourism has benefited construction and real estate conglomerates, who have been supported by Japanese ODA projects, rather than local businesses.

In recent years, there has been a shift in Japanese foreign investment from manufacturing to real estate and tourism. At the end of 1980, real estate and services accounted for less than one per cent of total direct foreign investment; by 1985, according to figures from the Japan External Trade Organisation (JETRO), service sector investment took up 8.3 per cent of the total and real estate 4.4 per cent, while in 1988 the proportions reached 9.7 per cent and 15.6 per cent respectively. In addition, overseas real estate acquisitions have risen in absolute terms and, by 1990, according to figures supplied by the Ministry of Construction, the proportion taken up by resort hotels had risen to 24.7 per cent (Inoue, 1991, p. 4).

At the time of writing, only about eight per cent of all Japanese overseas investment has gone to Asia (Rowley, 1991, p. 61), but Japan is already a significant presence in several South-east Asian countries and investment in tourism-related projects can be expected to grow. In addition, official statistics may underestimate the extent of such investment, with dummy companies sometimes being used to circumvent restrictions on foreign ownership (Inoue, 1991, p. 5).

Several developers who have profited from resort developments in Japan, especially golf courses, are investing in similar projects overseas. Indeed, it has been argued that they have been driven to do so by opposition within Japan, thus mirroring the industrial pollution exported from Japan in the 1970s. Since 1987, campaigns by numerous citizens' groups against such resorts have been publicised in special issues of several Japanese journals (*Agora*, 1991; *AMPO*, 1991). According to Kuji, a prominent critic of the 'political economy of golf', the construction of at least one hundred golf courses in Japan has been suspended as a result of opposition by groups of residents (Kuji, 1991, p. 51). In 1991, he estimated that Japanese companies owned 150 golf courses overseas, including those not yet completed (Kuji, 1991, p. 50). Because land and construction costs are lower in South-east Asia, clubs can charge lower membership fees than in Japan. As a consequence, even with air fares and accommodation costs, it may still be cheaper to play golf in Malaysia or the Philippines than at an élite club in Japan.

The case of Cebu in the Philippines

Cebu, an island in the Philippines, illustrates the relationship between manufacturing and other kinds of investment, and the links between private investment and ODA. With airport facilities developed at Mactan by the US military during the Vietnam War, and more recently upgraded with the support of Japanese ODA (Inoue, 1991, p. 3), the island was an ideal site for an export processing zone and in a good position to develop tourism (Tiglao, 1991, p. 61). The Mactan Export Processing Zone was established in 1979 and developed rapidly in the 1980s, when several companies fled south to escape labour unrest. The US-owned watchmaker TMK (Philippines) is the largest of these companies, of which approximately half are Japanese (Tiglao, 1991, p. 60).

Tourism was also developed in Cebu in the 1980s. Initially, allies of President Marcos received government loans for such projects as the Casino Filipino, the Cebu Piaza Hotel, and beach resorts (Tiglao, 1991, p. 61). More recently, Japan's OECF and the Asian Development Bank have pledged US $187 million in development aid for new roads and a new bridge to Mactan island (Tiglao, 1991, p. 60). The local government is also promoting tourism through the sale of government land, a policy which has led to inflation in land prices.

However, Japanese companies are often in a better position to cope with such inflation. In a project involving a golf course, marine resort and hotel on the West coast of Cebu, the Japanese developer initially bought 50 hectares of land from local landowners at 20 pesos a square metre. By the time the company tried to acquire the remaining 100 acres, landowners were demanding 50 pesos a square metre – more than double the original price. Nevertheless, when compared to prices in Tokyo, even this seemed moderate, and Inoue provides the following calculation of projected profits:

Calculating one peso at six yen and assuming a price of 50 pesos per square metre of land, the company will pay some 25 million pesos or 150 million yen to acquire the land. It will then in turn sell memberships in the resort for 2 million yen each, half going for the entrance fee and half for key money, a mere fraction of the 41.286 million yen average for golf course memberships in Japan as of September 22, 1990. Thus, it will be cheaper to go golfing in Cebu than in Japan, even when one includes the cost of travel and accommodations. Given this situation, the company can expect to easily reach its first stage recruiting target of 300 Japanese members, and it eventually hopes for a total membership of 1,600. With only 300 initial members, they can expect an income of 600 million yen, far more than their expenditure including the land price and construction costs (1991, pp. 5–6).

By 1991, Cebu was playing host to 50,000 tourists a year from Japan (the largest group), followed by 13,000 from the USA, 10,000 from Taiwan and 8,000 from Hong Kong. The Japanese can fly direct from Tokyo to the island, which provides for diving and other leisure activities, as well as such facilities as the Japanese-owned Coral Resort:

It is comprised of a golf course, marina, hotel and condominiums. The whole complex is tightly guarded by men carrying guns. The beautiful beach is accessible only to hotel guests, almost all of whom are foreign. (Inoue, 1991, p. 3).

In Cebu, the US military led the way through its creation of airport facilities. The expansion of the Mactan Export Processing Zone has been paralleled by the growth of tourism, which at all levels demonstrates the importance of the Japanese: as tourists, through technical assistance and ODA, and in private investment. Similar linkages have been noted in other parts of South-east Asia (*AMPO*, 1990).

The effects of Japanese tourism

Many of the effects of tourism in South-east Asia have been alluded to above. As elsewhere, tourism affects the environment, the economy and social relations.

Tourism and the environment

Much attention has recently been paid to the environmental effects of golf courses and resort developments, both in Japan and in such countries as Malaysia and the Philippines. In Japan, courses have been developed at the expense of agricultural land or forest areas. Every course requires approximately one hundred acres which must be cleared, often bulldozed, and remodelled. It then uses, every year, up to four tons of herbicides, fertilisers and other chemicals, which may have carcinogenic or other side effects, and which subsequently drain into rivers, ponds and swamps. By 1990, Japan's Ministry of Health had reported 950 sites where the quality or quantity of water had been adversely affected by golf course development. In addition, damage to flora and fauna has also been reported, leading to protests by environmentalists (McCormack, 1991a, pp. 126–7).

Similar criticisms have been made of golf course developments in Malaysia and the Philippines. In Malaysia, clubs are patronised by the Malay middle class and expatriates from Japan and elsewhere, some of whom are involved in business investment in Malaysia. Membership fees may be only ten to twenty per cent of the cost of membership in Japan. At the Templar Park Country Club, for example, which was developed by the Kyōwa Kankō Kalhatsu Company, 25 per cent of the membership was Japanese, while the Rahman Putra Golf Club has 30 per cent foreign membership, including many from Japan (Ling, 1991, p. 32). The Serandah Golf Resort, too, is to cater for golfing visitors to Malaysia. When completed, this 250 hectare resort will have 1,800 condominium units and 300 bungalows. By 1991, 40 per cent of the units sold were to buyers from Japan, Singapore and Hong Kong (Ling, 1991, p. 32).

Some economic effects of tourism

The economic effects of tourism development are complex, especially in the case of Japan and South-east Asia, where we must consider not only an influx of relatively wealthy tourists who may stay in virtual enclaves in the host country, but also the effects of foreign aid and investment on developing economies. When economic development is led by overseas investment, often in co-operation with local elites, the effects on other sectors of the economy may be limited. Although tourism brings foreign exchange to the host country, there is usually leakage of capital through profit repatriation, management fees, and the purchase of equipment for international-standard hotels (Mackie, 1988, p. 224; Truong, 1990, pp. 115–6).

As discussed above in connection with Thailand and the Philippines, the purchase of real estate by foreign investors may lead to inflation, making it harder for local people to participate in the industry and leading to the displacement of rural population as landowners sell agricultural land to developers and tenant farmers are evicted. As Inoue points out, 'developers derive their profits precisely from the difference between the Japanese and the local economies' (1991, p. 5).

Tourism is a notoriously fickle industry and expensive infrastructure may lie idle as international demand fluctuates. Although tourism continues to be Thailand's largest earner of foreign exchange, the number of foreign visitors to that country declined in 1991 and was not expected to reach the target of six million. The result was low occupancy rates in hotels, lay-offs and pay cuts of up to 50 per cent for hotel workers, and cancellation of some domestic flights between Bangkok and resort areas (Kelly, 1991, p. 44).

The drop in tourists visiting Thailand has been variously explained by reference to road and air accidents, perceived political instability, a general fall in travel in the Asian region because of the Gulf War, pollution and despoilation of the natural environment which forms the major attraction at many resorts, and negative perceptions of prostitution and the threat of HIV infection.

The fall in tourism to the Pattaya region of Thailand has been noted (Handley, 1991, p. 54), as have government attempts to attract new categories of tourist to Thai resorts (Kelly, 1991, p. 44). Indeed, Mechai Vivavaidhya, the Thai Minister of Tourism, is reported to be planning a Women's Visit Thailand Year for 1992 in an effort to change the negative image of Thai tourist resorts. The strategy is similar to that adopted by the Aquino government in the Philippines (cf. Richter, 1989, p. 79) and reflects a belated recognition that the (unofficial) promotion of prostitution may have lost the tourist industry 'untold others: couples, families, and culture-motivated travellers' (Richter, 1989, p. 100).

Tourism employment clearly has social implications. In Cebu, in the Philippines, for example, the local fishing industry has been displaced by hotel development. Fenced beaches deny access for fishing (Santos, 1991, p. 26). Although alternative employment may be created, it is often casual and temporary. Labour required to construct hotels and resorts may not be needed after completion, and the willingness of foreign developers to pay high wages for short-term employment may contribute to inflation. Indeed, resort developers on the Pacific island of Guam encountered a labour shortage, which they solved by importing construction workers from the Philippines and South Korea (Teeha, 1991, p. 21). In fact, most jobs created in resorts are likely to be service occupations, casual and with little or no career structure.

An influx of foreign tourists to developing countries, along with foreign aid and investment, inevitably influences class structures; gender relations, too, are said to be affected by 'the international movement of capital and relations of patriarchy within those countries' (Jennett and Stewart, 1987, p. 25). However, while the international division of labour in manufacturing, including the role of gender, has often been examined (Elson and Pearson, 1981; Lim, 1983; Ong, 1987), little work has been done in this regard on international tourism (Mackie, 1988; Truong, 1990).

It can be argued that tourism, like many aspects of manufacturing, is clearly based on an international division of labour, whereby knowledge- and capital-intensive sectors of the industry are controlled by companies based in such developed countries as Japan, in which many tourists originate. For their part, tourist-receiving countries specialise in providing a range of labour-intensive personal services:

The first characteristic of tourism is the combination of services (transport, accommodation, local services) whose quality is experienced essentially at the tourist destinations rather than at the place of purchase, i.e. travel agency bureaux. The salient feature of this 'experience commodity' is the replication in a commercial context of household-based services (hospitality, personal services, accommodation, personal and psychological fulfilment) (Truong, 1990, p. 124).

Tourism and gender relations

Much of the discussion of the relationship between tourism and gender relations has focused on prostitution, but this should always be discussed in the context of a whole range of personal services which are often gender-typed, including domestic service and aspects of the entertainment industry, and structural inequalities based on class, gender and ethnicity (Mackie, 1988).

Even in countries where open promotion of prostitution is eschewed, advertisements for airlines or hotels often focus on the attractiveness or nurturing qualities of female service personnel. In airline advertising, especially, the spotlight is on the feminine qualities of female flight attendants and their beauty may be linked with the 'natural' beauty of the country's resort areas, as in advertisements in editions of the *Far Eastern Economic Review* and similar publications for such airlines as Thai international, Singapore Airlines or Philippine Airlines. Gender is thus crucial to an understanding of the appeal of tourism, whether we consider the provision of services on the promotion of an image:

In this connection, the ways in which promotional campaigns focus on aspects of hospitality, such as female submissiveness, caring and nurturing as well as sexual temptation, may be considered as part of this discourse sustained by governments and enterprises (Truong, 1990, p. 125).

In the 1980s, the issue of 'sex tours' to South-east Asia received attention, both in Japan and elsewhere in the region. Although Japanese tourists did not form the largest nationality group of visitors to Thailand and the Philippines, male tourists formed a disproportionate number of these visitors. The situation is described by Richter, who quotes from the *Asia Travel Trade* of June, 1983:

In Bangkok, there are 400,000 more female than male residents, yet 89 per cent of all tourists are male. Nor can business travel, which is male dominated, account for the male imbalance, for it declined in 1981, though overall tourism grew. . . . 'The country's two largest sources of traffic – Japan and Malaysia, totalling a 29 per cent share in 1981 – account for a far greater proportion of male arrivals compared with the national average, than do other regional destinations. Only the Philippines have a higher male share than Thailand – and the Philippines has a similar reputation' (1989, p. 86).

At the time, joint demonstrations against prostitution tours were organised by women's groups in Japan and the countries affected (Mackie, 1988, p. 229). In Japan more recently, public discussion has centred on women from South-east Asia who enter the country as illegal immigrants and work in the entertainment industry (Mackie, 1988, p. 229).

Discussion of prostitution highlights the fact that tourism may have grave health implications. The high incidence of HIV infection and of other sexually-transmitted diseases in Thailand is one such social problem. Other health-related issues may involve environmental pollution, for example, the effects of pesticides and other chemicals used on golf courses (Ling, 1991, p. 33).

The political effects of tourism

Finally, we should consider the political effects of tourism. Richter, concerned with policy implications, and conscious that tourism may be promoted for political ends by particular groups, described how the industry was used to give legitimacy to the Marcos regime and how such policies were later modified by the Aquino government (1989, pp. 51–81). The recent promotion of overseas travel from Japan should also be understood in the context of foreign policy considerations, as detailed above.

However, where economic change is dependent on fluctuations in international tourist demand, on foreign aid projects, and on foreign investment, there is little room for autonomous development. Even when the relationship between foreign interests and local élites falls short of outright corruption, tourism is still likely to benefit these groups rather than the population at large, among whom regional disparities and inequalities of class and gender may be intensified or reconstituted in various ways.

In many South-east Asian nations there has been opposition to aspects of tourism, from women's groups concerned about prostitution, from environmental groups concerned at the destruction of forests and the natural habitats of flora and fauna, from victims of pollution caused by golf course complexes, and from farming and fishing communities displaced by resort developments. If such groups are to have a say in the direction taken by tourism in the future, it will be necessary to develop strategies for influencing decision-making, not only at the level of the nation state, but also by multinational corporations and international aid agencies. By examining the influence of Japanese tourists, investors and aid agencies in selected South-east

Asian countries, it has become apparent that the effects of unequal development in tourism operate on several levels. It is necessary to comprehend this complexity to develop strategies for more autonomous development within the region.

Note

1. Such issues have also interested Australian scholars examining Japanese proposals for a 'multifunction polis' – a combined resort and technopolis development – (cf. McCormack, 1991b; James, 1990) or when examining tourism development in Australia more generally (cf. Craik, 1991).

7 Tourism in Latin America: perspectives from Mexico and Costa Rica[1]

Sylvia Chant

This chapter examines international tourism in Latin America with particular reference to Mexico and Costa Rica, two countries where tourism has been an important element in national development in the post-war period. Following an overview of tourism in the continent in general, the chapter proceeds to a more detailed investigation of the industry in the two case study locations. Given the differences in nature and scale of Mexican and Costa Rican tourism, some time is spent accounting for major variations, after which selected aspects are highlighted for discussion. In the Costa Rican case, analysis focuses on the rising role of eco-tourism in national economic growth. For Mexico, attention is weighted towards the effects of tourism development on the Pacific coast on the employment and livelihood strategies of low-income groups, with particular attention to changing patterns of gender roles and relations in the fast-growing resort of Puerto Vallarta.

Tourism in Latin America

Tourism in Latin America is a highly variable phenomenon. First, its importance varies across different national economies. In Mexico, for example, tourism in the 1970s and 1980s has regularly held first, second or third place as a generator of foreign exchange, with oil and in-bond manufacturing as the other leading industries, and it is also a leading industry in terms of income and employment (Mathieson and Wall, 1982, p. 35). In 1977, for example, tourism generated 3.3 per cent of Mexico's GNP and in the same year constituted 26.3 per cent of total exports (Getino, 1990, pp. 108 and 112). Indeed, Mexico is, and for a long time has been, the unparalleled giant of the international tourist industry in Latin America (Getino, 1990, p. 91; Krause, Jud and Hyman, 1973, pp. 54–5; Jud, 1974). In countries such as Honduras, El Salvador, Surinam and the Guyanas, on the other hand, tourism's contribution to the national economy is negligible. In El Salvador, for instance, tourism was only 2.4 per cent of exports in 1977 (Getino, 1990, p. 112). Even in such countries as Costa Rica, where tourism has been actively promoted by the state, the contribution of earnings from international tourism to GDP in the late 1970s was still under 2 per cent (Jenkins and Henry, 1982, p. 505), and the industry's share of national exports only 6.6 per cent (Getino, 1990, p. 112).

Secondly, there is much variation in the volume and origins of foreign visitors. While Mexico and Brazil, for example, receive substantial numbers of tourists from North America and Europe, countries such as Argentina and Uruguay rely much more heavily on domestic tourism or on Latin American neighbours (cf. Morris, 1987, p. 157; Vasconi, 1991). Indeed, in South America generally, most foreign tourists are Latin American, with over three-quarters travelling from Chile, Colombia and Paraguay (Lea, 1988, p. 25). In the case of socialist countries such as Cuba, international tourists have traditionally come from the Soviet Union and the Eastern Bloc (cf. Lea, 1988, p. 11), as well as from other Latin American countries, such as Mexico, where friendly diplomatic relations have given rise to package deal holidays since the late 1970s.

International tourism in Latin America has increased since the post-war period and the index of visitors to the region has grown at more than the world average since 1950 (see Table 7.1). However, the continent's share of the world total of international tourists is still only 3.8 per cent, as compared to 3.2 per cent in 1950, and the overall proportion of world receipts received from international tourism actually declined from 15.5 per cent in 1950 to 4.3 per cent (of US $209,155 million) in 1989 (Table 7.1).

Breaking down the flow of foreign visitors by country, we can see from Table 7.2 that Mexico has by far the greatest share of the regional total, with most international tourists to that country coming from the USA or Canada. In 1987, for

Table 7.1 Arrivals of tourists from abroad and receipts from international tourism in Latin America

	Year	Tourists from Abroad (000s)	Index	Receipts from International Tourism (US $ million)	Index
Central America (inc. Mexico)					
	1950	391	100	103	100
	1960	749	192	694	674
	1970	2,919	747	525	510
	1980	5,652	1,446	5,893	5,721
	1989	7,199 (e)	1,841	4,625	4,490
South America					
	1950	410	100	223	100
	1960	426	104	212	95
	1970	2,422	591	321	144
	1980	5,767	1,406	3,784	1,697
	1989	8,199 (e)	2,000	4,375	1,962
Central and South America					
	1950	801	100	326	100
	1980	11,419	1,426	9,677	2,968
	1989	15,398 (e)	1,922	9,000	2,761
World					
	1950	25,282	100	2,100	100
	1980	284,841	1,127	102,372	4,875
	1989	405,306 (e)	1,603	209,155	9,960

(e) = Estimate

Source: World Tourism Organisation (1990) Vol. 1, Table 1, pp. 1–12

Table 7.2   Latin America: tourists from abroad, 1988

	Tourists (000's) 1988	% of Regional total
Argentina	2,119	14.0
Belize	142	0.9
Bolivia	167	1.1
Brazil	1,743	11.5
Chile	588	3.9
Colombia	829	5.5
Costa Rica	329	2.2
Ecuador	287	1.9
El Salvador	134	0.9
Guatemala	405	2.7
Guyana	71	0.5
Honduras	250	1.7
Mexico	5,692	37.6
Panama	199	1.3
Paraguay	284	1.9
Peru	359	2.4
Suriname	32	0.2
Uruguay	844	5.6
Venezuela	675	4.5
Total	15,149	100.0

Source: World Tourism Organisation (1990) Vol. 1, Table 9.1, p. 25

NB Percentages do not add up because of rounding.

instance, arrivals from these countries were 87 per cent and 6 per cent respectively, with 2.5 per cent from Europe and 4 per cent from other parts of Latin America (Economist Intelligence Unit, 1991, p. 25). By contrast, in most other Latin American countries, visitors from North America and Europe together account for less than half of all foreign visitors, as indicated in Table 7.3.

The third element in the differentiation in Latin American tourism is the resource base for the industry. Broadly speaking, three main types can be identified: sun-and-sea tourism, environmental/eco-tourism, and cultural/folkloric tourism (see also Schlüter, 1991). Countries with major beach tourism include Mexico, Brazil and Venezuela (cf. Getino, 1990, pp. 135–6). Eco-tourism, most notably expressed in Ecuador's creation of a preservation zone in the Galapagos Islands in 1964 (Getino, 1990, p. 136; Morris, 1987, p. 16) is also found in Brazil, Peru and Costa Rica, whose governments have all promoted national park systems with the twin aims of protecting indigenous flora and fauna and encouraging guided nature visits (Morris, 1987). Finally, some countries have promoted tourism which draws on such cultural and ethno-historical phenomena as pre-Columbian archaeological sites, colonial Spanish architecture, and contemporary handicraft industries and markets. Concentrated principally in Mexico, Guatemala, Peru and Ecuador, this kind of tourism appeals to 'international circuit travellers' or 'wanderlust tourists' (Pearce, 1989, p. 250), a market targeted by various South American countries with the so-called 'Andean route'. Further north, Guatemala, Honduras and Mexico are combining to

Table 7.3   Origins of international tourists: selected Latin American countries, 1987

	Total international tourists (000's)	N. America (USA & Canada) %	Europe %	Other Latin American countries
Argentina	1,951	4.00	10.63	80.73
Brazil	1,929	14.57	24.46	55.05
Colombia	541	16.93	11.40	69.21
Costa Rica	278	35.23	11.71	49.39
Ecuador	274	23.74	17.74	53.78
Guatemala	353	25.68	15.08	55.73
Mexico	5,407	91.65	4.04	3.49
Paraguay	303	3.79	11.34	78.91
Venezuela	615	36.74	37.51	10.16

Source: World Tourism Organisation (1990) Vol. 2, Table 1, pp. 1–135

Note: Data on the origins of international tourists to Peru and Bolivia are not provided in the source cited.

promote the 'Maya route' (Pearce, 1989, p. 250; Schlüter, 1991, pp. 10–11), a project recently boosted by an EEC grant of US £1 million (Hammond, 1991, p. 20).

Tourism in Mexico and Costa Rica

Although Mexican and Costa Rican international tourism differ quite markedly from one another, similarities do exist. Governments of both countries have actively promoted tourism as a development strategy, especially since the 1960s (cf. Jenkins and Henry, 1982, p. 501). Accordingly, both countries have various national and regional-level agencies concerned with stimulating tourist expansion. In Mexico, the main national agency is FONATUR (Fondo Nacional de Turismo/National Tourism Fund) and in Costa Rica, the ICT (Instituto Costarricense de Turismo/ Costa Rican Tourism Institute). The continuity of government initiatives has undoubtedly been facilitated by both countries' relative political stability in the post-war period. Indeed, political stability is viewed as one of the major reasons for the popularity of holidays here compared with other Latin American destinations (see for example, Huertas Alpizar, 1988).

Another similarity stems from the orientation of international tourism to the advanced economies of the world. Ninety-five per cent of Mexico's foreign tourists come from Nothern America and Europe; in Costa Rica the figure is around 47 per cent (see Table 7.3).

Beyond this, however, tourism in Mexico and Costa Rica diverges in both scale and nature. Disparities stem from numerous factors, including differences in size, ecological make-up, geographical position and distance from major international markets, historical/cultural legacies, and the length of their involvement in the international tourist industry.

Mexico is one of the largest and most populous countries in Latin America with around 85 million inhabitants, several well-developed intermediate cities, and the advantage of sharing a border with one of the richest sources of tourists in the world – the USA. Indeed, in the late 1970s and early 1980s, Mexico received a greater share of US foreign travel expenditures than any other country in the world (Stronge and Redman, 1982, p. 22). By contrast, Costa Rica is one of the smallest countries in Latin America, with a population of under three million, and much less urban development and infrastructure. Tucked away in the south of the Central American Isthmus between two historically politically unstable countries, Nicaragua and Panama, it is also less accessible and possibly somewhat less appealing to international travellers, even if in reality it is a very 'safe' country to visit. Not surprisingly, however, tourism in Mexico is developed to a much greater degree.

Mexico's extremely buoyant tourist industry owes its success to an extensive range of tourist resources, ranging from such natural attractions as beaches and volcanoes to an immense and diverse wealth of archaeological sites, as well as an equally varied range of ethnic and cultural features. Beyond this, it also has a tourism accommodation capacity unrivalled in Latin America, with 310,470 rooms in hotels and similar establishments in 1988, nearly one quarter of these being in the four- and five-star range (World Tourism Organisation, 1990, Vol. 1, p. 392).

Although Costa Rica has beaches, volcanic landforms and a rich vegetational diversity, it lacks the range of attractions and facilities offered by Mexico. For example, in 1987 it had only 5,289 rooms in hotels and similar establishments, less than two per cent of that of Mexico (World Tourism Organisation, 1990, Vol. 1, p. 374). Moreover, Costa Rica does not possess the vast archaeological and architectural heritage of Mexico and other longer settled parts of the continent. While Mexico was home to the great pre-Columbian civilisations of the Aztecs, the Mayas, the Mixtecs and so on, the physical legacy left by Costa Rica's small indigenous groups is minimal. Mexico was also one of the most extensively colonised areas of Latin America and was the focus of a massive wave of town foundation and the construction of churches, elaborate residences for the governing elite, and organisations of the state. As a result, the contemporary landscape is replete with fine examples of 16th, 17th and 18th century colonial architecture. Costa Rica, on the other hand, was largely by-passed in this respect. Since early in the 16th century, when it was found to be poor in minerals and precious metals (especially gold and silver), with a scarcity of labour, the colony was left in virtual stagnation, ruled somewhat disinterestedly from the distant seat of the Central American empire in Guatemala until Independence in 1821.

Beyond the unequal distribution of historical resources for tourism between Mexico and Costa Rica, other differences arise from contemporary cultural characteristics. While the indigenous populations of both countries were exposed to death, decimation or miscegenation over the course of the colonial period, Mexico still possesses Indian communities active in areas of cultural tourism attractive to international visitors, for example, art, handicrafts, dance and religious events. In Costa Rica, by contrast, there is no major indigenous presence.

Costa Rica: eco-tourism and national economic growth

Although wealthy relative to many of its Central and Latin American counterparts, Costa Rica's economy is heavily dependent on the export of a narrow range of tropical agricultural products. In the mid-1980s, for example, coffee, bananas, meat and sugar constituted 65 per cent of national exports (Gayle, 1986, p. 76). Costa Rica's small internal market and scarcity of raw materials for manufacturing have meant that industrial growth has been somewhat limited to date (cf. Hall, 1985; Izurieta, 1982; Sheahan, 1987). Indeed, the country relies on imports for nearly one-third of all goods consumed domestically (Gayle, 1986, p. 76). As a consequence, together with the mounting external debt arising from recession in the 1970s and 1980s, international tourism has come to represent an important arm of economic strategy, especially since the National Tourism Congress of 1987, when a major campaign to promote Costa Rican tourism abroad (mainly in the USA and Canada) was approved (Arguello Salazar, 1988).

While Costa Rica has beach resorts (some within the boundaries of national parks) and a few destinations of historic interest, the country's tourist industry revolves around its environmental resources. This is reflected in twenty-four national parks, which are situated in most of the country's major ecological zones (*Costa Rica Guide*, 1988, p. 34) (cf. Figure 7.1). Given Costa Rica's mountainous terrain, its maritime influence from both the Caribbean and the Pacific, and its location between 8° and 11° north of the equator, it possesses a wide range of climatic and vegetational conditions, from highland alpine vegetation to tropical rainforest (see, for example, Hall, 1985), making for a large number of distinct ecological environments over a relatively small area. Amongst the more notable natural attractions are over 1,000 kinds of orchids and over 825 species of birds (*Costa*

Figure 7.1   Costa Rica: major national parks, nature reserves and wildlife refuges

Rica Guide, 1988, p. 34). Sometimes, individual national parks themselves contain the fauna and flora of several different types of habitat. An example here is the Monteverde Cloud Forest Reserve in the north-west of the country (see Figure 7.1). Extending 700–800 metres down both sides of the Cordillera de Tilarán mountain range, the park covers eight different ecological life zones and has over 100 species of mammals (including jaguars and ocelots), over 400 species of birds (such as the three-wattled bell bird, and bare-necked umbrella bird, and numerous types of hummingbird), and around 2,500 species of plants, such as orchids, bromeliads, mosses and ferns (*Costa Rica Guide*, 1988, p. 15).

Arguably, Costa Rica's lack of tourist infrastructure when compared to larger Latin American countries may enhance its role in offering selective environmental tourism rather than mass tours (Schlüter, 1991, p. 10). Indeed, UK companies have recently begun to promote 'green holidays' for 'environmentally-friendly tourists' as an alternative to overcrowded beach resorts, and Costa Rica is noted as providing environmentally-sound and carefully-planned tourism. As this involves restriction of access, it also means higher prices (*Economist*, 1990, p. 103). However, although domestic visitors to the parks far outnumber foreign ones (227,300 to 161, 800 in 1989), the rate of international tourism is increasing substantially (Place, 1991, p. 187).

By 1988, the tourist industry in Costa Rica was worth US $165 million, compared with US $81 million in 1980, and is currently the country's third largest export commodity (Coffey, 1991, p. 2; Place, 1991, p. 187). From 1985 onwards a major programme to encourage private sector tourism investment through various concessionary measures has been in operation under the auspices of the Tourism Investment Incentives Law. This has provided for numerous tax exemptions for tourist-related enterprises (Coffey, 1991; ICT, 1988).

There are problems with this programme. There is no spatial component, so the process is not as directed as it might be to particular regional development needs, and interest rates on loans are not much below market rates, thus favouring foreign rather than domestic entrepreneurs (Coffey, 1991, pp. 9–11). However, there the law will undoubtedly enhance existing positive trends in the growing international tourist sector.

As in other parts of the world, eco-tourism in Costa Rica has received a major boost with increasing international concern over the destruction of rainforests, the extinction of plants and animals, and pollution. The creation of national parks from endangered environments of particular ecological interest protects the area concerned and generates revenue or employment to replace former economic activities. Indeed, several authors have emphasised the conflicts that may occur when territory traditionally used by local people for agriculture and grazing is taken out of their hands. Morris, for example, notes the problems in Ecuador of creating national reserves around volcanoes in areas which support large farming populations (1987, p. 16).

Costa Rica is no stranger to this problem, as Place (1991) documents in her detailed study of rural development in Tortuguero on the north-east coast of the country (see Figure 7.1). In 1975, Tortuguero National Park was designated a protected area to conserve the nesting beach of the green sea turtle (*Chelonia mydas*) and around 20,000 hectares of tropical rainforest (Place, 1991, pp. 190–1). It is a popular destination for both domestic and international tourists, receiving twelve times as many visitors by 1988 as in 1980, and attracting a growing proportion of international tourists. Foreign visitors to Tortuguero were 44 per cent of the total in 1981 and nearly 62 per cent in 1988 (Place, 1991, p. 194).

However, with the creation of the Park, the villages of Tortuguero were forced to curtail their exploitation of such declining resources as turtle eggs and lumber, and their agricultural subsistence also declined in the wake of an incipient cash economy. Moreover, as they lacked capital to invest in tourism, opportunities were taken up by outsiders. By contrast, most villagers involved themselves in informal services for the few permanent residents involved in tourism or scientific research, and for each other. These include childcare, the preparation of foodstuffs, washing, the thatching of roofs and so on (Place, 1991, p. 193).

Clearly, villagers could be involved more, and at a higher level, in the National Park (cf. Place, 1991, p. 198) but state intervention has at least been significant in putting the country on the international tourist map, even if some have argued that the Costa Rican Tourism Institute itself has been underfunded, and has occupied a rather uncertain position during various political administrations (see for example, Godinez, 1988).

Social and economic costs have been paid by local people as a result of national park initiatives. However, other aspects of environmental protection related to tourism development have been more positive, for example, Law No. 6043 on the Marine and Terrestrial Zone (*Ley Sobre la Zona Maritima Terrestre*). Passed in 1977, it aimed to stem unplanned coastal tourism and further the tourism potential of the country's 684 kilometres of beaches by conserving natural beauty. Although not without shortcomings – it does not cover national parks – the law creates a 200 metre-wide marine terrestial zone, which is divided into public and restricted zones. Development is generally prohibited in the former and regulated by government priorities in the latter, and lawbreakers are subjected to fines (Sorensen, 1990).

Not all ecology-oriented tourism initiatives in Costa Rica have had negative social and economic impacts on local people. A pertinent example here is the Monteverde Cloud Forest Reserve referred to earlier in this chapter. Although founded by North Americans, the group concerned were dairy-farming Quakers with a strong sympathy for protecting local customs. Thus while the Quakers dominate the ownership of tourist accommodation facilities in the areas, local people have been encouraged to continue making traditional crafts. These are made and sold to tourists in an on-site co-operative (*Costa Rica Guide*, 1988, p. 15). Moreover, the local Monteverde Institute, which fosters cultural, scientific and educational facilities for residents or visitors interested in tropical biology, is a non-profit association (*Costa Rica Guide*, 1988, p. 15).

In summing up, while the management of the development of tourism, and particularly eco-tourism, in Costa Rica has not been without problems, the country seems to have avoided the more deleterious effects of international tourism that have arisen in other developing countries. Much of this is because income generation has been coupled with a concern, and indeed an intrinsic necessity, to protect the environment and the small-scale selective nature of development, and because the visitors attracted by eco-tourism have a vested interest in preserving the landscapes they visit. Among the many tourists from the USA and Canada are scientists, educationalists, conservationists, ornithologists and so on. At the same time, future growth could pose certain difficulties. As Place points out, 'as mass marketing of ecotourism encourages larger numbers of visitors, it will become increasingly difficult to minimise their impact on remote populations and ecosystems' (1991, p. 189).

Notwithstanding the dangers of potentially large increases in environmentally-oriented tourist activity in future years, there is little doubt that Costa Rica needs to exploit the international tourism market in order to move away from heavy reliance on a limited number of agricultural exports for overseas earnings. Aside from the economic benefits of such a strategy, there may also be important environmental spin-offs: while the conditions of development of the country's main forms of export-oriented farming, especially cattle-ranching, have often led to the destruction of forests, the erosion of soils, and the reduction of species diversity, a rise in eco-tourism could provide a welcome counterbalance to this process.

Mexico: Tourism and the poor – the case of Puerto Vallarta

While Mexico also draws visitors on account of its ecological features, the nature of tourism here is much more diverse. As discussed earlier, the industry also revolves around such features as its beaches, pre-Columbian archaeological sites, colonial architecture and traditional Indian markets. Both international and domestic tourism have been vital to the national economy and actively promoted by the government since the 1950s, with positive results in terms of overall growth. During the period 1950 to 1972, the annual rate of increase in receipts from international tourism was around 12 per cent, and that of tourism exports between 1950 and 1970 was 7.2 per cent (Jud, 1974, pp. 20 and 29). Traditionally, a large proportion of tourism spending has been in the northern border area (57 per cent in the early 1970s – cf. Jud, 1974, p. 21), although tourism has increasingly extended further south, especially to coastal regions. Aside from generating significant amounts of foreign exchange, international tourism in Mexico has also given rise to dramatic expansion in employment. In the period 1960 to 1970, for example, employment in hotels and motels rose by 111 per cent and that in restaurants, bars and cafes by 147 per cent. This exceeded growth in both the total labour force and in the service sector at the time (Jud, 1974, p. 32). Indeed, some have argued that international tourism has been a saving grace for Mexico in the light of economic crisis and devaluation of the peso in the 1970s and 1980s, even if others have demonstrated empirically that this is not necessarily the case (cf. Stronge and Redman, 1982). For instance, Lea (1988, p. 24) maintains that high inflation in Mexico in the early 1980s and an overvalued exchange rate reduced tourist arrivals from the USA. Indeed, between 1974 and 1984 Mexico's share of earnings in the world tourism market fell from 2.5 to 1.5 per cent (Getino, 1990, pp. 96–7). However, large countries with diverse economies such as Mexico and Brazil are generally much less vulnerable to fluctuations in tourism than those where it represents the backbone of the economy, as in the Caribbean, for example (Lea, 1988, p. 2), even if Mexico itself is rather heavily dependent on the USA (Getino, 1990, p. 97).

In any case, downturns in international tourism to Mexico in the early 1980s have since reversed. For example, between 1985 and 1989 international tourist arrivals rose by nearly 50 per cent from 4.2 million to 6.3 million (Economist Intelligence Unit, 1991, p. 25). Total expenditure by international tourists correspondingly increased from US $1.72 billion to US $2.98 billion over the same period, with the overall balance from tourism income, calculated by subtracting expenditure by outgoing tourists from Mexico, increasing overall by 36 per cent from US $1.06 billion to US $1.44 billion (EIU, 1991, p. 25). In 1987, international tourists stayed a period of 11.3 days in Mexico and spent an average of US $474 (EIU, 1991, p. 25).

As stated earlier in this chapter, the Mexican government has played an extremely important role in the development of tourism in the country. In terms of beach centres, this has involved both the enhancement of existing tourist resorts (such as Puerto Vallarta and Mazatlán), and the creation of new ones (Cancún,

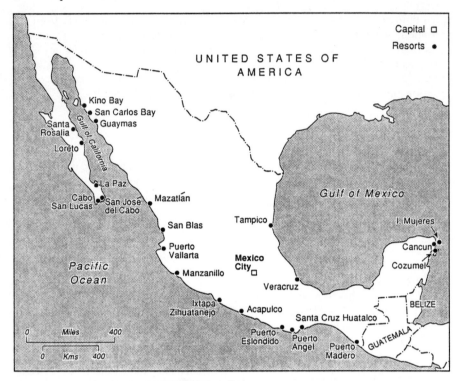

Figure 7.2   Mexico: major beaches and resorts

Ixtapa-Zihuatanejo, San José del Cabo/Loreta and Santa Cruz Huatalco, for example) (Stansfield, 1980) (see Figure 7.2). Government involvement has ranged from the planning and building of the infrastructure necessary for tourism such as roads and airports, to incentives for private investors, to the establishment of training institutes for the industry's workers.

The case of Ixtapa-Zihuatanejo illustrates the aims of government intervention in tourism. The project to create the planned beach resort of Ixtapa in the state of Guerrero, five kilometres to the south of the small fishing village of Zihuatanejo, dates back to 1972 and was designed to avoid the consequences of *ad hoc* development – for example, pollution and uncontrolled growth of unserviced, low-income housing, as had occurred in the large resort of Acapulco further down the Pacific coast (Reynoso y Valle and De Regt, 1979). The government aimed not only to develop tourist facilities, but also to provide amenities and training for the local populace, and favoured local participation in the process, the latter being reflected in the creation of a Community Development Team (cf. Reynoso y Valle and De Regt, 1979). Although the reality of the project fell short of its original aims, especially in the early years between 1972 and 1976 when the population of Zihuatanejo doubled, far outstripping local capacity to provide schools, health facilities, housing and other services, at least there has been some commitment to the principle of sensitive planning of tourist infrastructure. Indeed, Jud notes that the Mexican government has generally been concerned to protect and preserve local customs, even if present de-regulation and the opening up of the market to outside interests may undermine this (1974, pp. 40–1). Making direct investment to tourism even more attractive to foreign investors is one of the strategies pursued by the current administration of President Carlos Salinas Gortari, which aims to achieve a target of 10 million visitors and US $5 billion expenditure by 1994 (EIU, 1991, p. 25). Another strategy is to increase the number of international airline routes (EIU, 1991, p. 25). By 1988, Mexico possessed thirty-six airports of international standard, offering direct connections between Mexico and major cities in the United States, Canada, Europe, Australia and other parts of Latin America (EIU, 1991, p. 26). In the same year, the government sold off 'Aeroméxico', one of its two airlines, to foreign investors, and a year later permitted domestic and foreign investors to buy half of its 51 per cent of shares in 'Mexicana', its other company (EIU, 1991, p. 26). This is significant, since domestic investors have traditionally held 51 per cent of shares in the country's firms, including such international hotels as the Hilton, Holiday Inn and Western International (Jud, 1974).

Growth and development in Puerto Vallarta

Puerto Vallarta is an example of a Mexican tourist resort which does not owe its origins to government intervention, although the state has contributed to its expansion at subsequent stages of development (see Figure 7.2). It is currently the fastest-growing of the 124 municipalities which comprise the state of Jalisco in Western Mexico, and is itself the most rapidly-growing tourist resort on the Mexican Pacific (Chant, 1991a, p. 44). Lying in the country's largest natural bay, the Bahía de Banderas, until the 1960s Puerto Vallarta was a quiet town with small numbers of American tourists, some of whom had houses, apartments and small businesses. Although it was technically illegal for foreigners to own coastal homes in Mexico, many Americans 'borrowed' a name (*presta-nombre*) from a trusted friend or lawyer (Evans, 1979, p. 308). Following the filming in Puerto Vallarta in 1963 of Tennessee Williams' 'The Night of the Iguana', whose male lead, Richard Burton, was visited on location by Elizabeth Taylor, the town attracted even more interest from US tourists (Chant, 1991a, chapter 2). In the mid-1960s, recognising the potential of Puerto Vallarta to create employment in an otherwise mainly agricultural region, the government elected to foster further expansion (Evans, 1979 pp. 306–7). The two major projects funded by the federal government between the mid-1960s and mid-1970s were a paved road connecting the town to the west coast international highway, and an international airport (Evans, 1979, p. 312). In 1970, when the airport was completed, it received twenty-six international flights a week (Evans, 1979, p. 310). In 1969, the government also created a major regional planning agency to oversee development in Puerta Vallarta itself as well as the southern coast of Nayarit, the state to the north. The main responsibility of this agency, the Fideicomiso Puerto Vallarta, was the regularisation and organisation of land tenure.

During the 1970s, population growth reached an unprecedented rate of 11.9 per cent per annum. By the early 1980s, it was 12.3 per cent, at which time the average growth of Jalisco state itself was only 2.7 per cent (Fideicomiso Puerto Vallarta, 1985). By 1986, the town's population was in the region of 160,000 (see Chant, 1991a).[2]

Social impacts of tourism development on the poor

Although a study of the attitudes of Argentinian university students towards tourism in their country alleged that their response was generally favourable, recognising the economic importance of the industry and emphasising its potential for 'fostering international understanding and world peace' (Var, Schlüter, Ankomah and Lee, 1989, p. 434), generally speaking, people have tended to focus on the negative social impacts of tourism (cf. Getino, 1990, pp. 121ff; Jud, 1974, pp. 40–1). When it comes to women, these impacts are usually seen as even more serious, for example, in the growth of exploitative sex work in various South-east Asian countries (Graburn, 1983; Lee, 1991; Truong, 1990). However, in the context of Puerto Vallarta, some changes would appear to be rather positive.

One of the most significant elements noted in the development of tourism in resort localities in developing countries is the creation of employment for women (Getino, 1990, p. 116; Wilson, 1979). The Mexican Pacific is no exception, with increased female labour force participation noted for Ixtapa-Zihuatanejo (Kennedy et al., 1978; Reynoso y Valle and De Regt, 1979), as well as for Puerto Vallarta (Chant, 1991a).

The entry of women into paid jobs in Mexico is significant because traditionally Mexican women have represented a fairly low proportion of both the rural and urban labour force (at least in terms of 'visible' employment or that which gets recorded in official statistical documents). Reasons for historically low rates of female employment in Mexican cities range from discrimination by employers to restrictions operating from within the home (especially in the case of married women, who generally have exclusive responsibility for childcare and domestic labour, and whose husbands have often resisted the idea that their wives should work) (Chant, 1991a, Chapter 1).

Certainly, such tourist resorts as Puerto Vallarta seem to have higher rates of female labour force participation than towns based on different types of economic activity. An in-depth comparative study carried out in 1986 in Puerto Vallarta and two cities in the central highlands – León, a major centre of footwear production, and Querétaro, a modern manufacturing city – revealed that women's involvement in the workforce in Puerto Vallarta was highest of all three. The conclusions were based on census figures, a survey of local employers, and also on a sample of women in low-income settlements in each town (Chant, 1991a, p. 136, Table 4.8). According to the census, the percentage of the workforce made up by women in Puerto Vallarta was 32.3 per cent; the author's own survey of employers in selected commercial enterprises, hotels, restaurants and catering establishments in the town showed that women were an average of 37.4 per cent of those employed; and among adult women (wives of male household heads or household heads in their own right) in two low-income communities on the outskirts of the city, 58.7 per cent had some form of income-generating activity (Chant, 1991a, p. 136).

To explain why Puerto Vallarta (and other Mexican Pacific tourist resorts) display higher than average rates of female labour force participation (cf. Kennedy et al, 1978; Reynoso y Valle and De Regt, 1979), it is necessary to note several issues. First, most tourism-related employment is labour-intensive. In this respect, it is likelier for local labour markets of this nature to recruit women and men, especially where workers are in scarce supply. This is certainly the case in Puerto Vallarta where, at particular times of year, there are labour shortages (notably the 'high season' between December and April); at these times, women are often employed in jobs that are normally the domain of men. Although restaurants often prefer to employ only men, women are sometimes recruited as dishwashers and cooks if there are no male applicants for the jobs (Chant, 1991a, pp. 47–8).

Secondly, much tourism-related employment consists of low-skilled tertiary work, where a disproportionate number of women are usually concentrated. This is certainly the case in Mexico generally, and even more for resorts such as Puerto Vallarta where segments of employment are distinctly 'feminised' – especially those which represent an extension into the marketplace of skills generally acquired by women during gender socialisation in the home. Typical jobs here include chambermaiding, laundrywork and the preparation of food.

Thirdly, women's involvement in the so-called 'formal sector' of the tourism labour force creates space for others to perform household tasks they can no longer do effectively themselves, at least on a full-time basis. For example, some women in Puerto Vallarta's low-income settlements charge a small fee to look after the children of neighbours; others cook snacks that provide the basis of the evening meal for women who are out at work all day. As such, two main 'tiers' of female employment appear to arise from tourism: one consisting of the feminised sectors of the formal labour force itself, the other emerging to cater for the workers involved in it.

The generally favourable context for female employment in such tourist resorts as Puerto Vallarta has a number of implications for the social organisation of low-income households, with particularly marked effects in the spheres of household form and gender roles and relations.

One of the most notable features of Puerto Vallarta's low-income neighbour-hoods is the high incidence of households headed by women. According to the author's survey, 19.6 per cent of households in Puerto Vallarta's low-income settlements were female-headed, compared with only 13.5 per cent in Querétaro, and 10.4 per cent in León (Chant, 1991a, p. 137, Table 3.8).[3] The high incidence of female household heads relates very much to the availability of work for women in Puerto Vallarta. Resorts such as Puerto Vallarta tend to attract women who, lacking male support as a result of divorce, desertion and so on, need to find a source of income themselves; as such, a disproportionate number of female heads of household seem to move into the city from outside (Chant, 1991a, p. 172). The other important point is that, for women natives and migrants alike, the knowledge that they can find work if they want it seems to produce a situation in which they are less likely to get married and/or to stay with a man if a relationship does not work out.

Indeed, rates of formal marriage among women in male-headed households in the survey settlements in Puerto Vallarta are only 79.7 per cent, compared with 91.6 per cent in Querétaro and 97.1 per cent in León (Chant, 1991a, pp. 172–3). Although many women in Puerto Vallarta wanted children and had them, several would also, in their own words, 'try their partners out' before committing themselves to a formal union. A common pattern is to live with a man and to have one or two children before deciding to 'tie the knot'. This is important since, generally speaking, 'free unions' are frowned upon in all social classes, and elsewhere in Mexico pregnant single women are usually subject to family pressure to marry the fathers.

According to interviewees, and with confirmation from case studies and work histories (Chant, 1991a), the existence of paid work helps explain the situation. Because women can be financially viable without a husband, they are less likely to enter a marital relationship in the first place or tie themselves to a partner who may be problematic (see below). This idea finds support from other academic analyses (cf. Blumberg, 1978; Safa, 1981).

However, other factors are also significant. Major migration to Puerto Vallarta commenced only in the 1970s and, compared to longer-established cities such as León and Querétaro, people are not surrounded by kinsfolk. Consequently, young people apparently face less pressure to conform to established social norms (Chant, 1991a, p. 173). Many women regarded this lack of kin as extremely positive, arguing that too many girls married young, before they experienced life, and that marriage should be entered into only when sure of one's partner.

In addition, the social ambience of Puerto Vallarta seems freer and more relaxed than that of the conservative cities of the central highlands. Women in Puerto Vallarta's settlements seem far happier to talk openly about sex and relationships than women in León and Querétaro. Moreover, people are less embarrassed and reluctant to disclose their status as single parents than in other cities. Indeed, single parenthood in Puerto Vallarta does not seem to bear the same stigma as it does elsewhere in the country, and even reports of such local planning authorities as the Co-ordinating Commission of the Development of the Ameca River Basin emphasise how tourism development in the city has brought with it greater personal liberty for women and an acceptance of unmarried motherhood (see COCODERA, 1980, pp. 515–18). The same organisation attributes this situation to women's access to work in the resort, and to contact with foreign customs and behaviour. The tourist industry brings women from other parts of the world (especially the United States and Canada) into close contact with their Mexican counterparts, and appears to have made a strong impression. Several interviewees in the survey settlements expressed approval for more casual Western styles of dress and had themselves taken to wearing shorts and sleeveless T-shirts in the street (a rare sight in the interior of the country, even at home or in the local neighbourhood). Several also commented favourably on the fact that North American women had their own money and sometimes openly paid the bills in hotels and restaurants, and how even married women came on holiday without their husbands and children. Those interviewees who, in their younger days, had also worked in the United States with a family they first met in Puerto Vallarta, were even more convinced that Mexican women (and men) should draw some lessons from their North American neighbours.

Where households have a male head, it is noteworthy that working women appear to have more egalitarian relationships with their partners than in other parts of the country, where women have lower rates of labour force participation and where 'machismo' seems a more prominent cultural characteristic.[4] Certainly, women in Puerto Vallarta have a considerable role in household decision-making, expenditure, and also in influencing household membership. To alleviate the burden of women working full-time, for example, female relatives are often invited to live with the family and share the workload (see Chant, 1991a, Chapters 4, 5 and 7). Moreover, husbands tend to have greater respect for their wives and treat them accordingly, possibly recognising that their wives can leave them if they want. Challenges to male dominance over women in tourist resorts have also been noted for Ixtapa-Zihuatanejo by Kennedy, Russin and Amalfi (1978) and Reynoso y Valle and De Regt (1979).

Having emphasised some of the more positive social impacts of tourism development on low-income women, it is also important to note the existence of certain counter-tendencies. These fall into two main camps: the first relates to home life and the second to the wider labour market.

In the domestic sphere, there are two main problems. First, women employed in the formal sector who lack domestic help from adult relatives pay the cost of a 'double day' of paid and unpaid work. Although some husbands assist with chores, women are generally left with exclusive responsibility for housework and child-care. Consequently, they often pass tasks to children (especially eldest daughters) which is also unsatisfactory when the latter have their own jobs or studies to consider. The 'double day' is particularly hard on women in low-income settlements which lack such essential services as piped water and sanitation networks. Certainly women in Puerto Vallarta have little time for themselves if they do have jobs.

In addition, some men have reacted to women's increased financial autonomy by reducing their own contributions to household income. The Ameca River Development Commission suggests that men accustomed to being breadwinners with dependent wives may find it extremely difficult to adjust in a town where women have abundant work opportunities and may be the only ones in the household with a secure wage (see COCODERA, 1980, pp. 518–19). Such men may begin to withhold financial support and let their wives provide the bulk of the resources for family consumption. Some also begin to indulge in flagrant displays of drinking, gambling and card-playing. However, while this situation obtained for a small minority of households in the survey settlements, women who had received negative treatment usually left their husbands, or successfully managed to re-negotiate the balance of domestic obligations.

In the local labour market, other problems are apparent. While women have access to employment in Puerto Vallarta, they still tend to occupy inferior positions in terms of the status and remuneration of their jobs. As mentioned earlier, the tourism labour force is highly gender-segmented, with men tending to occupy the more prestigious branches of employment, and/or posts at higher ranks in firm hierarchies.

In non-administrative hotel work, for example, women are usually limited to areas that require no further training in skills beyond those they have picked up in the context of their domestic roles within the household, such as chambermaiding and laundrywork, whereas men may be found in portering, gardening, waitering, bar work and sometimes in kitchen work. While the legal minimum wage for chambermaids and laundryworkers is actually 20 per cent higher than for bell-boys, groundsmen, waiters, bar attendants and so on, the tips received in female jobs are much lower, with male jobs bringing in about five times as much in gratuities per week as those followed by women (see Chant, 1991a, pp. 76–7).

Men also tend to occupy the more 'visible' posts involving direct contact with the public in restaurants and catering establishments, whereas women provide behind-the-scenes support. There are few waitresses and cooks, for example, but numerous female dishwashers and kitchen assistants (see Chant, 1991a, Chapter 3). Again, this affects the tips received, which in more visible posts can be three times as much as the basic weekly wage. In Puerto Vallarta, the advantages of a 'male' job, such as waitering, are exemplified by the fact that a number of professionals from big cities such as Mexico City and Guadalajara move to Puerto Vallarta during the high season to make money, whereas it is virtually unknown for professional women to move to take jobs as bed-makers and linen-keepers.

Beyond this, the feminised segments of employment into which women move tend to have little career structure. The organisation of housekeeping departments in hotels, for instance, tends to consist of a group of chambermaids overseen by one supervisor, and perhaps a deputy, whereas waitering has a greater range of ranks and specialisations. A large restaurant, for example, may have supervisors, chief waiters, section waiters, wine waiters and commis waiters. Given that employment opportunities in the city are also more abundant for men, they have greater bargaining power in negotiations for promotion; if an upward move is impossible within one enterprise, they can always leave and take employment in another. As such, men tend to ascend to jobs with higher pay and status at a much faster rate than women. Further light on the disproportionate representation of men at supervisory levels may be gained from the observation of some employers that men accustomed to power in domestic life found it difficult to take orders from women (cf. Chant, 1991a, Chapter 3).

Finally, women in Puerto Vallarta tend to face more barriers to entering employment than men on the grounds of age and marital status. Employers generally prefer young single women for shop work, hotel work, restaurants and so on, because these women are less likely to be prone to absenteeism and/or have fewer distractions as a result of family commitments, whereas men can generally find work at any age (see Chant, 1991a, Chapter 3, especially Table 3.4, p. 75).

On balance, then, while such tourist resorts as Puerto Vallarta seem to be characterised by labour market circumstances that extend certain aspects of women's personal freedom and allow them to make fairly crucial decisions in terms of their domestic arrangements, there are still several forces, operating from within the home and at the workplace, which maintain them in an inferior and subordinate position. However, some employers in Puerto Vallarta claimed to be experimenting with women in areas of employment usually occupied by men. It was said that, despite their family commitments, women were often more reliable than men, arriving for work on time, tending not to become drunk on the job (in bar work), and proving more trustworthy with money (cf. Chant, 1991a, Chapter 3). It will be interesting to see whether the development of international tourism in Costa Rica, just as it has tended to marginalise the lower-income groups into jobs at the lower end of the skill and productivity spectrum, will also, over time, come to be characterised by similar segmentation on grounds of gender.

Notes

1. The author is grateful to the Leverhulme Trust and Central Research Fund for supporting work in Mexico, and to the Nuffield Foundation and Economic and Social Research Council (Research Award No. R000231151) for funding research in Costa Rica.
2. Fieldwork in Puerto Vallarta in 1986 was carried out as part of a comparative study of women, work and low-income households in three intermediate Mexican cities (the other two cities being León and Querétaro in the central highlands). Data collection was carried out by means of a household survey directed to women in low-income settlements, and an employer survey with a sample of firms in each town. Ninety-two women were interviewed in Puerto Vallarta, 77 in León and 20 in Querétaro. In the latter city, a larger survey of 244 households had been carried out in 1982–3 under the auspices of a doctoral programme (Chant, 1984). The household survey comprised two main components: a questionnaire survey, and in-depth semi-structured interviews with a sub-sample of women. These were aimed at gathering socio-economic data on household units with particular reference to women's work in household survival strategies and its relationship to household composition (Chant, 1991a: Appendix 1). The employer survey was based on interviews with recruiting personnel in a range of enterprises characteristic of the locally dominant branches of formal economic activity in each city. In Puerto Vallarta the survey consisted of twenty-one hotels, restaurants and commercial establishments; in León, fourteen firms relating to shoe production (including footwear manufacturing itself, as well as cardboard box-making, rubber sheet production and so on) were surveyed, and in Querétaro, the sample covered fourteen firms in the four dominant types of industrial activity: capital goods production, food and drink manufacture, chemicals and parachemicals, and metal-mechanical production. The employer survey gathered basic data on the composition of the

workforce, paying particular attention to the role of gender in recruitment policies and practice (Chant, 1991a, Appendix 2).

3. The figures for Puerto Vallarta and León relate to the survey carried out by the author in 1986 and those for Querétaro in 1982–3. This is because the 1986 survey in Querétaro was non-random and based on only a small number of households (twenty), whereas the 1982–3 survey was random and covered 244 households.

4. Although there is considerable debate on the precise meaning of the term 'machismo', there is a broad agreement that it is a form of patriarchy characteristic of Spanish-colonised Meso and South America. The root of the term is the Spanish word 'macho', meaning male, and it is generally utilised to describe a situation where men dominate women ideologically, physically and sexually (cf. Brydon and Chant, 1989, pp. 16–18).

8 Tourism development in Cuba[1]

Derek R. Hall

'. . . we still have an awful lot to learn about tourism . . . (it) will be the leading industry, and since we haven't found those big oil deposits, it is marvellous to have at our disposal these extraordinary deposits of natural resources for tourism' (Fidel Castro, 5 May 1990, quoted in *Granma Weekly Review (GWR)*, 27 May 1990, p. 3).

'. . . tourism is not only part of the spinal column of our economy but also it is an opening through which we may view the world – hear new voices, break down insularity and the blockade' (Eusebio Leal, official Historian of the City of Havana, quoted in Barclay, 1990).

Introduction

If there is a guiding theme for this chapter, it is the paradox of persistence and change. At the turn of the century, Cuba's political economy moved from Spanish colonialism to US semi-colonialism and thence in mid-century to a form of state socialism. Yet despite these very considerable superstructural changes the country remained dependent upon markets for Cuban sugar and upon sources of fuel and energy, particularly petroleum, in which the island is crucially deficient. Reinforcing this dependency, Cuba was the first and most important focus for international tourism in the Caribbean until the late 1950s. United States territories excepted, no other Caribbean island had closer ties with the US. Since the 1959 revolution and the imposition of a US economic embargo from the early 1960s, none has had fewer contacts with the US.

As a major vehicle and symbol of dependence, international tourism was initially spurned by the revolutionary government, which had more pressing political and economic priorities. By the mid-1980s, a succession of disappointing sugar harvests and low world prices for sugar, tobacco and nickel resulted in crucial shortages of hard currency and a significant reduction in economic growth. Repayments on debts to the West (estimated at three billion dollars) were suspended in July 1986. With declining economic and ideological support from the Soviet Union and its (former) allies, and with no little irony, the country's leadership decided in 1987 to give priority to tourism development, albeit of a quality different from that of the pre-revolutionary period.

The nature of the country's resource base and profound changes in external relations have thus conditioned Cuba's political economy in general (White, 1987; Zimbalist, 1982; Zimbalist and Eckstein, 1987), and its attitude towards international tourism development in particular. Set within a context of uncertainty over Cuba's future, the interrelationship of these factors provides the focus for this chapter.

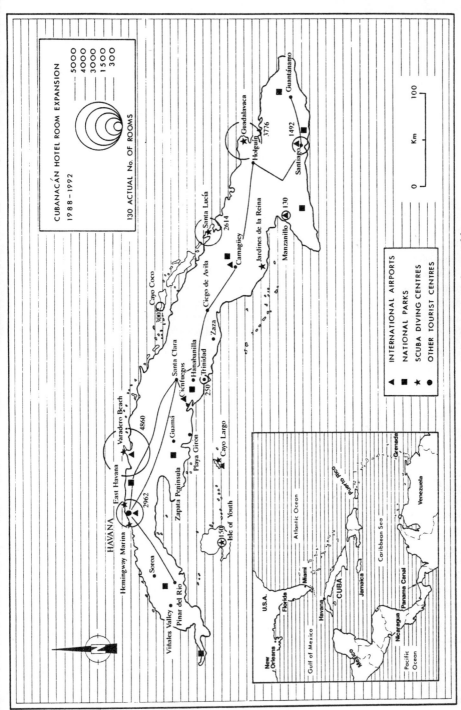

Figure 8.1 Cuba: major features of tourism development. Inset: Cuba's location in the Caribbean

The regional context

Roughly the size of England (114, 524 sq km), Cuba is the largest country in the Caribbean, comprising almost half of the region's island area. Yet many assessments of the country's development overlook its regional setting. As a Spanish-speaking society with a particularly colonial heritage, Cuba is often placed in a Latin American rather than a Caribbean perspective. Since the 1960s, Cuba's position within the Soviet bloc has added a further dimension to the comparative framework. This implied 'un-Caribbeanness' is perversely reaffirmed by the numerous Western tourism guide books to the Caribbean which omit Cuba (American Automobile Association, 1990; Blume et al., n.d.; Jamison and Jamison, 1990; Peterson, 1990; Runge, 1990; Schwab, 1988; Tucker, 1989; Zellers, 1990). This partly reflects the US government's ban on its citizens visiting the island. However, volumes on the Caribbean by Birnbaum (1988), Box and Cameron (1990) and Henderson (1990), do encompass Cuba in their tourist assessments, while recent guides specifically focusing on the country include Calder (1990), Gébler (1988), Rann and Geide (1985), di Perna (1979) and Gravette (1988), the latter two receiving official Cuban sponsorship.

Although Cuba is only 145 km from Florida (Figure 8.1), the country's relative political isolation in the hemisphere, reinforced by the US embargo, has largely precluded the level of tourism activity experienced elsewhere in the Caribbean. Consequently, Cuba attracts only around three per cent of all Caribbean tourist arrivals (Table 8.1). This figure actually declined during the second half of the 1980s

 Do

Table 8.1   The Caribbean and Cuba: tourist arrivals (millions)

Date	Caribbean Total	Caribbean Cruise passengers	Cuba Total	Cuba Cruise passengers	Cuban arrivals as % of Caribbean arrivals
1980	6.880	3.603	0.094	nd	1.37
1985	7.765	4.026	0.240	0.002	3.14
1986	8.203	5.032	0.282	0.003	3.44
1987	9.301	5.733	0.293	0.003	3.15
1988	9.797	6.404	0.309	0.005	3.16
1989	10.846	6.710	0.310	nd	2.86
2000a	12.930		0.455		3.52
2000b	15.680		0.659		4.20
2000c	23.790		1.333		5.60

Notes: a projection based on 1979–89 last quarter decade rate
　　　 b projection based on 1979–89 last half decade rate
　　　 c projection based on 1979–89 decade rate

	1980–9 Average annual % increase	Overall % increase	Share of world market 1989
Caribbean	5.2	57.7	2.69
Cuba	14.2	229.8	0.08

Sources: World Tourism Organisation 1990, Vol. I, pp. 14, 24, 28 and 41; Sobers et al., 1990, pp. 167, 175, 177, 180–1, 194; author's calculations

Table 8.2 The Caribbean and Cuba: international tourism receipts

Date	Caribbean $ million	Caribbean Annual % change	Cuba $ million	Cuba annual % change	Cuban international tourism receipts as % of Caribbean total
1984	4,415	–	84	–	1.9
1985	4,958	12.3	96	14.3	1.9
1986	5,611	13.2	123	28.1	2.2
1987	6,531	16.4	145	17.9	2.2
1988	7,059	8.1	189	30.3	2.7

	1984–8 Average Increase Annual %	Overall %	% Share of World Market 1984	1988
Caribbean	12.5	59.9	4.02	3.63
Cuba	22.7	125.0	0.08	0.10

Sources: World Tourism Organisation, 1990, Vol. I, pp. 16, 128 and 132; author's calculations

after a rapid increase in the first half of the decade, although tourist income continued to rise (Table 8.2). The current re-emphasis on tourism development has, however, produced projections of visitor numbers which could see the island's share of Caribbean tourism increase significantly by the end of the century. Nevertheless, any change in the political complexion of Cuba, with its reverberations on relations with the United States, could render current figures meaningless overnight. For example, the minimal role Cuba plays in the lucrative Caribbean cruise trade (Table 8.1) largely reflects the dominance of the US market in this sector and that country's current boycott of Cuba.

Although tourism in the region accounts for just 2.7 per cent of the world market and for just $7bn of the $200bn expended globally (Table 8.2), it is the major, and sometimes the only, hard currency earner for many Caribbean island economies, with profound economic, social, cultural and environmental implications (Archer, 1985; Beekhuis, 1981; Bélisle, 1983; Bryden, 1973; Caribbean Tourism Research Centre, 1976; Erisman, 1983; Momsen, 1985; Potter, 1983; Sealey, 1982; Seward and Spinrad, 1982). While transnational corporations may be major beneficiaries of this process, this is not so in Cuba. Indeed, only since the passing of joint venture legislation in 1982 have West European, Canadian and Latin American companies been able to participate in Cuba's tourism development, albeit on a minority basis. However, this dimension was upgraded in 1987 with the declared aim of increasing hard currency tourism earnings to a billion dollars by 2000. Although, since 1980, an overall upward trend has been observed (Curtin and Sobers, 1988, p. 16) (Figure 8.2), tourism receipts remained relatively low (Tables 8.2 and 8.3). In Table 8.3, the low proportion of Cuban GDP derived from visitor expenditure could be interpreted optimistically as reflecting a relatively wide economic base and lack of dependence on tourism, as compared to several other Caribbean countries, coupled with considerable potential for tourism expansion. In practice, the entire Cuban economy has been dependent and, as overall GDP declines in deteriorating economic circumstances, tourism is increasingly seen, in desperation, as at least a short-term economic palliative.

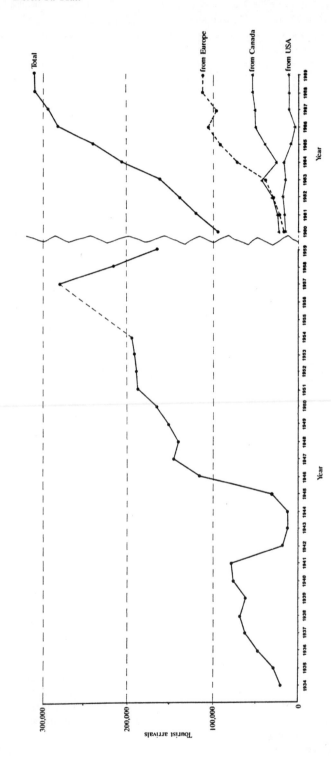

Figure 8.2   Cuba: growth in tourist arrivals, 1934–1989

Sources: Curtin and Sobers, 1988; Schroeder, 1982, p. 462; Sobers et al., 1990; World Tourism Organisation, 1983, 1985a, 1990

Table 8.3 Selected Caribbean locations: visitor expenditure as a percentage of GDP

	1980	1985	1986	1987	1988
Bermuda	58.6	74.7	83.0	87.7	84.9
Br. Virgin Islands	87.6	121.0	138.6	143.3	na
Cayman Islands	na	27.9	27.3	28.6	31.9
Cuba	0.2	0.4	0.5	na	na
Puerto Rico	4.1	3.6	3.4	3.7	3.9
Suriname	2.4	na	na	na	na
Trinidad and Tobago	2.4	2.7	1.7	1.9	1.8

Source: Sobers et al, 1990, pp. 150–1

Tourism and socialist dependency

The relationship between state socialism and international tourism has always been problematic. Whilst international tourism may be a key linkage in core-periphery relationships and a vehicle for the generation of dependency relationships with transnational corporations and 'first world' governments, an appropriately structured tourism development programme can help achieve such 'socialist' objectives as increasing spatial equalisation of opportunities and imbuing visitors with a sense of the superiority of the socialist system (Hall, 1990a, 1990b). However, the inflexibility of state socialist bureaucracy has often compromised the achievement of its own objectives (Hall, 1991).

Cuba's pre-revolutionary political economy contained the essential ingredients of classic dependency: the economy was dependent upon international economic and political circumstances, economic surpluses were largely directed to developed countries, particularly the United States, while an economic and social élite enjoyed most of the domestic benefits of the Cuban dependent economy. Since the revolution, however, Cuba has continued to be highly dependent upon external, controlling factors for securing sugar markets and sources of fuel and energy: economic circumstances which have given rise to ideological and conceptual debate.

Although Cuba did not join the Soviet bloc Council for Mutual Economic Assistance (CMEA) until 1972 (Bosakova, 1987; Shearman, 1987; Smith, 1988), Soviet credits had begun as early as 1960 (Bach, 1987). The two-way flow of Cuban sugar to the Soviet Union (and to other CMEA countries) and Soviet oil to Cuba provided both an assured market for around sixty per cent of Cuba's annual crop at relatively stable, guaranteed prices, and an important and regular source of fuel. Cuba was able to use this relationship to its financial advantage, re-selling a proportion of its subsidised Soviet oil at market prices for hard currency to prop up its own foreign exchange stocks (Pérez-López, 1987, 1988a). When world market sugar prices were lower than Cuban production costs, Cuba bought cheaply on world markets to sell, as its own sugar, to the Soviet Union and other CMEA members for guaranteed higher prices (Pérez-López, 1988b). These transactions contributed over half of the country's annual hard currency earnings (Duncan, 1986). Attempts at economic diversification (Hall, 1981a) and the use of limited indigenous oil could not free Cuba from a dependent economic relationship which such manipulations only helped to reinforce (Smith, 1985).

By the mid-1980s, Soviet investment in Cuba was estimated to be up to five billion dollars per year, representing over half of all Soviet aid to developing countries (Duncan, 1986, pp. 46, 51). The USSR had been involved in over 400 joint industrial projects (*GWR*, 14 February 1988, p. 6), and employed some 19,700 Soviet military and civilian personnel on Cuban soil (Erisman, 1985). Now, with political change and internal disruption within the Soviet Union reducing absolute oil production levels, cutting exports, changing trade attitudes and requiring hard currency payment from 1991, and with the end of East–West tensions in Europe aiding a Soviet cut-back of military spending, Cuba finds itself in both an ideologically and economically confined position.

Under these circumstances, attempts at understanding both Cuba's 'socialist dependency', and the likely consequences of its transformation are important in helping to place the role of international tourism development in perspective. However, the literature is at best ambivalent. LeoGrande (1979), in a methodolog- ically flawed analysis (Mesa-Lago, 1981, Packenham, 1986) argued that if the high level of Soviet trade and aid was to be seen as 'dependency', then it was a 'strikingly different form' from the accepted capitalist model (LeoGrande, 1979, pp. 27–8). Packenham (1986) examined nine major indicators of Cuban dependency. Of these, six had shown no change since 1959, two had revealed increased dependency, and only one, a comparison of trade partner concentration with the USSR since the revolution and with the USA before 1959, could be interpreted as expressing less dependency. Other observers have argued that Cuba has not been subject to long- term capital outflows, deteriorating terms of trade, or extraction by the core (Roca, 1988; Zimbalist, 1988), and have stressed the convergence of interests between Cuba and the Soviet Union, claiming Soviet influence to have been positive for Cuban development processes (Fagen, 1978a; Brundenius, 1984). Packenham, by contrast, considering Cuba as an 'economic liability' yet 'political asset' (Blasier, 1983) for the USSR, concluded that an 'alliance of Cuban and Soviet élites' had systematically dominated and exploited the Cuban people (Packenham, 1986, p. 88). The reality lies somewhere between these poles.

Data sources and problems

Until the early 1980s, official Cuban statistical data in several fields were at best sketchy. But from the 1982 issue of *Anuario Estadístico de Cuba*, published by the State Committee for Statistics (Comité Estatal de Estadísticas – CEE), data relating to a number of sectors, including tourism, were improved. *Cuba en Cifras*, a summary of the *Anuario*, has included a section on tourist numbers and accommodation since 1981. The CEE annual English language publication *The Cuban Economy in 19..* only introduced a tourism section in its issue for 1989 (State Committee for Statistics, 1990). The Cuban National Bank, jointly with CEE, publishes an annual *Economic Report* and the *Cuba Quarterly Economic Report* (*CQER*), but only since March 1989 has a separate section of one or two paragraphs on international tourism appeared. The *Boletín Estadístico Mensual de Cuba* is a monthly statistical bulletin published since January 1983. An English language offshoot, *Cuba Economic News*, which appears six times a year, has included a separate tourism section since its May/June 1987 issue.

Lingering problems with most of these official sources, however, include changing definitional bases, a lack of any data in such areas as tourism-related employment, and an often considerable time lag between compilation, publication and availability. The major alternative source is the World Tourism Organisation's annual *Yearbook of Tourism Statistics*, the 1989 issue of which appeared in the summer of 1990, containing national data up to 1988. In the case of Cuba, data are found in some nineteen separate tables in this two-volume 1,300-word compendium; useful comparative Caribbean data appear in a further four separate tables. The Caribbean Tourism Organization, based in Christ Church Barbados, also publishes an annual statistical report (e.g. Sobers et al., 1990), placing Cuba within its regional context although, compared to most other territories, the data available for the country are somewhat limited.

Pre-revolutionary tourism development

The historical perspective

Cuba's first international tourist was Christopher Columbus. Arriving in October 1492, he is claimed to have described the island as 'the most beautiful land ever seen' (*CTN*, March 1989). Conquered by Spain in the early sixteenth century, Cuba soon became a stepping stone for further ventures in Central and South America, serving as a focal point for merchant vessels and attracting many visitors. By mid-nineteenth century, the imperial process had turned almost full circle: Spain had lost all its American colonies except Cuba and Puerto Rico. After the Louisana and Florida purchases, Cuba appeared to American expansionists as the next logical territorial incorporation. This appeared to be reinforced by the symbolic way in which the Florida peninsula pointed towards the island's heart, and by the country's strategic location in relation to the yet to be completed Panama Canal. With substantial economic interests in the island to protect, the United States quickly defeated Spain in their 1898 conflict.

Though proclaimed in 1902, Cuban independence was limited by the Platt Amendment. This maintained the United States' right to intervene in Cuban affairs, which it did several times before the Amendment was repealed in 1934. The impact of this imposition laid the basis for a lasting anti-American feeling which was most forcefully expressed in the 1959 revolution.

Cuba as a playground for North Americans

From the early 1900s, Cuba had been a major recreational attraction for North Americans. Not only was it easily accessible, but its winter climate was considered healthy, and even capable of providing a cure for consumption. By 1915 there were seventy-two hotels on the island, twenty-seven of them (37.5 per cent) in Havana (Sims, 1916, p. 31). In the 1930s, the annual average tourism income of over twelve million dollars represented the country's third most important 'export' commodity after heavily dominant sugar ($116 million) and tobacco ($14 million), with visitors annually numbering over 130,000 (Schroeder, 1982, p. 454) (Figure 8.2) In 1938, for example, Cuba received 37 per cent of all tourists visiting the Caribbean (Anglo–American Caribbean Commission, 1945; Momsen, 1985).

Cuba remained the tourist hub of the Caribbean region well into the early post-war period. A wide range of recreational opportunities were made available: mineral springs, swimming and other beach activities, yachting, fishing, hunting, horse racing, polo, golf, tennis, jai-alai and baseball (Schroeder, 1982, p. 451), as well as gambling, prostitution and related pursuits. The demonstration effect of this process saw the Cuban élite seeking North American lifestyles and reinforcing dependency by stimulating the import of goods to meet such aspirations (Hall, 1989). Despite wartime depression, tourism expanded with US promotion, reaching its peak in 1957, when 355,805 foreign tourists and excursionists visited the country, 87 per cent of whom were from the USA. But with increasing domestic instability, decline set in thereafter.

Inter-war and early post-war public works projects on tourism-related infrastructure included improvements to highways, public buildings, water supplies and airports. Between 1951 and 1958, of the 172.6 million pesos expended on specific tourist zones, 76.9 per cent was channelled into Havana, with Varadero the next most important centre, receiving 8.7 per cent, and Santiago 5.3 per cent. However, a further 167 million pesos were also used for the upgrading and provision of new roads to promote tourism throughout the island, thus spreading investment distribution a little more widely (Schroeder, 1982, p. 458). An accommodation building boom was fostered by the Hotel Act of 1953 and financed by government credit institutions. Between 1951 and 1958, hotel capacity rose by a third, with Havana Province increasing its dominant share from 63.3 to 69.4 per cent of the country's total bed-place capacity: increases were concentrated at Vedado (2,030), downtown Havana (1,186) and Miramar (1,016), whilst elsewhere, only Varadero (372), Santa Clara (280) and Ciego de Avila (144) saw increased capacities of more than a hundred during this period (Schroeder, 1982, pp. 455, 458–9). Indeed, 78.1 per cent of all hotel capacity expansion undertaken between 1952 and 1958 took place within Havana city, virtually ending with the 25-storey Havana Hilton, opened in March 1958.

Even so, not until 1956 was the annual balance of tourism account in the black: between 1947 and 1955, official figures record that Cuban tourists travelling abroad – predominantly to the United States – continued to spend more than foreign tourists in Cuba, thereby exacerbating economic dependency. The biggest deficit was recorded for 1950, when the shortfall was $14.5 million. The peak tourism year of 1957 saw a positive balance of $25.9 million and total foreign tourist expenditure within Cuba of $62.1 million (Schroeder, 1982, p. 463). Such figures, however, excluded disbursements and other leakages.

Pre-revolutionary tourism was therefore concentrated in and around Havana, with a secondary concentration at Varadero. This reflected the socio–economic and spatial disparities within the country at that time: most professional services and major educational and health facilities were located in the capital. Strong US controlling influences in the tourism industry mirrored Cuba's dependency relationship with that country, while the undercurrent of vice and organised crime reflected the close spatial proximity of the two countries and the US perception of Cuba as the nearby underdeveloped sub-tropical playground where 'anything goes'.

The impact of the Cuban Revolution

When victory was attained in 1959, the revolutionary struggle, while strongly anti-American, was aimed essentially against the inequalities of Cuban society. A range of general social welfare and economic measures was introduced to improve the well-being both of Afro–Cubans and poor white groups. Socio–economic equality in domestic leisure and recreation was sought through the eradication of Cuba's exclusive white associations and an opening up to all groups of private beaches, luxury night clubs and hotels (Azicri, 1988, p. 52). Varadero Beach, for example, Cuba's best and most important tourist centre, developed from 1880 by the

American textile millionaire Dupont family, excluded native Cubans. Somewhat ironically, the commercialisation of Afro–Cuban culture for tourists at the Tropicana night club and elsewhere continued.

Following the US boycott imposed in 1961, a debate ensued concerning the country's future economic strategy. This was similar to that over Soviet industrialisation undertaken in the 1920s (Carciofi, 1983). Tourism had little part to play in this: an industry without chimneys and heavy machinery could not generate the same feeling of achievement and progress that socialist dogma derived from a new cement plant; it also carried the stigma of being the vehicle for pre-revolutionary corruption and vice and a symbol of socio–economic inequality.

As in other countries attempting to follow Marxist–Leninist principles, Cuba's 'early socialist' period was characterised by severe constraints on international tourism and an emphasis on domestic or 'social' tourism. Families were encouraged, through collective institutions, to gather knowledge about their motherland and its socialist achievements by taking subsidised holidays organised by their trade union or workplace. Such vacations, often granted to groups who had not previously enjoyed paid holidays, were taken in key cultural, historical and ideological centres, with available accommodation ranging from former international tourist hotels to spartan hostels and school buildings. Under-privileged groups, such as large families and peasants from remoter areas of the country, were given priority alongside such favoured groups as veterans of the revolutionary war and model workers. The emphasis of such 'tourism' was educational. It complemented national programmes of illiteracy eradication and the need to reduce urban–rural and regional socio–economic inequalities (and to transform the resulting attitudes of superiority and inferiority).

The 1960s saw an emphasis upon mass labour mobilisation and the idealism of moral incentives. But it was not successful economically. Consequently, in the 1970s and the first half of the 1980s there was a move to economic rationalisation and the need to exploit comparative advantages rather than to pursue too rapid a policy of diversification. Such comparative advantages included tourist attractions: beaches, mountains and other natural features, as well as the island's cultural heritage. Cubatur, the state tourist agency, began to expand and refurbish its infrastructure, and a National Institute of Tourism (Intur) was created to regenerate the industry. Foreign tourist numbers quadrupled in the mid-1970s, aided by the Carter administration's lifting the ban on US citizens visiting the island in 1977. But this was re-imposed by the Reagan leadership in 1982 (Rudolph, 1985, p. 221), and has especially restricted Cuban efforts to tap the growing cruise-ship holiday market (Table 8.1).

In 1986, with increasing economic pressures, a re-emphasis was placed upon moral incentives and mass mobilisation within a national 'rectification of errors' campaign. Diverging from the new direction being taken in Moscow, Cuba's leadership declared *perestroika* and *glasnost* to be irrelevant to their country's situation.

Cuba's tourism resources and activities

Coastal and water-related tourism

With 5,746 km of coastline, 1,600 cays (keys) and islets, coves, bays and inlets, as well as coral reefs, Cuba boasts 289 recognised beaches, the largest number of any

Caribbean country. Varadero, the most popular beach resort, possesses more than 20 km of white sand; other major coastal areas are indicated on Figure 8.1.

Although modern watersports can be found only on the most developed tourist beaches, the majority of those so designated are equipped for a limited range of activities; eight scuba diving centres have been established (Figure 8.1). The country has built up an international reputation for sport fishing – as championed by Ernest Hemingway – both in its varied seas and freshwater lakes and rivers. The semi-independent Cubanacán tourist corporation has sought a more extensive water sports market based around the annual marlin tournament. The recently developed Hemingway Marina to the west of Havana attracts a limited number of sea-going yachts and fishing enthusiasts.

The heritage industry

Since the revolution, the focus of Cuba's tourism, after its beaches, has been the country's historic sites. While the Spanish colonial area of Old Havana acts as the prime attraction (Barclay, 1990), the cities and many smaller towns contain a variety of historic monuments; baroque cathedrals, colonial palaces, forts and mansions, cobbled streets and squares, and catalan style haciendas (cf. Castillo, 1981). Many older buildings have only recently begun to receive due attention.

Trinidad, one of the most notable cities, located on the south coast, was founded in 1514. Designated a city-museum, and, since December 1988, a UNESCO 'world heritage site', it was an important residential location for plantation owners and one of Spain's richest colonial settlements in the New World.

Mostly comprising two- and three-storey Spanish colonial buildings fringing narrow, grid-iron streets, Old Havana has suffered from a rudimentary infrastructure, physical deterioration, demolition, infilling and congestion (Judge, 1989; Torrents, 1989). In the mid-1960s, a National Monuments Commission began to study its problems but not until a decade later, following the declaration of the area as a 'national landmark', was indiscriminate demolition halted and preparations for a comprehensive restoration programme commenced (Capablanca, 1985). The 1982 UNESCO declaration that the area was of 'world cultural heritage' status has had a knock-on effect for the greater care of other historic assemblages in the country (M'Bow, 1985; Hamberg, 1986).

Activity tourism

The island's interior presents a variety of natural environments, being divided by mountain ranges, plains, forests, farmland and river valleys, with spectacular waterfalls, 25 kilometres of explored mountain caves, botanical gardens, wildlife parks and marine reserves. Facilities exist for camping, trekking, horse riding, climbing and caving. Mountain resort holidays are particularly popular amongst Cubans themselves. The country hosts some 380 species of birds, twenty-one of which are indigenous. The Soledad Botanical Gardens near Cienfuegos contain many of the island's plant species, while Soroa's orchidarium nurtures over 700 examples. In all, some 8,000 species of flora are represented, many of which are indigenous. In 1963, the Academy of Sciences set aside land for six national parks, including such diverse environments as the swamps of the Zapata peninsula and the limestone stacks of the Sierra de los Organos (Figure 8.1). In such areas, which cover four per cent of the country's land area, hunting and tree felling are prohibited. They are overseen by the National Committee for the Protection and Conservation of National Treasures. Controlled hunting is mostly pursued in the country's wetlands (Gravette, 1988, pp. 105–7), where accommodation can be spartan (eg. see Gébler, 1988, pp. 48–9).

Health tourism

Affluent Latin Americans who may once have gone to the United States for medical treatment have been attracted to Cuba by relatively low cost, high quality health care in such areas as heart surgery, kidney transplants and other specialised therapies, for example, vitiligo skin disease. By the end of the 1980s, about 2,000 tourist patients were being treated, and through Cubanacán's joint venture activities it was planned to establish a number of health-care resorts. Nestling at an altitude of 800 metres in the Escambray Mountains some 27 kilometres from Trinidad, and refurbished in 1988, is the Topes de Collantes sanatorium, said to be the only one of its kind in the Caribbean. Containing over 200 rooms, both the sanatorium's accommodation and activities are being expanded as a cluster of hotels are being developed around it (*GWR*, 8 July 1990, p. 12).

Conference and business tourism

As a major global tourism growth activity, conference and business tourism is being promoted, with attention focused on providing services for those attending conventions at Havana's International Conference Centre. Tourism-related business activities themselves have contributed to this process; for example, the World Tourism Organisation's seminar on tourist marketing strategies for the Americas was held in June, 1989, and the Ninth Congress of the World Association of Tourist Personnel Training was held in November 1990. Previously sponsored by a number of former Soviet bloc countries, Cuba has maintained its support for the study and use of Esperanto, with several events being regularly held in the country. Recently, the notion of 'scientific tourism' has been promoted with the completion, in July 1990, of the 110-room Biocaribe Hotel in Havana. Built for Cubanacán, this hotel has been aimed exclusively at professionals and scientists, particularly those in transit. However, Aeroflot's announcement late in 1990 that it was intending to shift the hub of its flights between Europe and Latin America from Havana to Miami is likely to considerably reduce the viability of such a venture.

Current priorities

The expansion of tourist numbers and income

In 1987, with deteriorating economic circumstances and rapidly diminishing external ideological support, past prejudices were cast aside and the country's leadership assigned tourism Cuba's top economic priority, aiming to extract $1 billion from more than 500,000 tourists by 1992. Major resources were allocated to semi-competitive state tourism enterprises; joint venture promotion was re-emphasised while necessary improvements in construction, gastronomy, tourist products, recreation, environmental protection, transport and services were to be encouraged.

A sum of $395 million was set aside for Intur to develop and upgrade facilities at such 'key' resorts as Varadero and Cayo Largo, and for an aggressive promotional campaign to be undertaken. In 1986, Publicitur, the Intur enterprise for tourism promotion and marketing, launched a campaign in major long haul markets, emphasising Cuba's competitive prices compared to the rest of the Caribbean. In Europe, the UK and Scandinavia received special attention, with Cubatur and state airline Cubana de Aviacíon offices opening in London. The initial response was encouraging, with such large tour operators as Thomson UK offering package holidays in Cuba. However, there were no direct flights from Britain, from which country Cuban tourism representation was later removed. Greater success was achieved in West Germany and Italy, where direct scheduled flights were available. However, the continued US trade embargo has seriously restricted Cuban efforts to exploit the growing cruise-ship holiday market (Table 8.1).

By 1988, Canada was still the major single source of tourist arrivals, although its share had fallen from a peak in 1986 of 17.9 per cent (50,415 arrivals) to 17.1 per cent (53,000 arrivals). The Spanish were the next most numerous group, representing 9.9 per cent (30,663) of the total (WTO, 1990, Vol. 2, p. 147), reflecting historical links, direct air access and business and investment activity. By contrast, the UK, France and the Netherlands have stronger ties in other parts of the Caribbean with former colonies and dependencies. Arrivals from Eastern Europe and the Soviet Union made up almost a quarter of 1988 arrivals – 24.4 per cent (75,557). Visitors from this region have subsequently diminished dramatically; for the first nine months of 1990 they were a mere four per cent of the total.

Accommodation upgrading

The industry aims to increase its accommodation capacity to 28,000 rooms for 522,000 tourists by 1992 and, by the turn of the century, to 40,000 rooms for 1.5 million tourists (McManus, 1990). Until recently, the backbone of international tourism accommodation has been the large hotels in Havana and Varadero Beach, which were build before the revolution – for example, the Havana Nacional or the International, Varadero. Before recent refurbishment, these were rather antiquated compared with hotel accommodation in most other Caribbean resorts. During the 1970s, rather drab, similarly-styled hotels were built in several provincial capitals. These newer hotels have either been located in the more popular beach resort areas or provide supplementary accommodation in hunting, sporting and country resorts. At Varadero Beach, Cuba's prime beach resort 250 kilometres from Havana, there are plans to build 3000 rooms annually up to a total of 30,000 by the year 2000, as well as for substantial infrastructural upgrading.

Although most tourist class hotels in Cuba are three-star establishments, some larger hotels in the capital and the more luxurious resort establishments rate either four or five stars. By contrast, several forms of accommodation, such as the 'cabañas', some self-catering units, log cabin and camp sites, are relatively spartan.

Joint ventures and international capital

Cuba's first joint venture law was introduced in February 1982, providing for up to 49 per cent foreign ownership (Pérez-López, 1986), but it remained largely in abeyance until Cubanacán was created in 1987 to seek tourism development with foreign partners willing to provide capital, expertise, experience, computerised technology and management techniques.

In the mid-1980s, Canada's Export Development Corporation helped to finance improvements at the José Martí international airport and, by the late 1980s, five joint ventures had been set up to develop new hotels, four with Spanish partners and one with a West German partner. Another joint venture was established with a Mexican firm to refurbish seven Havana hotels. However, the denial of hard currency repatriation for foreign partners in particular has constrained the effectiveness of the joint venture legislation.

A Specialised Tourism Division was established within Cubatur to undertake agreements with foreign agencies for special interest tourism, and appears to have achieved some success. For example, arrangements have been established with Italians to promote sports hunting, and with (West) Germans for fishing visits. In 1987, as part of the Cuban Railways' 150th anniversary, three groups of Spanish railway enthusiasts undertook specialised visits of the island by train.

Upgrading service training

Responding to a significant deficiency in tourism expertise and training facilities, Intur's training schools and colleges now teach skills for hotel, catering and transport services in such important resort areas as Varadero Beach. However, training efforts are hampered by a lack of infrastructure and materials. The most important tourism training centre, the Rubén Martínez Villena Polytechnic Institute of Hotel and Tourism Services, founded in 1977, has an enrolment of over 900 students. Since 1987, Cubanacán has set out to retrain the tourism staff it inherited and to establish schools for new recruits. In 1989, an international catering school was opened, and the corporation's first hotel school was established in the refurbished Comodoro in Havana. At that time Cubanacán was supervising 1,256 catering and 849 hotel administration students (*GWR*, 7 May 1989, p. 5). In January 1990, it was announced that the United Nations Development Programme would provide assistance in hotel management, public relations, computer systems and other areas of training for the tourism industry (*GWR*, 18 February 1990, p. 4).

Reflecting on the shortcomings of past practice, the manager of the first Spanish joint venture hotel at Varadero Beach pointedly indicated a preference for staff without previous hotel experience 'to avoid any pre-established vices or bad habits' (*GWR*, 24 June 1990, p. 12).

Transport improvements

Tourist transport to Cuba is almost invariably by air. The country has been regularly linked to twenty-five cities in twenty-three countries in Latin America and Europe, with charter flights from several more. Cubana de Aviación, now with an annual passenger capacity of 400,000 (*GWR*, 5 June 1988), Air Canada, Iberia, Mexicana de Aviación, Interflug, CSA, TAAG, and Aeroflot have been the major carriers, but at the time of writing the full impact of the changes in Eastern Europe had yet to be felt. Significantly, however, as noted earlier, late in 1990 Aeroflot announced an intention to substitute Miama – centre of the Cuban exile community – for Havana as its hub for flights to Latin America.

Up to 1979, only Havana's José Martí airport handled international flights; now, eight other airports have international status (Figure 8.1). A CMEA protocol of March 1986, on the comprehensive development of airports, entailed agreements to help Cuba remodel its main airport and to foster an improvement in the country's air transport infrastructure. The future of this plan is now doubtful.

As Table 8.1 revealed, Cuba's share of the Caribbean cruise trade has been very small since the revolution, although vessels of both former German states have called at Havana, and more are to be encouraged. Facilities for handling cruise ships were re-established in the early 1980s (Fraser and Hackett, 1985).

The national highway system has received some degree of renovation: whereas between 1959 and 1985, 382 kilometres of new highway were built, for the 1986–90 period 566 kilometres were planned for completion, including a new major road link to Varadero Beach. In justifying an upgrading to meet new tourism requirements, the country's leadership argued that the additional roads and causeways needed were being built at a cost of 90,000 tonnes of oil – the amount Cuba previously gave annually to the Nicaraguan Sandinista government (McManus, 1990).

The impact of tourism

The economic impact

Tourism revenue more than doubled during the second half of the 1980s (Table 8.2). While offering Cuba much-needed hard currency to help offset the fall in revenue from traditional exports, and helping to upgrade infrastructure and modernise the economy, tourism development has exposed two major economic problems. First, within Cuba there exists an extensive second economy and black market. In 1988, only half of the accumulated four billion pesos circulating was placed in savings banks, and a growing dollar economy brought in by tourism and emigrant remittances has added to inflationary and social tensions (Ridenour, 1990).

Secondly, the problem of economic leakages appears to be serious: for example, around 40 per cent of the hotel fittings in recent constructions, including air conditioning units, lifts and kitchen equipment, are imported (Hurtado, 1989). In 1986, the president of Intur estimated that plans up to 1992 would require an external expenditure of $200–250 million on equipment and materials alone (EIU, 1986, p. 77), yet recent estimates place Cuban hard currency reserves at only $40 million (Lane et al., 1990). In 1989, the proportion of Cuban produced goods sold in Intur tourist shops declined to 24.5 per cent; this was followed by an increase in the dollar budget for Suchel, the Cuban manufacturer of cosmetics, toiletries and perfume, and for Cuban handicraft organisations (*GWR*, 22 October 1989, p. 4). Somewhat ironically, a programme of constructing new shops, craft markets and entertainment areas has been accompanied by the acceptance of American Express and other credit cards.

Indigenous industries, however, are receiving a boost from tourism development. The most notable beneficiaries are those dealing in building materials, furniture, linen, ironwork and mattresses, and specialised food producers and, as a consequence, the employment multiplier is improving. Import substitution in these sectors is receiving heavy emphasis, as in other sectors of the economy. In 1989, for example, an enterprise to produce bathroom fixtures – some 200,000 units a year – was completed in Holguín. However, new plant and key requisites still need to be imported. When Fidel Castro opened the first joint venture hotel at Varadero

Beach, he noted that glass, copper and other necessary metalware imports were very expensive, and that although Cuba had an elevator factory, the quality of its output was not yet good enough for four- and five-star hotels (*GWR*, 27 May 1990, p. 2).

Detailed employment data are not available, although the Cuban leadership has recently quoted a figure of 250,000 jobs in tourism (*GWR*, 22 July 1990, p. 9).

Environmental impacts

In 1990, while arguing that Cuban tourism should be promoted, given its natural comparative advantages, United Nations Development Programme spokesmen emphasised that this should not be at the environment's expense (*GWR*, 18 February 1990, p. 4). Limited research on environmental degradation in the Caribbean (Archer, 1985; Beekhuis, 1981; Gormsen, 1988) has suggested the operation of three interdependent processes – coral damage, beach sand loss, and contamination of coastal waters. The destruction of coral reefs through sewage pollution, fertiliser residues, pleasure craft and human trampling removes their breakwater effect, thereby permitting beach erosion to take place. Water adjacent to Havana Bay, for example, is heavily polluted from maritime and industrial discharges, and smaller scale impacts can be seen around the island. Research on coral conservation and the prevention of beach erosion has been undertaken at Varadero Beach by the Oceanographic Institute of the Cuban Academy of Sciences (*GWR*, 15 July 1990, p. 4), although little official indication of environmental deterioration, least of all from tourism impacts, has yet been given.

The social impact

Attempts to establish a more even spread of tourism within the country bear a superficial resemblance to earlier idealistic spatial policies (Gugler, 1980; Hall, 1981b, 1989; Slater, 1982; Susman, 1987a, 1987b). Currently, extra hotel capacity is being developed in virtually every province to meet new international and growing domestic tourism demands. As part of this process, some accommodation previously set aside exclusively for domestic use has been upgraded for international tourism, such as the 150 concrete cabins fronting the beach at Playa Girón (Bay of Pigs). Hitherto, domestic tourists had dominated the non-hotel accommodation sectors, while foreign tourists had been disproportionately represented in hotel accommodation (Table 8.4).

To avoid the more immediately traumatic impacts of the glaring inequality tourism brings to a relatively poor developing society, Cubans appear to have been implicitly refused access to some of the more up-market hotels (and restaurants and clubs), not least because they are forbidden to hold convertible currency. Within such edifices as the four-star Hotel Nacional, the wide range of luxury goods on show in hard-currency shops and the relatively opulent food supplies available around the clock contrast markedly with the rationing and general impoverishment of the domestic economy of shortage.

Questions concerning the segregation of international and domestic tourists and the squeezing out of the latter to make way for dollar generation – for example, their exclusion from tourist taxis and certain hotels – were raised at the July 1990 session of the National Assembly. Fidel Castro argued that segregation was not the official policy but admitted that there may have been cases of ill-treatment of Cuban

Table 8.4   Cuba: international and domestic tourist nights (in millions)

	Hotels and similar accommodation		Supplementary accommodation		All nights	
	No	%	No	%	No	%
Tourists from abroad						
1987	1,949	27.5	1,148	18.6	3,097	23.4
1988	2,053	30.8	1,010	16.7	3,063	24.0
Domestic tourists						
1987	5,141	72.5	5,016	81.4	10,157	76.6
1988	4,623	69.2	5,053	83.3	9,676	76.0
All nights						
1987	7,090	100.0	6,164	100.0	13,254	100.0
1988	6,676	100.0	6,063	100.0	12,739	100.0

Source: WTO (1990), Vol. 1, pp. 63, 65, 71; author's calculations

tourists (*GWR*, 22 July 1990, p. 9). In practice, given continued currency inconvertibility, increasing economic difficulties and domestic shortages, this process is liable to increase in the short term, as hard currency generators are given higher priority and as the black market attempts to divert increasing amounts of potential tourist income into private pockets.

Domestic tourism grew in popularity during the 1980s, with more Cubans aspiring to take holidays away from home. This reflected government encouragement, the availability of new facilities and the demonstration effect of increasing international tourism.

Arguably, domestic tourism led the way in the geographical diffusion process, and represented over three-quarters of all tourist nights in 1988 (Table 8.4). In that year, there were over a million domestic tourists, 521,026 of whom took advantage of group excursions and tours (*CTN*, March 1989). By contrast, few Cubans are allowed out of their country, a proscription that will prove a source of heightening social tension as further direct contact with the outside world is brought about with increasing numbers of foreign tourists on Cuban soil. In 1984, for example, Cubans took just over 12,000 holiday trips abroad, all to countries then in the Soviet bloc (WTO, 1985b, p. 56). Even this outlet will now be disappearing. Coupled with continued rationing in an economy of shortage, the cultural impact of increasing numbers of more affluent, essentially consumer-orientated tourists with virtual total freedom of travel is likely to be immense, and eventually to have a severe impact on Cuba's political processes.

Such 'demonstration effects' can only increase currency speculation and the growth of a black economy, further fuelled by the heightened life-style aspirations of an increasingly knowledgeable and sophisticated host population. The authorities may therefore wish to reinforce segregation between tourists and hosts to minimise such impacts. This may be seen at a general level in the emphasis upon developing and consolidating self-contained beach complexes on the peninsula of Varadero, to produce an 'ocean liner' effect (Sampson, 1986). There is also now a close circuit television channel provided exclusively for tourists – Canal del Sol. However, the likely consequences of current trends in increasing segregation may be just the reverse of those intended. Although rarely discussed openly in the country's media, the question of Cuban exclusion from tourist facilities has now been taken up in popular music. At the time of writing, the song *Tropicollage* by Carlos Varela, protesting precisely against the discrimination the revolution was meant to eliminate, was beginning to take on a symbolism for the new generation of questioning Cuban youth.

Conclusions and future prospects

While large-scale tourism generation could provide a palliative for Cuba's economic problems, it raises fundamental social and ideological paradoxes. At the end of the 1980s, Cuba, the largest Caribbean country, was acting as host to just three per cent of all tourists visiting the region. If this position is to change substantially, two ingredients may be necessary: enterprise and Americans. Cuba once had the largest entrepreneurial business class in the Caribbean; many remain just 110 kilometres away in Miami, and some could well be induced to return with investment if appropriate incentives were offered. Some sixty per cent of tourists to the Caribbean are American yet, apart from returning Cuban exiles, only an illicit trickle find their way to Cuba. With such an enormous and wealthy market on its doorstep, can the present (or subsequent?) Cuban leadership afford not to build bridges with its larger neighbour (in a manner which would need to avoid a loss of face)? Yet such a development would represent a substantial turn-about, and Cuba's historic and geographical relationship with the United States has established a very particular set of parameters within which the current leadership has only limited room for manoeuvre.

Certainly, a thoroughgoing appraisal of Cuba's development path is urgently required to fill the vacuum now being left by the withdrawal of economic and ideological support from the erstwhile Soviet bloc. Since 1989, the reduction of Soviet oil shipments to Cuba has cost the country about $150 million a year in foreign currency re-sale earnings. From 1991, Cuba has had to assume petroleum shipping costs, variously estimated in the West at between $50 and $160 million annually. In January, 1991, a five-year Cuban–Soviet trade agreement expired, to be followed by trading strictly on hard currency terms, with agreements having to be ratified annually by the Supreme Soviet. As a consequence, at the time of writing no new five-year plan existed for the 1991–5 period, and senior Cuban officials were admitting that the future beyond 1992 was uncertain (Halebsky and Kirk, 1990; Halebsky et al., 1991).

Not surprisingly, economic links with Spain, which had been maintained even under Franco, became proportionately more important for Cuba as former ideological allies withdrew economic assistance. By 1990, such links amounted to $2.5 million in annual aid, $100 million in soft loans over the previous four years, and millions more in private investment in tourism. But in July, 1990, tensions were created when asylum-seeking Cubans took refuge in the Spanish and other European embassies in Havana. The Cuban leadership then precipitately compromised the island's growing tourism programme by haranguing Spain over this episode: the country which, virtually alone, had been prepared to give the Cuban tourist industry a major boost. Canada and West Germany, other major sources of tourists to Cuba, were also admonished. As a consequence, Madrid suspended all further assistance to Havana, and EEC aid, which had been little more than symbolic, was also curtailed, halting a tourism promotion scheme. This took place when Cuba most needed to cultivate the few Western governments willing to offer support for the country's faltering development programme. Furthermore, in 1991, Cuba faced a high-profile and economically costly agenda, hosting the Pan American Games and a papal visit, as well as staging the country's fourth Communist Party Congress.

At the time of writing, therefore, a sustained international tourism development programme appeared vital to ameliorate the country's parlous economic circumstances. Yet it was being compromised by the very dogmatic approach which the country's former East European allies were abandoning. Cuba's existence as one of the last bastions of state socialism might itself be a tourist attraction – perhaps portraying the country as a sub-tropical Brezhnevite theme park. But can the country's virtual survival programme be realistic when the US market is still closed? Either way, the paradox of international tourism promotion under state socialism will inevitably bring social change. And with increasing tourism influences on domestic social attitudes, can changes to Cuba's leadership and unconstructed political economy be far behind?

Note

1. Grateful thanks are due to Vivian Kinnaird for comments on an earlier draft of this chapter, and to Pat Juliasson and Neil Purvis for the artwork.

9 The politics of tour guiding: Israeli and Palestinian guides in Israel and the Occupied Territories

Glenn Bowman

Introduction

The so-called 'Holy Land' constitutes one of the chief goals of European and North American international tourism. Most tourists, in accord with the Israeli Ministry of Tourism, call the land 'Israel', but in United Nations terminology the land is 'Israel and the Occupied Territories'. This variance in nomenclature reflects a deeper issue of identity; Israel and the areas it occupied in the 1967 'Six Day War' constitute a deeply, and violently, divided country. Sixty per cent of its population is Israeli and very much 'First World' in its cultural, political and economic links with the West, while 40 per cent is Palestinian and profoundly 'Third World', both in its cultural affiliation with the 'Arab World' and in its engagement in a national liberation struggle against the Israeli State and its Western allies (Israeli Central Bureau of Statistics, 1988).

The civil strife between the two populations, like the gross inequities of standard of living, political representation, and civil rights underlying it, is in large part rendered invisible to the touristic gaze. Tourists, most of whom embark for the 'Holy Land' with little sense of its contemporary traumas, are likely to return from their travels either with images of the land as an iconic rendition of their imaginings of the 'Bible land' or with a sense of 'Israel' as an oasis of Western democracy surrounded by bellicose wastes of 'Arab' tyranny. As others have shown (Benvenisti 1976, Hirst 1977, Lustick 1980, Morris 1987, Said and Hitchins 1988, and McDowall 1989), such representations are considerably less than accurate, but my main concern is how people who have actually seen the place are able to so selectively represent – or misrepresent – it, and I examine the discursive construction of touristic images of the 'Holy Land' as they are mobilized and modified in guided tours of the country. I argue that, in the eyes of the tourists, 'Israel' is a composite image put together not only from presuppositions they bring to the area, but also from assertions and representations presented to them by people and agencies in contact with them during their travels. Israeli and Palestinian guides offer tourists very different images of the character of the land, and this chapter examines the determinants of the nature and circulation of those differing images and the ways they are received by tourists.

Tourism to Israel and the Occupied Territories

The focus of this chapter is mainly on Christian tourists, who tend, more than Jews, to visit the country in groups. Among them, interest in the 'Arab/Israeli Conflict' is generally uninformed, diffused, and tangential; they come to the land to view sites with allegedly little connection with present-day politics. Two other categories of visitor are considered only for comparative purposes, since both arrive in the country with a strong sense of what they want to know and clear ideas of how to go about finding it out.

First, there are Jewish visitors, who come to visit friends and relations or to witness for themselves the first avowedly Jewish nation since the collapse of the Kingdom of Israel more than eighteen hundred years ago. The state of Israel plays an important role in twentieth century Jewish identity and Jews outside Israel are likely to have learned a considerable amount about the country before even considering a visit.

The second category of visitor is the Christian pilgrim, who is not interested in relations between Palestinians and Israelis. Pilgrims prepare for their visits by meditating on sacred texts which elaborate the spiritual significance of the biblically-valorized sites they will visit. Since July 1981, these 'real pilgrims' have had the legal right to be guided in the 'Holy Land' by guides (usually priests or monks) accredited by their own sects rather than by those licensed by Israel.

During the two years of my field research (1983–1985), as earlier (cf. Table 9.1) 'real pilgrims' were a small proportion of foreign visitors to the region. Furthermore, there had then been virtually no Muslim tourists to Israel since the 1948 war or to Jerusalem and the Occupied Territories since the Six Day War of 1967. In 1984, of a total of 1,259,000 visitors, only 150,000 were strictly religious Christian pilgrims. Of the rest, 519,000 were Jews from the diaspora, and the remaining 590,000 visitors were largely North Americans and Europeans of Christian backgrounds. Of these 270,000 came on 'Holy Land Tours', defined in contradistinction to pilgrimages as 'other tours which stressed visiting Christian sites' (Fisher and Bar-on, 1983, p. 1), while another 320,000 came for the primary purposes of studying, working, attending conferences, playing, or visiting friends or relations (Fisher and Bar-on, 1983 and Israel Central Bureau of Statistics, 1986).

In practice, the distinctions between the various categories of non-Jewish visitors to the land become blurred. Like pilgrims, tourists from abroad are likely to tour the country during their stays, and the itineraries followed do not diverge substantially. Indeed, trips to the area by non-pilgrims of Christian background are marked by two key characteristics. First, Israel and the Occupied Territories are already pre-

Table 9.1 Tourists to Israel, by purpose of visit and religion, April 1979–March 1980

Main purpose of visit	Jews (%)	Non-Jews (%)
study/work	8	10
conventions/missions	5	11
religious (pilgrims)	6	20
leisure	6	12
visiting	39	7
touring	28	36
other/unknown	8	4
	100	100
	(n = 413,000)	(n = 473,000)

Source: Bar-On, 1982 pp. 56–57. (Wives and children of people coming to work, study or attend conventions are listed by census officials under the 'other' category)

defined as significant through the cultural resonance of the names of the region's cities and sites. Second, nearly seventy per cent of these non-pilgrim visitors view the land as members of organized tours led by Israeli-licensed guides rather than priests (as calculated from Bar-on, 1982, p. 89, and Fisher and Bar-on, 1983, p. 1). The combination of these factors provides space for a substantial inculcation of novel, potentially ideological, information into tourists' perceptions.

Guides in Israel

It is useful here to distinguish between two types of guide: the pathfinder and the mentor. Cohen, acknowledging that the modern tourist guide can combine elements of each, defines the pathfinder as a 'geographical guide who leads the way through an environment in which his followers lack orientation or through a socially defined territory to which they have no access (1985, p. 7), and distinguishes this from the mentor who is akin to the leader of a religious pilgrimage – 'a specialist [who] services as a "guru" to the novice, adept, or seeker, guiding him towards insight, enlightenment or any other exalted spiritual state' (1985, p. 8). The former facilitates access whereas the latter builds on that to which the traveller has access, integrating what is seen into a coherent and meaningful image of place.

In a territory as well developed for tourism as the Holy Land, the pathfinder is rarely needed. Foreign visitors can, and often do, visit tourist sites in the Holy Land without assistance. However, they will rarely achieve a coherent sense of what they visit, whereas a guide encourages them to develop a sense of having visited the 'real' place. With real pilgrims, guides (who are normally male) decode an already ascribed significance, and in secular tourism they not only introduce elements of a landscape considered by them to be significant, but also construct for tourists an interpretative framework, 'conceptions of a general order of existence' (Geertz, 1973, p. 90), enabling them to share his sense of the place's significance.

The process involves the guides in selecting, glossing and interpreting sights (Cohen 1985, p. 14–16). Interpretation is not, however, simply a facet of the process but its entire impetus. The guide must translate '. . . the strangeness of a foreign culture into a cultural idiom familiar to the visitors' (1985, p. 15), thus offering tourists unambiguous signs of a particular ideological order. As an Israeli guide remarked:

What they see they see because I point it out. Herod could be walking down the street, and if I didn't point it out they wouldn't know it. . . . They're dependent on you to create their experience for them. This creates an enormous dependence of all kinds, and when this is coupled with the fact that they're Christian and we're Jewish – and most [guides] are chauvinistic – you get to the point that the Christian is seeing his holy land through a Jew. . . . This has political implications. Israel needs public sympathy very badly, especially in Europe and America. How do you get through to them [travellers from Europe and North America]? Give them an Israeli guide; we'll sneak propaganda in through the back door . . .

Israeli law requires that a licensed guide accompany any tour group that makes use of commercial transport (coaches or mini-buses). While agreement was reached in 1981 between the Ministry of Tourism and the Pastoral Commission for Pilgrims and Tourists exempting certain categories of pilgrim from this regulation (Commission of Christian Pilgrims, 1984, pp. 109–121), most non-Jewish foreign visitors to the area are not classified as pilgrims and travel in groups large enough to require commercial transport. Consequently they must have their impressions mediated by an Israeli or Palestinian trained as a guide by the state. The forms such mediation takes differ according to the 'national' allegiance of the guides, both in terms of the 'vision' of place each wishes to promote and in accordance with the restraints on that mediation effected by the tourists, the guides and the state.

There is a considerable difference between the way most Israelis view the land they consider to be Israel and the way Palestinians, whether in Israel proper or in Territories occupied in 1967, regard what most of them call Palestine. In the Zionist vision, the establishment (and expansion) of the State of Israel is the fruit of a long, perhaps divinely guided, struggle of a dispersed people to return from a two thousand year exile to its original home. For Palestinians, Israelis are usurpers who have come to a land on which the Palestinian people have lived for thousands of years to drive out or enslave its indigenous people and take the land for their own. Each side demonizes the other: the majority of Israelis consider all Palestinians as active or potential terrorists and most Palestinians see Israelis as 'settler colonists' dedicated to the eradication of all traces of the Palestinian nation.

These two visions are as totalizing, and as resistant to alternate interpretations, as those of Christians who claim the Holy Land as territory integral to their own ontological projects (Bowman 1991). Nonetheless, if they are not to alienate those they guide, Israeli and Palestinian guides leading Western non-Jewish tourists through their respective and coincident national territories need to accommodate their nationalist visions to what tourists want to see and hear. To do so, guides can follow one of two strategies. The first, effectively the only option for Palestinian guides, is to avoid manifesting any trace of their national vision and to restrict their presentations to what tourists want to perceive. The second, available to Israeli guides, is to establish bridges between the cultural discourses of guide and tourist so as to present a nationalistic reading of the land as an extension of the religio–cultural vision of the tourists.

Until recently, the Palestinian approach, while not allowing guides a forum for presenting their political opinions, at least offered them a substantial share of the tour guiding industry. Until around 1980, according to one tour agent, Israeli guides addressed mainly Zionist topics and evinced a degree of anti-Christianity. Consequently, there was a strong demand by agencies catering to non-Jewish tourists for Palestinian guides who, having worked since the 1940s with foreign Christian visitors to the holy places, were more liable to address tourists' interests and sensibilities. Since then, Israeli guides have developed a better rapprochement with tourists from Christian cultures, not through changes in the official training programme, but through their own realisation that such programmes were inadequate and threatened to drive business into Palestinian hands. As a guide remarked:

[the course] needs more thorough training for guides on how to deal with Christian groups . . . [the teachers have a mistaken] belief in a simple universal Christian doctrine [but we] need as much Christianity in our course as we do geography.

Despite these shortcomings, the content of tour guide presentations in Israel is not regulated from the top as it is in some totalitarian societies (Hollander, 1981, pp. 348 and 375). Although there are limits, which affect Palestinians more than Israelis, guides are relatively free to construct discourses they deem appropriate to the groups they guide.

You'll tell them [the tourists] what they want to hear, and not what any Ministry will want you to say. . . . I don't have a feeling that the Ministry of Tourism has a certain doctrine as far as what we say here. We feel perfectly free.

Evaluation commences even before groups arrive and continues when the guide meets the group. One guide, catering for evangelical Christians, summarised the secret of successful guiding: 'Pump them for what they want to hear. Learn what their wavelength is [and] feed them information on that wavelength'.

By fashioning their presentations to their audience, guides not only supplement their rather low salaries, which are fixed by government, through tips, but also – if they are Israeli – benefit their nation. Tourists disappointed with the modernity of a heavily populated and over-touristed region can bring bad publicity. Alternatively, sensitively guided travellers may be convinced that a visit to Israel and the Occupied Territories is a spiritually rewarding way of gaining new insights into old beliefs, and advertise that belief to friends and acquaintances at home.

Orientalist discourse

Non-Jewish visitors from Western countries share with Jewish Israelis certain cultural assumptions about the Middle East. 'Orientalism', a perspective based on the assumption that the people of 'the Orient' are not like those of 'the West' (Said, 1978), creates a ground of aversion to and distrust of 'Arabs' on which Israeli guides and secular and religious tourists can meet. There may be exceptions, but every Israeli-guided group with which I toured was regaled by its guide at numerous points with comments about the 'otherness' of 'the Arab'. The effect of these 'descriptions' was to confirm tourists' beliefs that 'Arabs' are inscrutable and 'not like us' and thus offer validity to guides' assertions that tourists should give no credence to what 'Arabs' say, avoiding altogether, if possible, any contact with them. By contrast, Israelis, despite living in the midst of the alterity of the Middle East, are to be seen as 'Western' and thus deserving of tourists' trust and support.

The following story illustrates the strategy. One Israeli guide, leading a 'Holy Land tour' through the Jordan Valley, told the group a joke about an 'Arab' named Suleiman who had thirty-seven wives yet always lusted for more:

One day Suleiman approached the well at Jericho and saw a beautiful young woman he immediately wanted to marry. He went up to the woman and asked her for her father's name because, like all Arabs, he would bargain with her father to have her. The woman looked at him with surprise and said 'but father, don't you recognise your own daughter?'

Two hours later, the coach pulled up in front of a contemporary house with a small, but well-tended, garden, in a *moshav* (an Israeli co-operative settlement in which members own their own land and houses) in Southern Galilee. The house was the guide's, and he invited the people on the coach to come in, meet his wife and two children, and have tea. Some tourists toured the house with the guide while the others chatted over tea and biscuits with his wife in the garden. Afterwards, as the coach drove off, I overheard one of the tourists comment to her friends: 'Isn't it wonderful? His house is just like ours – the children's rooms, what's on the shelves in the kitchen . . .'

The promotion of sympathy for Israel by presenting tourists with images of Israelis as being 'the same as' themselves is carried further. 'Bridges for Peace', a Christian Zionist organization run out of Jerusalem, was, in 1985, offering

Americans 'Christian tours to Israel'. These tours, with Israeli guides, took people through all the 'traditionally important' places but added to their itineraries a one day trip called 'Bridges'. As one of the co-ordinators told me,

> people see so many churches they get turned off by them. To meet people doing the same work in the modern times, that's what moves them. . . . 'Bridges' people get to meet Israelis of their own professions (doctors meet doctors, teachers meet teachers, F16 pilots meet F16 pilots!). So many people come here and never meet Israelis [but] this is the highpoint of the trip. . . . We want the tourists to go back and tell the story of Israel as it is . . . to clarify politics and what it means to a Christian, to understand how to decipher the news in terms of the issues facing this country . . .

By contrasting Israeli familiarity with an unseen but allegedly primitive and threatening Palestinian culture, travellers are encouraged to feel they are 'in good hands' with their Israeli guide, who is correspondingly accorded more interpretative authority (Van den Berghe, 1980, p. 581; Almagor, 1985, pp. 45–46). At the same time, Arabs wishing to speak of the land and its politics are discredited.

Furthermore, tour guides 'establish their expertise and authority by telling their clients . . . that the environment is a complex and potentially dangerous place' (Schmidt 1979, p. 458). Such an emphasis not only leads tourists to depend more on the guide's authority but also to adopt his attitude towards the source of danger. The 'Arab' is thus not merely considered an anachronistic buffoon happiest living in desert tents and following the dictates of his indiscriminate lusts; he also incarnates the forces threatening to extinguish the values binding Israeli guide and Western tourists together in imagined community.

Israeli guides thus frequently warned tourists of Palestinian 'dangers'. The 'friendly' Arab shopkeepers in the old City of Jerusalem were really terrorists, intent on robbery or rape. Garnished and inaccurate accounts of the desecration and destruction of synagogues, along with other 'historical' events, were provided, and access by foreign Christians to their holy places was linked to the continuation of the Jewish state. Tourists were encouraged to believe that what they thought of, initially, as a place of monuments to Christianity was, in fact, a community of people whose values and antagonisms they shared. The director of Israeli's Ministry of Tourism made this equation explicit in a speech to representatives of Western travel agencies at the 'Pilgrimage 1984' conference:

> There is a dark wave of fanaticism which we as children of God will fight. We will fight to squash the fanaticism which threatens freedom of access to holy places. The more pilgrims the more chances that peace will come. There is no tolerance or respect for human lives in the lands around us. You are carrying on a mission of peace, understanding and love between people and land [by sending tourists to Israel] – a torch to assure that our people can live in the land in peace and tourism.

Legitimation through religion

In addition to mobilizing orientalist assumptions shared with Western tourists, Israeli guides can establish links between the cultural repertoire of Judaism and the religious discourses of Christians. The attraction of Israel and the Occupied Territories to Christian visitors is ultimately based on the land's relation to religious texts which have transmitted the 'message' of Christianity across the centuries. These texts, collated in the Christian Bible, not only refer to places in and incidents from Ancient Israel, but also assimilate the Jewish Scriptures. Israeli guides can therefore appeal to a shared sacred text in calling on Christians they conduct to support Israel, the present-day avatar of the biblical kingdom.

One guide I accompanied led his group to the remains of the Solomonic gate on the Temple Mount (Haram al-Sharif) and quoted a passage from 1 Kings 6 about Solomon's building of the Temple. Telling them to lay their hands on the stones referred to in the passage, he said 'if anyone ever tells you the Jews don't have a right to this land, you tell them you touched these stones'. Similar links of biblical references and the latter day Kingdom of Israel are made throughout the Holy Land. Christians know the land as Israel because it is referred to as such throughout their Bible, and thus the association of the land, the Bible and the modern day state of Israel appears commonsensical. As one Christian group leader remarked, 'the people [in my group] come to visit Israel, not Palestine. Israel is in the Bible, the Israelites are in the Bible. Palestine is not in the Bible, and neither are the Palestinians'.

If the Holy Land is read through the Bible, it nonetheless remains nearly as open to varying interpretations as is its master text. While some religious tourists approach the land as a museum which celebrates the biblical past, others envisage it, as they do the Bible, as a means of seeing the future (Bowman, 1991). One guide told me that although many 'pilgrims' come to Israel to see monuments to ancient events and have no interest in what is happening in the land today, many Christian visitors come

because they are disenchanted with what the churches tell them. They don't want to believe that [sacred] history stopped in the first century A.D. but want to know what God is doing in the world today. We can show them that here . . . we don't just trot them around the holy places but give them a wide overview of modern Israel.

Guides who recognize in their groups a tendency to interpret contemporary history as a fulfilment of biblical prophecy can provide their clients with the required evidence of divine intervention. One guide told me that 'Bible-believing fundamentalists' resist being taken to churches ('there are no churches in the Bible'):

For them I read the newspaper like Holy Scripture. I tell them at Qumran [where the first century Dead Sea Scrolls were found] 'those parchments were stuffed into the jars in a hurry. Remember, Qumran was destroyed as the Romans were marching on Jerusalem to destroy Jewish independence in this land. For 1900 years they've lain unseen until the day the UN voted for the partition of the land and established the State of Israel. Isn't that a coincidence?' [They shout] "Hallelujah!". I show them the Israeli air force over the plain of Armageddon. They're looking for this. That's what they've paid for! That's the merchandise!

Many such members of fundamentalist Protestant and charismatic Catholic movements may come to the land to see, and assist in, the present day fulfilment of biblical prophecies related to Israel (Halsell, 1988). According to one Christian Zionist:

This makes a wonderful place for the past but for us it's a great place for the future – we're futurists. Our role is to speed up the day in which the ultimate destiny of the day is realized.

Mainline pilgrims, as well as fundamentalists and charismatics, promote tourism, which is claimed to be Israel's second largest source of earned foreign exchange. The former may publicise the country as a sympathetic, safe and spiritually invigorating milieu, whereas the latter may also provide substantial political and economic support, in line with their belief, confirmed on their visits, that Israel's work is that of God (cf. Wagner, 1985).

The rhetoric that aligns Jewish settlers, members of the Israel Defence Forces, Christian tourists and God is not, however something reserved only for fundamentalists and charismatics. One group, with which I travelled extensively, was neither; half its members were Anglican and the other Congregationalist. Throughout the week we spent together, our guide continually emphasised that both Israel and the West were threatened by 'the Arabs'. On one occasion, while passing the ruins of a Palestinian refugee camp, he told us: 'We try to stop them from destroying Israel. They tried to destroy us, but there are miracles in Israel. Who is looking after us? Maybe it is Jesus Christ who protects us.'

It is hard to know what people really think, and what thoughts promulgated in the rush from site to site will survive the return home. However, during a visit to the Church of the Nativity in Bethlehem, when a military curfew was in operation and only tourists and soldiers were on the streets, no-one demurred when the guide stood before the site where Jesus is supposed to have been born and called upon us to join him in singing 'Israel, You Have Brought the People Peace'.

Palestinian guides and the constraints of discourse

The strategies open to the few Palestinian guides with licences to guide foreign tourists to Israel and the Occupied Territories are severely limited. They are constrained by agents and agencies of the state from presenting foreigners with 'Palestinian' readings of Israel and are unable to manipulate Western orientalist assumptions or the biblically-inspired ways travellers interpret their surroundings to convince non-Jewish travellers that Palestinian visions of Israel and the Occupied Territories are credible.

In fact, Palestinian guides are themselves objects of orientalist discourse rather than subjects using that discourse to characterise others. Many travellers are predisposed to see an Arab guide as they would see Arabs in general: duplicitous, inscrutable and backward. Furthermore, many European or North American travellers equate 'Palestinian' with 'terrorist' and are deeply suspicious of a guide who presents himself as Palestinian. The moment a guide locates himself as a Palestinian Arab qualified to talk of the situation for his people, he distances himself from tourists so they cannot 'hear' him.

Palestinian guides therefore tend, in their relations with Western groups, to veil their Arabic or Palestinian identities and to emphasise identities or characteristics to which tourists will prove more sympathetic. Many guides are actually Christian, and some who are Muslim present themselves to travellers as such. Others strive to render their alterity invisible and earn the approval of clients by delivering exact images of the Holy Land travellers wish to see. While such strategies serve to gain guides the approval and patronage of non-Jewish groups, they simultaneously lose for them the chance of speaking to foreign tourists of their situation under occupation.

Even such self-concealment, which in the past ensured tourist trade for Palestinian guides, no longer serves as a strategy for promoting business. Traditional pilgrims, who seek a vision of the Holy Land unsullied by politics, rarely call on the services of the Palestinians they had demanded before the rapprochement between the Ministry of Tourism and the Commission of Christian Pilgrims gained them the right to be guided by their own priests. Fundamentalist Christians do not want to be led by 'Arabs' now that their brand of Christianity is characterised by pro-Zionist rather than anti-semitic positions. All 'Arabs', regardless of their actual religious affiliation, are considered to be Muslim – for example, materials distributed by the International Christian Embassy describe the population of 'Israel' as 'Jewish, Christian, and Arab' – and thus to constitute a demonic opposition to the re-establishment of Israel, the rebuilding of the Temple, and the return of Christ. In addition, fundamentalist, charismatic and millenialist groups now consider doing business with Israeli firms an essential part of manifesting their support for Israel and the prophetic fulfilment it represents, and avoid the East Jerusalem (Palestinian) tourist agencies, which are the only agencies to employ Palestinian guides.

There are, furthermore, constraints on what a guide can communicate about the politics of the situation. Presentations that say 'look what they are doing to us' expose guides to the risk of losing their guiding licences when tourists presumed sympathetic prove not to be. On 29th June, 1984, the Palestinian weekly *Al Fajr* reported that the licence of a Palestinian guide had been revoked by the Ministry of Tourism because he had made 'political' comments. These were not cited in the article, but an Israeli guide I subsequently interviewed said of the incident: 'Oh, all of us know the story. He took people into Yad Vashem [the Museum of the Holocaust] and said "here you'll see what the Germans did to the Jews, and now the Jews are doing it to the Palestinians".' There were two Jews in the group, and they complained to the Ministry.

The head of an East Jerusalem tourist agency told me that the case was unusual in that the guide's licence was revoked after the first offence, whereas the first reported instance of 'anti-state comments' normally led to a three month suspension of the right to guide, with permanent revocation occurring only after a second offence. Yad Vashem (the Holocaust Museum) plays an important role in the politics of Israeli tourism, however, which may explain this severity. One Israeli tourist agent, who organises pilgrimages and school tours for Irish and English visitors, said that visits to Yad Vashem, where tourists are shown graphic illustrations of Nazi genocide against European Jews, are always placed early in her itineraries so that non-Jewish visitors 'can see how the Bible has been interpreted [by Christianity]'. Diplomatic delegations to Israel are taken through Yad Vashem prior to talks with representatives of the State, and the impact of the experience is clearly meant to weaken both the resolve and the moral position of negotiators who may intend to query or oppose political projects the Israeli state claims are vital to the survival of the Jewish 'remnant'.

It is difficult for a guide to know how his audience will respond to political statements. In any group there may be Christians offended by an admixture of politics and religion and others who, being pro-Israeli, are loath to hear the state criticized. Jews often tour with Christian groups, either because others in the groups are friends or because some tour agents will mix groups without regard for religious sensibilities. People unhappy with their guides are able to report them to the Ministry of Tourism's Ethics Committee. Complaints against Israeli guides – for example, for taking Christian groups to Yad Vashem immediately before taking them to the Church of the Nativity – rarely lead to more than a notice of the complaint being sent to the guide, but complaints against Palestinian guides can lead not only to the guide's licence being revoked but also, on occasion, to the revocation of the licence of the agency employing him. To protect themselves and their employers from such contingencies, Palestinian guides tend to confine their presentation to what they know tourists will consider natural material. When, for instance, I asked a Palestinian guide leading a group from Jerusalem to Hebron why he had said nothing when we passed squalid refugee camps huddled in the shadow of affluent Jewish hilltop settlements, despite a tourist's question regarding the difference between the two communities, he replied:

Occupation has to be pointed out to be seen properly. I can only talk of settlements as 'beautiful rich buildings so different from those of the people who live in the valleys'. [In this case] I can't say a word because he [the coach driver] is an Israeli driver . . .

There are, however, other strategies of presentation open to Palestinian guides. Israel and the Occupied Territories are polarised, and their bifurcation is reflected in the road networks, especially on the West Bank where many Christian holy places are located and through which travellers usually have to pass *en route* from Jerusalem to sites in the Galilee. Recent and proposed Israeli roads parallel existing roads linking Palestinian towns and villages to each other and to Jerusalem. This duplication ensures that Israelis do not have to travel through Palestinian-populated areas to reach Israeli centres:

. . . the New West Bank road system can be defined as a dual system. There are new "Jewish roads", serving Jewish settlements and regions, and "Arab roads", the old pre-1967 network, that will continue to serve Arab towns and villages. The interaction between the two networks is intentionally kept to a minimum (Benvenisti 1984, p. 23; cf. Benvenisti and Khayat 1988, pp. 14 and 36).

Whenever possible, Israeli guides circumvent Palestinian areas completely by using the Israeli network to reach tourist sites, sometimes arguing that insurance cover is difficult to obtain for travel through Palestinian areas. If complete evasion is rendered impossible by the location of site visited (the Church of the Nativity in Bethlehem, for instance), Israeli guides shepherd their groups along routes that provide the least contact with Palestinians. In Bethlehem, Israeli-guided tourists disembark from coaches in front of the Church of the Nativity and, after their visit to the Church, are picked up immediately afterwards at the same place. Guides tell the tourists that the town is too dangerous to walk in and that, if they want to buy tourist goods, they will be taken to 'safe' shops, endorsed by the Ministry of Tourism, on Bethlehem's outskirts. Avoidance of Palestinian areas serves two purposes: it renders invisible the substantial presence of Palestinians on the land and allows Israeli guides to characterise that invisible population as dangerous.

Palestinian guides counter this elision and demonisation by exposing travellers as much as possible to Palestinian communities. They use roads that pass through Palestinian areas and lead tourists through areas in which Palestinians live and work, such as the Old Cities of Jerusalem, Bethlehem, and Hebron. In coaches which seem to have no problems with insurance cover, they take their groups along 'Palestinian roads' to Palestinian cities Israeli guides are loath to visit. Afraid of losing their licence, guides are reluctant to provide commentary on such journeys (thus weakening their own credibility), but feel people should be exposed to 'their side' of Israel and the Occupied Territories. On a visit to Hebron's 'Tomb of the Patriarchs', the guide remarked, 'my American visitors don't like to go to Hebron or Nablus, but if they don't see these places they don't see the West Bank'. Such visits not only expose tourists to Palestinian communities and indicate their close links to the holy places in their midst, but also show the naked face of a military occupation which, in more frequented tourist areas, remains masked. On the above-mentioned visit to Hebron, a woman remarked: 'So many guns, so many soldiers. I have never seen anything like this. This is supposed to be the Holy Land.'

The demise of the Palestinian guide

Israeli and Palestinian guides attributed a statement to Moshe Dayan which they felt characterized the Israeli attitude to Palestinian guides: 'I'd rather an Arab bomber pilot over Tel Aviv than an Arab tour guide'. It seems unlikely, given the constraints on political communication they operate under, that Palestinian guides are threats as real to the state of Israel as high explosives, but they do expose foreign tourists to elements of life in Israel and the Occupied Territories which contradict the favourable image of Zionism the Ministry of Tourism is anxious to promote. An official in the Israeli Tour Guide Licensing Office told me tourism is important to Israel because it promotes in non-Jewish visitors a

. . . curiosity about place – it takes them out of the wholly religious perspective . . . [and leads them to ask] "who lives in the places? What's happened with them?".

Clearly, such curiosity benefits Israel only if it is directed at the Israeli people and bypasses Palestinians. It was the ability of Palestinian guides to 'explode' the myth of a benevolent Israel by introducing tourists to 'backstage' areas (cf. MacCannell, 1973) that prompted an apparently systematic attempt by the Ministry of Tourism to ensure the demise of the Palestinian guide. As Moshe Sharon, Begin's Arab Affairs Advisor, wrote in a *Jerusalem Post* article entitled 'The Propaganda War' (14 June 1983), Arab tourist guides are in the best position to spread propaganda and must therefore be 'neutralised'.

In June 1967, when Israel took possession of East Jerusalem and the rest of the West Bank, it 'inherited' a thriving Arab tourism industry. Prior to that time, most sites revered by overseas Christians had been in Jordanian hands; in Israel proper, only Nazareth and a few secondary sites scattered through the Galilee (Mount Tabor, Cana, Caphernaum, and Mount Carmel) had figured on Holy Land itineraries. In 1967, there were 260 Arab guides licensed by the Jordan Ministry of Tourism to lead tourists through West Bank and Jerusalem sites; by 1984, only thirty-eight Palestinians held 'general' licences permitting them to guide throughout Israel and the Occupied Territories. In the meantime, tour guiding had become a major growth industry for Israelis and, by 1984, 3,356 Israelis had passed through the Ministry of Tourism guides' course and received general tour guiding licences (Israel Central Bureau of Statistics, 1986, p. 196). By 1984, then, Palestinian guides from the Territories occupied in 1967 made up one-tenth of one per cent of the pool of guides licensed to lead tourists throughout the Holy Land.

Since the 1967 war, no new Palestinian guides have entered the industry from East Jerusalem or the West Bank. An Armenian has graduated from the guides' school and, at the time of writing, another is taking the course, but the Israeli state does not consider Armenians as 'Arabs'. In 1973, when the Israeli Ministry of Tourism was persuaded by tourist agencies strapped by a shortage of guides into offering a course (in English) enabling licensed guides resident in annexed East Jerusalem to upgrade their general Jordanian licences to general Israeli licences, only fifty-six Palestinian candidates were permitted. The thirty-eight Palestinians with general licences in 1984 were the rump of this fifty-six. The youngest of them was forty three years old.

Thirty-three additional Palestinian guides hold local licences, which permit them only to guide tourists on the West Bank and within the confines of the Haram al-Sharif (which, as a Muslim holy place, is a *waqf*, or pious endowment, and thus nominally free from the jurisdiction of the state). They had once held Jordanian general licences but, as residents of the occupied West Bank rather than annexed Jerusalem, were not allowed on the Ministry of Tourism course. Possession of a local licence does not guarantee employment. As agency-organised tours must employ one guide for the entire visit, to retain their licence to operate agencies must engage guides licensed to work throughout Israel and the Occupied Territories. This regulation prevents agencies from hiring Palestinian guides with local licences and such guides have to promote themselves by hanging around tourist sites and badgering unguided tourists. They are rarely employed.

Such a conclusion is supported by research carried out by Masouda (1984). Although he does not distinguish between Palestinian guides with general licences and those with local (West Bank) licences, his general conclusion is clear:

... the most common problem was lack of work, followed by falling income due to increasing unemployment, decreasing number of days worked, and lack of work opportunities .... [Guides] ... cannot meet their children's school and university fees, health insurance and expenses, and (for many) rent demands (Masouda, 1984).

The fact that two guides with general licences had emigrated between 1982 and 1984 is symptomatic of the trend of decline. Not surprisingly, one East Jerusalem tour agent told me 'in ten years there will be no Palestinian guides'.

The decline in the number of Palestinian guides is not due to Palestinian indifference. Rather, the system ensures that few, if any, are granted the right to guide tourists. Although the Ministry of Tourism initiates several guiding courses a year (approximately 150 new guides are enrolled each year at training centres in Jerusalem, Haifa and Tel Aviv), places for Palestinians are difficult to obtain. First, all applicants must have graduated from certified secondary schools and be citizens of Israel. Since the start of the *intifada* in 1987, Palestinian schools in Gaza, Jerusalem and the West Bank have been closed by military order so, at present, there are no new Palestinian graduates. However, between 1983 and 1985, when most of my fieldwork was carried out, education was not the problem. Then, as now, Israeli citizenship was a barrier. Since Jerusalem and its suburbs were annexed by Israel in June, 1967, very few Palestinians resident there have applied for Israeli citizenship. For those outside the annexed areas, the option was never offered (Aronson, 1990, pp. 10–12). Thus the few Palestinians able to qualify to apply are almost exclusively 'Israeli Arabs' (i.e. Palestinians resident within the 1948 borders of Israel). One East Jerusalem agent told me the only Palestinians licensed since 1973 are from Northern Israel, but pointed out that these fifteen 'have the additional disadvantage that they live in Galilee and are not near the only people likely to give them work, namely the Palestinian agents in Jerusalem'.

For those permitted to apply for the courses, expenses are high. In 1984, the eighteen-month guides' course cost $1500 (at the time of writing it was $2500). Applicants also had to pay a $150 unrefundable application fee as well as another $100 for a psychometric test at the Institute for Vocational Guidance. This test not only examines applicants in Hebrew and in their knowledge of the country's geography and history (as taught in Israeli, but not Palestinian, schools) but furthermore evaluates the 'suitability' of applicants in terms of criteria which are not specified. Those few Palestinian applicants judged to possess sufficient Hebrew and an adequate knowledge of geography and history inevitably fail, according to an

East Jerusalem agent, to overcome the hurdle of 'suitability'. They thus lose both application and testing fees.

Not only are courses taught exclusively in Hebrew (there has never been a course in Arabic), but the framework within which materials are presented is strongly biased towards Jewish culture and Israeli nationalism. The courses are based on a method of gaining 'Yediath Ha'Aretz' (knowledge of one's native country) developed from an early twentieth century Zionist programme for resocializing Jewish immigrants and integrating them, through a 'de-neutralizing process' (Katz, 1985, p. 63), into the nationalistic Jewish community in Palestine.

This nationalistic bias excludes Palestinians who, national feelings apart, are unfamiliar with the Jewish and Israeli discourses within which materials are presented. As a Palestinian who had taken the course and dropped out explained, 'the entrance course involves lots of Judaism, and I didn't know enough to follow'.

Furthermore, throughout the course there is a strong element of communal bonding and Palestinians, a tiny minority among the participants, are unable to join in the communal atmosphere. As described by an Israeli:

You have a certain mood in the class, [an] atmosphere, and in 99 per cent of the cases an Arab will not feel good there. I remember the beginning of the course that we had with a Palestinian, and he left after two, three weeks. Why? We had our own slang, our own jokes, even singing what we call Israel songs, and he just didn't feel at home there. . . . A tour guides' course is something very intimate – it's a real reference group – and if you don't belong to that reference group it can be very difficult for you to stay there socially. But of course the government is not really trying to do anything about it, and why should they?

As succinctly expressed by a tourist agent, 'the guiding course . . . is a closed shop for the Jews'.

In future, fewer and fewer Palestinian guides will introduce foreign visitors to the country. This prospect troubles very few non-Palestinians in the tourism business of Israel and the Occupied Territories. Those concerned with tourism and pilgrimage in the largely foreign churches are struggling to defend the right of their priests and monks to expose pilgrims and tourists to their churches' visions of the Holy Land, while state organisations controlling the tourism industry want to ensure that tour guiding serves the interests of their (Israeli) constituencies and the state. For each, Palestinian guides are an irritant; they take (a small amount of) business away from their own guides and, despite severe operating constraints, manage to make visible a complex moral and political terrain which advocates of an iconic Holy Land and a triumphant modern state would prefer foreign visitors not to see. By so doing, they come to be seen as combatants, and are treated as such by the Israelis, if not by the foreign churches. One Israeli guide told me: 'You should be amazed that there are any Israel government licenced Palestinian guides, not complain that there are so few. There is a war on here.'

The existence of a war, and the implication of tourism in the hostilities, is demonstrated in an August, 1989 newspaper report of covert activities allegedly carried out by the Israeli Defence Force. Entitled 'Israeli Agents, Disguised as Tourists, Shoot Arabs', the report describes an incident of 21 August in which several men, who 'wore shorts and backpacks, carried guidebooks and maps, and conversed in English, drew pistols from their packs and opened fire' on Palestinian demonstrators, killing a twenty-four year old man (Diehl, 1989, p. 18). A local man told the reporter, 'now the boys will have to check every tourist who comes into the market. . . . Everyone who comes in will be under suspicion' (Diehl, p. 18). Such suspicion will poison relations between Palestinian residents and those few tourists who, disregarding warnings in Ministry of Tourism handouts and the statements of Israeli guides, enter Bethlehem city. This will strangle one of the few remaining channels of communication between indigenous Palestinians and foreign visitors.

Conclusions

Tourists' experiences of Israel and the Israeli-Occupied Territories are discursively structured not only by touristic pre-dispositions to 'see' a particular Holy Land, but also by the strategies of tour guides, who fashion tourists' experiences of sites and of the land as a whole. Whilst introducing tourists to particular sites, guides also provide interpretative frameworks which tourists use in determining the significance of those sites and in constructing generalised images of the character of the land and its peoples.

By shifting the focus of the study from images of the tourists' destinations constructed in their home culture to the way such images are re-worked in tourists' contacts with the host culture, attention has been drawn to the powers possessed by host societies, so often portrayed as powerless victims of international tourism. As the example presented here reveals, the discursive setting up of an image of place can involve a substantial input from local interest groups involved in the organisation of the tourism industry. The 'place' tourists see is not simply a reified image of their expectations, or a real terrain, but the result of a dialogue between tourists and those persons and institutions which mediate between the tourist gaze and its object. The study of such 'places' should enquire carefully into what takes part in such dialogues, and who is excluded from them.

Note

1. Field Research for this chapter was funded by grants from the Palestine Exploration Fund, the Lady Davis Foundation, the Deya Mediterranean Area Research Centre, Oxford University and the University of Kent at Canterbury. The Sociology and Social Anthropology Department of Hebrew University (Jerusalem) generously provided office space and library access during the early stages of my research.

10 Life in the informal sector: street guides in Kandy, Sri Lanka

Malcolm Crick

Introduction: International tourism in Sri Lanka

Between 1966 and 1982, international tourism was a leading growth sector in the Sri Lankan economy. From 18,969 foreign visitors in 1966, international arrivals grew to 407,230 by 1982. Over the same period, tourist-derived receipts escalated from US $1.3 million to US $146.6 millions. In 1982, tourism became the fourth largest foreign exchange earner, pushing such a traditional export as rubber into fifth place. Directly and indirectly, 64,262 people were employed in the industry (Ceylon Tourist Board, 1982a, pp. 5, 8, 14).

Since 1983, ethnic violence has shattered the image of Sri Lanka as a tourist paradise and by 1987 tourist arrivals had already declined to 182,620 (Central Bank, 1987, p. 190). However, even without widespread civil strife, Sri Lanka might not have sustained the impressive rate of tourist development of the previous decade and a half. Before 1982 tensions were already acute in the industry and many in Sri Lanka were realising that the 1960s 'manna from Heaven' view of tourism was naive and one-sided.

The original aims of tourism development were obtaining foreign exchange, employment stimulation, and regional diversification. The industry was not regarded as capital-intensive, being supposedly based on existing assets such as the beauty of Sri Lanka and the natural friendliness of its people. Over two decades later, after much heavy infrastructural investment, with a foreign exchange leakage rate in excess of 30 per cent, and recognition of the menial, seasonal nature of much of the employment, the economic arguments were appearing less compelling. Many had also become aware of the social and cultural problems which often follow tourism development (Mendis, 1981), 'costs' about which the Ceylon Tourism Plan (Harris, Kerr, Forster and Co., 1967), like most others of the period, was significantly silent. Sri Lanka had acquired, among other ills, a drug problem, and a reputation for child prostitution. The 'friendliness' of many locals was also far from evident in 1982.

Industry decision-makers also had to decide whether to allow ever-increasing numbers of international arrivals or to restrict numbers and maximise foreign exchange revenue by admitting only high per diem spenders who would use the relatively expensive approved accommodation sector. As occupancy rates in hotels and licensed guesthouses had fallen in the late 1970s with more budget travellers staying in unlicensed premises, the Tourism Board considered eliminating those engaged in tourism services outside its own controls by formulating a Specified

Tourist Services Code. This would enable its officers to inspect, examine, fine and even close establishments considered unsatisfactory. Already, in 1982, 'Operation Overstay' was under way as police raided well known hippy haunts to round up, fine and deport those overstaying their visas while living on a pittance. In Kandy, Sri Lanka's Hill Country 'cultural capital', another conflict was apparent as newspapers ran stories about the 'stranglehold' touts allegedly held on the city's tourism. And the Minister of State (whose portfolio included tourism) was warning the industry that high pricing made it vulnerable to competitors offering similar attractions. The Minister was also broadcasting a different message. His Vice-Presidential address to the World Tourism Organisation conference in Manila was entitled 'Tourism – the greatest movement for world peace and understanding' (de Alwis, 1980), a viewpoint which, over the last few years, seems to have captured a number of devotees.

In contrast to such elevated, abstract rhetoric, this chapter is an anthropological account (based on seven months of fieldwork in 1982) which stays close to actual events and specific relationships. It focuses on the 'informal' tourism sector, that arena beyond the effective control of the tourism authorities – street corners, unlicensed guesthouses, cheap cafes, and so on. I concentrate particularly on the ties linking street guides (disparagingly referred to by the authorities and well-to-do as 'touts'), the guest house proprietors, shopkeepers, and the sort of tourist who avoids 'package holidays' and expensive accommodation.

In Sri Lanka, as in other countries, the 'tourist industry' is highly segmented. As well as its luxury hotels and plush private homes, Sri Lanka also has spare rooms in modest homes almost unmodified for foreign guests and, at the bottom of the range, sleeping space on verandahs. The spectrum of foreign visitors is similarly wide.

Clearly, there is some correlation between types of accommodation, controlled or owned by different strata in Sri Lanka society, and different categories of tourist, although it would over-simplify matters to state that the less well-off tourists stay in the more modest accommodation whereas the more affluent stay in establishments owned by wealthy Sri Lankans. Package tourists often have to save hard for their holiday, while others opt for more modest accommodation for non-financial reasons. However, the more modest guesthouses will normally be owner-occupied, and most tourist expenditure in this sector will stay in the local economy. This cannot always be said of the hotel sector. First, 'package tourists' pay for their holidays in advance, and much foreign exchange never reaches the destination country. Secondly, like other Third World countries, Sri Lanka encouraged foreign investment in its tourist industry and, consequently, many of the more luxurious hotels have a foreign equity compartment, which acts as a source of foreign exchange leakage. The foreign equity component in the hotel sector was estimated at 15 per cent in 1983, so Sri Lanka has certainly avoided the fate of those tourist destinations where the industry is almost entirely foreign-owned (Attanayake et al., 1983, pp. 275–7). Legally, a local partner must have the majority share holding. Furthermore, many establishments are owned by the Ceylon Hotels Corporation, in which the government is the major investor. Some graded hotels are completely owned by Sri Lankans. Several in Kandy, for instance, are owned by local businessmen or members of a single family.

In 1982, Kandy, with its surrounding villages, had a population of approximately 100,000. Site of the famous Temple of the Tooth, and venue for the *Asala perahara*, one of the largest Buddhist pageants in Asia, the city was visited by virtually all international tourists to Sri Lanka, although many stayed only a day or two *en route* to the beach resorts. During 1982, Kandy contained eleven hotels, eleven guesthouses and thirty-four addresses with paying guest accommodation (Ceylon Tourist Board, 1982b, pp. 62–4, 79–82). Official statistics, however, represent only the tip of the iceberg. Kandy was widely known as the 'guest house capital' of Sri Lanka, and there were probably at least another hundred addresses, not licensed by the Tourist Board, catering to tourists. While operators of such premises avoid municipal charges and taxes, they also fail to run their establishments in accordance with standards set by the Tourist Board. Similarly, although the Tourist Board has a comprehensive training programme for guides, in the streets of Kandy were numerous untrained and unlicensed 'guides'. In such respects, Sri Lanka is not unusual. Throughout the Third World, where a tourism industry has developed, a similar 'informal' sphere has grown up around its margins.

As the discussion in this chapter is confined almost entirely to the informal sector and restricted to the city of Kandy, there is no overview of the entire tourism industry in Sri Lanka. However, in the unlicensed guesthouses and the streets of Kandy much interaction between foreigners and locals occurred; services were performed and money changed hands, contributing neither to the official tourism statistics nor to the industry's glossy image. This is an arena, indeed, many would like to see eliminated. It is a niche of insecurity and frequent violence. But, somewhat sordid and shrouded in ambiguity, it is intrinsic to Third World tourism.

It would be over-simplistic to describe what goes on in this arena as 'deceitful' and 'hypocritical'. Arguably, Sri Lanka cultural codes and roles are simply extended to involve foreigners. Much in the relationship between a street guide and a tourist, for instance, could be termed 'brokerage', and displays similar features to transactions elsewhere in Sri Lankan life. Guides are essentially 'middlemen' who profit by bringing others into a relationship (van den Berghe, 1980, p. 381). The practice of creating obligations in others and of expecting gifts of favours instead of specific payments for specific services is certainly not confined to tourism; it is common to exchange relationships in other areas of Sri Lankan political and economic life.

The informal tourism sector in Kandy

The concept of 'informal sector' (Tokman, 1978) has frequently been employed in accounts of Third World tourism. For some (Davis, 1978, p. 303), it is very much the locus of the 'underemployed residue' one finds in the service sector as a result of dualistic development involved in modernisation. In tourism, for instance, hotels employ room boys, waiters and receptionists, whilst outside on the pavements there are hawkers, 'black market' profiteers, pimps, guides, prostitutes and thieves. As in other countries (Wahnschaft, 1982, p. 431), this informal sector operates without government sanction or registration procedure (Bromley, 1979); in some countries it is strictly illegal, falling outside the regulations that protect the formal, approved sector (Davies, 1979, p. 91). Not surprisingly, those in the formal sector are often antagonistic towards those on their margins. In many parts of the world, for instance, hotels provide brochures for their guests, warning them about touts who may badger them during their stay (Cleverdon, 1979, p. 73). In Sri Lanka, tourists are certainly warned about unscrupulous touts by Tourist Board literature, and guide books may explicitly mention Kandy as a tout's paradise (Wheeler, 1987, pp. 135–6). Indeed, some guest houses actually request tourists to phone them from the station, preferring to pay for a taxi than have their guests arrive with a guide (Wheeler, 1987, p. 136).

Image is all-important in tourism and, clearly, badgering and deception jar with notions about 'friendly, smiling people', or 'relaxing in paradise'. Tourism authorities frequently resolve this dilemma by attributing all ills to very specific groups of local mischief-makers, even to specific types of tourist, who are then hounded, with varying degrees of energy, out of the industry or the country. However, such manoeuvres lend weight to partial and misleading representations of tourism; in Sri Lanka, while many agreed that street guides tarnished the country's image, it was also commonly held that highly respectable people with political connections and police protection were investing in hotels to launder profits nefariously gained elsewhere. Strong negative images certainly existed about and among people in the informal sector, and street guides and guest house proprietors commonly maligned one another's reputations. However, in focusing on relations between guides and proprietors, especially of unlicensed premises, it must be recognised that they rely upon each other, just as some shops are also highly dependent upon the activities of the guides. Possibly the rhetoric is so negative precisely because these are relationships of mutual, if reluctant, need.

While the position of individuals and the nature of their involvement in the tourism industry vary considerably (Dogan, 1989, p. 225), most Third World governments assist more expensive developments and either fail to encourage, or actively discourage, grass roots activities, where locals of fairly modest means offer accommodation. As Samarasuriya states for Sri Lanka, to tourism planners and policy makers the poor are normally just a nuisance (1982, pp. 6–7). Economic gains that remain within the lesser developed countries tend to flow to the local élites and the poor therefore have to use their limited resources to tap this flow. Many of the roles available to some sections of the population, particularly women, are highly demeaning (Samarasuriya, 1982, pp. 33, 46, 77–8).

The informal sector has been regarded by some as rich in entrepreneurial opportunity (Henry, 1982, p. 460) and, despite the odds stacked against the poor, we must recognise how their assets are creatively used (McGee, 1979, pp. 56, 61). These strategies are linked to the behaviour and needs of tourists involved in the informal sector, and without understanding their circumstances it is not possible to grasp the street guide's 'middleman' role.

Two features of the tourists' situation particularly lend themselves to intermediary operations. First, touristic encounters tend to be transitory. Even on holiday, most tourists are in a hurry. Many, spending no more than two weeks in Sri Lanka, stay only a day or two in any one place, although much longer stays are the norm at beach resorts. In fleeting transactions, then, norms associated with durable relationships are absent. As a sales assistant remarked, business was simply business, occasionally including 500 per cent profit margins. Tourists were at fault if they failed to learn the value of things, a point also made by several street guides, who added that foreigners would think them stupid if they did not seek to maximise their income.

Secondly, while tourists have economic resources to spend, they possess very little 'cultural capital' in the sense of knowledge of the local language, price levels, or local customs. By contrast, most street guides lack subtantial economic assets but are rich in cultural capital, especially in a practical understanding of how to meet the needs of the many tourists who, choosing not to experience a country from inside the protective environment of a 'package tour', need to decide, on a daily basis, where to eat, where to stay, and so on.

At this point, one might acknowledge the guides' insightful, if essentially pragmatic, understanding of human nature, their ability to read a social situation, and their skill in turning it to their advantage. Guides have a set of general conceptions about tourist motivation, national stereotypes and tourist types, which they employ in their encounters. As a guide explained, one has to 'catch the eye' and engage in 'tactics talk'. Tourists wary of being cheated in a foreign country may react gratefully to 'Hello friend', a common conversational opening by the street guides. The term 'friend' used between locals and foreigners, however, is highly ambiguous (Wagner, 1982, p. 93), and tourists are frequently ignorant of the commercial elements bound up in such an overture (Cohen, 1982a, p. 246).

In a sense, the informal sector is an arena in which strategies are employed to channel whatever 'free floating' resources are found there. The chief asset of the guest house owner, for instance, is clearly a home in the right location and with certain kinds of facilities. Resources are channelled mainly in this context, where part of the cultural capital will be a reasonable command of English, and other middle class refinements and comforts. Although some unlicensed guest houses in Kandy were rented by their operators, most such services were provided in owner-occupied homes. By contrast, the assets of most street guides were of a different order. Their arena of operations was not the home but the streets and the cafes. Most spoke, at best, broken English and few had any substantial knowledge of Sri Lankan or even local history. However, they did possess knowledge of drugs, prostitutes, and the cheapest places to eat and stay, information which could be obtained neither in Tourist Board publications, nor in most travel guide books.

Above all, guides have two basic resources: wits and time. Street guiding is very much a matter of living off one's wits, seizing opportunities as and when they occur, without going too far. While the well-to-do often referred to touts as 'lazy idlers', they are perhaps more accurately viewed as the 'spurious leisure class of the unemployed' (Hannerz, 1969, p. 105). What appears as idle time is, in fact, a major asset. One has to 'hang around' to catch stray tourists in the informal sector. Having nothing else to do is vital in this 'hit and miss' game.

Street guides and tourists: making a living from the streets

On any day in Kandy during 1982, guides would be strategically positioned in shop doors, outside cafes, on street corners, near hotels. At the station, they emerged from the train with tourists caught during the journey, steering their charges through the groups of guides at the station entrance who tried to attract tourists with offers of cheaper accommodation. Tourists proceeding alone from the bus or railway station, evidently tired after the three-hour journey from Colombo, inevitably ran the gauntlet of several guides. Rebuffing one, they would move on quickly, only to be approached further down the street by another. For tourists on their own or in pairs, particularly women, it could be quite intimidating. Many resorted to telling anyone who approached them to 'fuck off', and the guides often replied in kind. Often, too, when a tourist was 'caught', unsuccessful guides followed, hurling abuse at the successful guide and alleging that he was a 'robber'. Older onlookers would denounce these 'young semi-literates out of the drain', as they put it.

The hundred or so street guides of Kandy came from diverse ethnic and social backgrounds. Most were men in their late teens and early twenties, generally poorly educated and speaking only broken English. Many were physically small and appeared very young, and some were reputedly physically attractive. I was informed that there were so many small, youthful guides because tourists felt safer with them than with more robust-looking characters, and that many Europeans, men and women, had a strong desire for sex with youngish boys.

Despite the preponderance of young men, Kandy's street guide population included others not fitting the above description. A few middle-aged or elderly men were guides, one of whom even had a municipal guide's licence, but of the dozen or so municipally licensed guides in 1982, he was the only I knew to work the streets. Another middle-aged guide, apparently constantly drunk and seemingly incapable of knowing what he was doing, spent most of his time abusing other guides for stealing his 'clients'; in seven months I never saw him actually catch a tourist.

Some occasional guides were local University students from 'good' homes, trying to earn a little money. Others were school-aged children, playing truant for the day or permanently absent from school. One young teenaged girl, supporting her unemployed father, had developed a working knowledge of three European languages over the years and combined shopping with tourists with occasional sex. Apart from her, most females constantly in the streets were very young children who followed tourists, begging for money. One or two guides appeared to border on severe emotional disturbance, including one well-educated man in his late twenties who had allegedly been introduced to drugs by a German woman some years previously and, after becoming ill, subsequently became an alcoholic. He hung about in the streets in an extremely dishevelled state, trying to escort tourists to Kandyan dance performances. One or two tourists taken to a show would earn him 20 to 30 rupees (just over US $1.00), enough to keep him in alcohol for a day or so.

Is there a 'social structure' to the street guide population in Kandy? In the sense of 'structure' used by Whyte for Cornerville (1955), there is not. In Kandy, we are not dealing with large gangs with established leaders routinely performing a number of joint activities. Although some spend most of their time on the streets, the guide population in the informal sector is not well circumscribed; for many, it is an instantaneous and short-lived role. Furthermore, many services provided by street guides were occasionally provided by others in Kandy. Waiters in cafes, for instance, sometimes tried to find accommodation for tourists and taxi drivers, too, attempted to meet their needs, not only for accommodation but also for drugs and prostitutes. Because of the proximity of the bus and fire stations, off-duty firemen would also convey tourists to accommodation and guides told me that even off-duty policemen tried to get into the act. People going to work sometimes engaged tourists in conversation and suggested places to stay or shop, and businessmen, too, would 'accidentally' bump into a group of tourists, warn them about the guides, and then offer to guide them around the town.

Clearly, in these circumstances, the question of how many guides there were in Kandy cannot be answered. Given the opportunity, on the spur of the moment, anyone can become a guide. The size of the 'latent' guide population was brought home to me late one night when I assisted an elderly American woman with her suitcases, only to find I was regarded by other guides and apparently casual observers as a competitor, and receiving considerable abuse for my pains. In 1982, in fact, several European tourists had set themselves up as guides in Kandy, and were making money from other tourists who felt safer hearing their own tongue spoken fluently than being ferried around by a local.

A second factor to bear in mind when discussing any 'structural' dimension to guiding activities is that, whereas in Whyte's Cornerville definite hierarchies were identifiable, street guiding in Kandy is normally a highly individualistic occupation. Although small groups of guides would congregate in cafes or on street corners (partly for protection, I suspect), business was overwhelmingly an individual affair. Some guides were always on their own. Others would leave their peers when business seemed likely and, on occasions, there was acute rivalry between them.

There was, indeed, a strongly 'atavistic' quality to life on the streets, similar to that described for ghetto-like situations. Myth-making, exaggeration and bravado abound, personal failures are converted into heroism, and exaggerated amity is quickly undone by the need to survive (Hannerz, 1969, pp. 86, 105–7; Liebow, 1967, pp. 176, 206–7, 213–4, 217).

Although there is little Cornerville-type 'structural' quality to the guides' activities, there is a degree of territoriality. Some guides work the bus station, others around the lake, others congregate in specific cafes and some have special relationships with particular guesthouses. For new guides from out of town, a rough welcome was frequent. Felix, normally a fairly amiable informant, could not contain his anger when a Tamil from Jaffna decided to 'do some tourism' in Kandy one weekend. The appearance of this well-spoken university graduate trying to make money on 'his' pitch made Felix explode with rage, and he made life difficult for the newcomer, telling him to go back where he came from, that he owned land and had money, and should not come to Kandy to deprive poor people of their living.

In addition, although this should not be over-formalised, there was evident specialisation among the guides. Some simply accompanied tourists to guest houses to obtain the commission; others avoided that role but tried to escort tourists on shopping sprees. Yet others specialised in taking tourists to the Kandyan dance performances. Some guides were drug specialists. Many street guides provided sexual services for some of their 'catches'. Indeed, 'sex mad' was how many described tourists, male and female, of most nationalities. Individuals who specialised in homosexual prostitution were reticent about their trade. Not so others, who would brag about their sexual conquests with European women, although acknowledging that often they had to perform with women they did not want. But 'making it' with a strikingly attractive European was a source of great kudos, power in the sexual arena perhaps compensating for the lack of status elsewhere (Bowman, 1989). At the same time, sex was still very much of a tactic. One self-assured guide, who certainly enjoyed his sexual liaisons, told me: 'I spend 100 rupees (approximately US $5.00) on them and sleep with them and in return I get back 1,000 rupees or more'.

At the outset, a street guide does not know what a tourist is after. A guide may thus spend half a day escorting someone around town, only to find that they spend nothing – thus earning the guide nothing. Alternatively, a conversation may start around buying batiks and then move to drugs. A guide who takes tourists to a guest house may end up escorting them around the island for a ten-day trip, being fed and housed by the tourists. Occasionally, guides obtain business they know will occur only once in a lifetime. A young man, who for over a decade had specialised in taking tourists to Kandyan dance performances, once approached me in a highly excited state. He was hoping to obtain 100,000 rupees (US $5,000) for arranging the marriage of a Dane to a local woman, which would enable him to stay permanently in Sri Lanka. In 1979, a tourist car driver had almost paid off his mortgage from commission obtained by taking three South American women to a jewellers in Colombo, where they made the largest gem purchase he had ever experienced.

Although reliable quantitative data on guides' earnings is not available, their income is certainly irregular. Windfall gains are made, but guides may go for weeks without business. Over the long term, partly because of the tourist lifestyle in which they must, to some extent, participate, few were secure. Theirs was an 'easy come, easy go' existence. Some claimed to save money but, for many, the proceeds of a lucrative catch would soon disappear on beer, cafe food, and so on. Some of the younger guides lived with their parents, indeed, some came from extremely respectable homes; others slept on the streets or in alleys, sometimes going for days without food.

Along with the unpredictability of income, making a living from the streets involves difficult relationships with the authorities. Occasionally, street guides were arrested and fined under the Vagrancy Ordinance, but some achieved a *modus vivendi* with the police by bribing them. Nevertheless, guides were sometimes 'roughed up' and there were also cases of extortion. Although I witnessed only one fight and several scuffles, I was informed that violence occurred daily, perhaps leading to serious injury, taking place off the tourist circuit. Such incidents are not unique to tourism. Violence, corruption and coercion are part of daily experience in many areas of Sri Lankan life. During the 1983 riots, gangs of thugs allegedly operated under the control, and even in the pay, of some Members of Parliament, while monks and even police looked on. (Obeyesekere, 1984, pp. 159–60, 163–4; Kapferer, 1988, pp. 232–3). After elections, strong-arm tactics are often employed by businessmen, using groups of thugs to drive out business rivals who supported the losing party.

I have emphasised some of the less savoury aspects of guiding in the informal arena. Felix described 'friendship' in tourism as a 'tactic', as 'business', and no doubt he is right. But some guide/tourist relationships do acquire other characteristics. Felix had a short list of addresses of tourists with whom he had been friendly over the years. He still wrote to some, and was distressed one day to find that he had lost his wallet which contained the address list. Most on this list were women with whom he had been on trips around the island. At the start of such trips, he would state the price of his company, but if he grew to like his companion, he would tell them at the end that they could give him whatever gifts they liked. Of course he would have enjoyed several days travel, good food, good accommodation and probably sex, but he made a qualitative distinction between such relationships and a simple business arrangement. As has been recognised in other cultures, such relationships with foreigners can have a profound psychological significance, which terms like 'tout' or 'prostitute' do not adequately convey (Cohen, 1971, 1982b, 1986). Gifts given by tourists to Felix and to other street guides in Kandy meant a great deal, even when in monetary terms they were comparatively worthless. Umbrellas, cast-off clothes, and other unwanted goods were often given to guides. Despite the hand-to-mouth existence which many of them lead, such gifts were frequently treasured as mementos of relationships, and guides told me that they would never sell them.

Felix had had ten years of guiding experience. His earlier enthusiasms for things foreign had waned appreciably and his view of Europeans had become somewhat jaundiced. He used to tell me that one could not 'do tourism with an honest heart'. Although he hoped that 'one day God will smile upon my face', he was well aware that those years on the streets meant he would not be able to marry a local woman and he despaired of finding any other kind of employment. Whilst admitting the calculating nature of guide behaviour, Felix felt that many had too harsh a view of the guides. Of all the street guides in Kandy, he claimed, only about six would rob a tourist or do them real harm. Tourists wanted to be shown around in a short space of time and the guides could do this and keep them safe from criminals. He added that, if guides were 'rogues', guest houses were also out to take the foreigner's money, only they were 'robbers in a gentlemanly way'; they were, in his words, 'rogues behind a curtain'.

Street guides, shopkeepers and guest house proprietors: tensions and transactions

Newspaper headlines during 1982 about touts running tourism in Kandy undoubtedly exaggerated the situation. First, street guides normally have access only to independent, budget travellers. Those on 'package tours' or in chauffeur-driven hired cars are usually beyond their reach. Secondly, major hotels and the more expensive private guest houses have almost nothing to do with them. Nonetheless, concern was widespread, for the street guides were powerful, and clearly able to direct certain types of tourist towards or away from specific shops and guest houses, and to influence what went on inside such establishments between their proprietors and the foreigners.

A guide escorting a tourist into a shop claims a percentage of a priced article or influences the bargaining process between shopkeeper and tourist. Indeed, a shopkeeper is sometimes forced to bargain simultaneously with the guide and with the customer. Because the guide has to be paid, tourists will normally pay more than if they had arrived on their own. Furthermore, a guide may demand, in Sinhala, that a shopkeeper substantially raise his prices so that he can receive a large commission. If the shopkeeper refuses, the guide may persuade the customer to leave. Some shopkeepers resist such pressures. One semi-retired businessman stated that he would not 'rob Peter to pay Paul', thus refusing to allow the guide's demands to lead to the tourist being cheated. The tout who, in his eyes, did virtually nothing to earn his money could have 5 per cent, and if he did not accept that he could leave empty handed. Other shopkeepers felt far less confident, fearing the trouble that might follow an argument with a guide. For a shopkeeper, a heated argument in the presence of a customer can be very embarrassing, and he is therefore in a somewhat compromised position. If the price is too high, the tourist may not purchase; if the commission level is high, the trader's profit margin is significantly reduced; if the commission is too low the guide may leave in a huff, taking his catch with him and threatening never to bring any more tourists to the shop.

The situation above understates the bravado of guides in Kandy, for some tried to obtain commission from shopkeepers without having made a catch at all. They simply watched tourists going into shops, followed them in a few seconds later, spoke to them briefly, and later in the day asked the shop assistant for commission on any sale. Sometimes guides even waited for tourists to emerge with their purchases, and then claimed to have sent the tourist into the shop.

If this scenario looks one-sided, guides have their own view of the matter. As Felix explained, if shopkeepers did not want any dealings with guides they needed only to put over their doors a notice 'No guides allowed'. Few shops had such a notice, because many were partly reliant upon tourists brought by the guides. Not all shops were centrally located and, with limited time at their disposal, tourists could not see all available establishments. In these circumstances, directing tourists into a shop is a significant service. Felix suggested that many shopkeepers who complained about touts were really aggrieved because guides did not visit their particular shop, rather than because they did so.

A similar pattern is evident in the relationship of guides and unlicensed guest house owners. Hotels and registered guest houses do most of their business with groups on package tours, or with tourists in hired cars booked into accommodation in advance by travel agents in Colombo. Little of their trade consists of individual tourists searching for accommodation. Some hotels have a standard rate of 10 per cent commission to guides bringing such people, but others give no commission at all to discourage street guides from frequenting their premises. Some larger licensed guest houses adopt the same policy. The story is very different, however, for unlicensed guest houses, which cannot advertise in Tourist Board literature and, being small, lack contacts with travel agents. The source of their guests, therefore, is somewhat variable and, for many, tourists picked up by guides while casually wandering around the streets of Kandy are a significant source of custom. That, however, does little to change the rhetoric of opposed interests between guest house proprietors and guides.

At one guest house, I received the standard story about guides being 'good for nothing'. However, staying there on a semi-permanent basis were at least two individuals who were always catching tourists in the streets of Kandy. I later discovered that they were actually employed by the guest house, frequently sleeping there and, in fact, possessed rail passes purchased by the owner so they could go daily to Colombo to bring tourists. When asked about tourism in Kandy, another guest house owner told me guides were dishonest, that she would have nothing to do with them and that I should avoid them, adding that the foreigners staying with her were friends of her son in England. The claim was curious, given that they were all French or German. On leaving the guest house, I was given a receipt with the wrong address and a false name, and my guide received no commission, the owner claiming that someone else had brought me. Some weeks later she walked past a group of guides, including mine, and in my earshot told them to bring her more tourists.

When a street guide takes a tourist to a guest house, he is entitled to commission. Whereas a hotel might give a guide 10 per cent for every day that a tourist stays, guest houses often give 25–30 per cent for one day and, if a tourist stays for three or four days, the entire rent received for the first day. Commission to the guide does not always mean higher room rates to the tourist. Some guest house proprietors have a fairly fixed idea of charges for their rooms, and this is paid by a tourist whether he/she arrives with a guide or alone. In the former case, it is the guest house owner whose income is reduced, as some of the rent is pocketed by the guide. Where room rates are not in writing, however, the arrival of a new tourist is an opportunity for bargaining and many guest house owners raise their charges to take account of the guide's commission. Indeed, some proprietors allege that guides have arrived at the front door and demanded, in Sinhala, that the room prices be doubled so that they have a high commission. Not unnaturally, this might mean that the tourist refuses to stay, but owners also found it embarrassing because it made them look greedy. It also infuriated them because it seemed to allow those they regarded as the hoi polloi to dictate to them.

Because room rates are normally not fixed, and rules concerning commission are also loose, there is much room for misunderstanding or deception between guide and guesthouse proprietor. I heard guides complain that commission they deserved was refused, with the proprietor claiming either to have already paid it, or that the guide did not really help the tourist. Sometimes proprietors force guides to come back several times before they give them any money. There are also disputes about the agreed percentages or even over how long a tourist stayed in an establishment. Some guest house owners are convinced that guides deliberately move tourists on, even when they would like to stay longer, because it is in the guide's interest to receive several commissions of 25 per cent, rather than to have a full day's rent, collectable only at the end of a period of several days.

It is not only room prices that lead to conflict between guide and guesthouse owner, for more is involved in the relationship of guide and tourist and of tourist and guest house proprietor. For instance, Felix once arrived at a guest house with a young woman, only to be refused entry because, according to him, the owner wanted to have sex with her. The tourist was unwilling to comply and, three days later, when she left, her bill was much greater than she had been led to expect. There was an argument and, when Felix arrived, he told her a reasonable figure and suggested she pay that and leave.

In a somewhat different context, Ali, another informant, recounted how he befriended an Italian couple visiting Sri Lanka to learn about street vending before establishing a business back home. They wanted him to export goods to them in Italy. Arriving at their guest house to work out the details of the business arrangement, the proprietor refused him permission to enter. The tourists explained that their business dealings had nothing to do with the guesthouse and a row erupted. The tourists immediately left with Ali, who then arranged alternative accommodation.

Another potential source of conflict involves the arrangement of transport for tourists. Siri, a teenage guide, delivered a group of tourists to a guest house and then, at their request, arranged for them to visit the Veddah (aboriginal) people, living in the jungle an appreciable distance outside Kandy. The guest house owners tried to dissuade the tourists, saying that it was not safe and that they should go in the guest house's own vehicle, a much more expensive mode of travel than the one Siri intended, namely, a car driven by a taxi driver friend who would give Siri commission of one rupee per mile. Siri protested to the guest house owners that whereas they had a right to room rent, anything else the tourists wanted to do was his concern and not theirs. He told me that it was unfair for wealthy proprietors to try to deprive him of his livelihood. Siri insisted on taking the tourists, for which he was well qualified, having been on several such trips before and even having a slight knowledge of the Veddah language. The guest house owners were incensed and Siri reported that for weeks after the incident he went in fear of reprisals, graphically describing several 'close shaves' when they tried to run him down with their car.

Guest house owners sometimes claim that their profits come less from room rents than from the provision of meals. Some, in fact, deliberately offer low room rates to attract tourists, aiming to compensate by providing relatively expensive meals. If a street guide delivers a tourist to an establishment with the intention of meeting the tourist later, to show him/her around the shops, to have a cafe meal, and so on, the proprietor clearly risks losing income. Furthermore, he may himself wish to escort the tourist around the town, picking up commissions on shopping purchases, thereby depriving guides of a lucrative source of income. In such circumstances, the tourist becomes the recipient of conflicting advice, receiving cautionary tales from both parties. A guide will tell the tourist not to eat at the guest house because it will be expensive and, as soon as the guide has departed, the guest house owner will endeavour to ensure that the tourist spends no more time with the guide by blackening his character.

Whilst this may be a genuine expression of concern for the tourist, the guest house proprietor may simply want to monopolise the tourist's time and expenditure to maximise his income. Guide informants related a new pattern developing during 1982 which particularly irritated them, where owners sent their guests on shopping expeditions escorted by their own teenaged daughters. Guides clearly could not do business with a tourist accompanied by someone from a guest house; indeed, in every shop, the daughter would simply tell the shopkeeper to send the commission to the guest house. I witnessed one instance where a young woman had to walk briskly through Kandy, followed by numerous guides hurling abuse at her, while she tried to ignore the whole affair so that the tourists would not understand what was happening.

To avoid such confrontations, many guest house owners deliberately confined their role to their own premises and took no interest in tourists' other activities. Escorting tourists shopping not only means that owners have to venture into the streets – the territory of the guides – thus risking potential conflicts, but also that they expose themselves to public opinion. Although some of the well-to-do and respectable in Kandyan society were involved in tourism, it was still an activity looked down upon by many. Conscious of their reputations, people simply avoid accompanying tourists in case onlookers make adverse comments about them.

Aggrieved street guides and proprietors of unregistered guest houses have no easy means of satisfactorily resolving their disputes. Both are engaged in activities on which the Tourist Board and local authorities frown, so there is no ready resort to the tourist police or municipal officials. There are some sanctions, of course. Guest house owners can tell a guide never to bring tourists again, but then risk receiving fewer tourists or having to rely more on other guides. Indeed, some guides have been so upset by the demeaning treatment they have received from guest house proprietors that for long periods they have refused to take tourists to certain establishments. The manager of a well-known arts and crafts establishment told me that he admitted no guides because if he did, and subsequently offended any of them, they would combine in a boycott.

Such a fear is exaggerated, just as the proposal that all shopkeepers put up notices forbidding street guides to bring tourists is unrealistic. Neither guides nor guest house owners act in concert. Certainly, conflicts between proprietors and guides are conflicts between the relatively affluent and the predominantly poor, between owners of property and those with only their time and labour to sell, but the two categories do not normally act as antagonistic classes. Neither category is closed: anyone can become a tout and any home owner can try to let rooms to foreigners; and giving up guiding and ceasing to be involved in tourism can also occur very quickly. Furthermore, the class basis is the less obvious because particular individuals in each category are interdependent. Vertical linkages are more visible than solidarity (Bromley, 1979, p. 113). Guest house owners are fiercely competitive and jealous of one another and among street guides, too, it is ultimately everyone for himself.

On one occasion, however, some Kandyan shopkeepers tried to act as a group. In 1982, a local newspaper reported that a petition, drawn up and signed by twenty-two of them, had been presented to the local Inspector-General of Police (*Sun*, 30/6/82). They argued that the touts were so ruining tourism in the city that their businesses were suffering and demanded that police eliminate the guide population from the streets. Although this incident reveals that a group of shopkeepers was able to act in concert, I doubt that guest house owners would take similar joint action, even though conflicts will certainly continue between individual guest house owners and individual guides. Late in 1982, a proprietor suggested at a tourism seminar held in the Town Hall in Kandy that guest house owners should work together to boost tourism in the city. The idea fell on deaf ears and the speaker did not expect even a few of his colleagues to act together. As he put it, they were too busy jealously competing with each other to sense that they had interests in common.

Concluding thoughts

During 1982, there was considerable pessimism in the streets of Kandy. Many guides felt that tourism had peaked, and those with whom I regularly spoke readily conceded that there were then so many at work in Kandy that guiding was becoming impossible. Indeed, the 'catching zone' already extended to Colombo, where some Kandy guides would lurk outside the station and try to intercept tourists before they even boarded the Kandy train. One or two guides commented that 1982 was the worst year they had experienced, and that in previous years tourists had been considerably more generous. They also felt that tourists would increasingly tell them to 'get lost' because of the number of cheap travel books which had become available.

Nonetheless, many were still sustained by one of the 'founding myths' of the guides, that 'doing the tourism' was relatively easy. Some of the first generation of street guides in Kandy were still around. During the early 1970s, a few had received overseas air tickets from tourists and at least one had married a European woman. The continued affluence of one was evident from his style of dress and the motor cycle he used to ride around the streets. No doubt during 1982 some street guides were still being attracted by the 'bright lights' of tourism, but most were involved simply because they were without regular, or indeed any, employment.

I once asked Felix what street guides would do if tourism came to halt in Kandy. He replied that they would either move elsewhere or become robbers. I do not know how the decline in tourism since 1982 has affected them or what impact the enactment of the Specified Tourist Services Code in 1984 has had on those operating without the approval of the Tourist Board, unlicensed guest house operators and street guides alike. For many, activity in the informal economy is a vital means of subsistence and legislation, therefore, might not bring fundamental change.

Some tourists in Kandy alleged that touts in Sri Lanka were the most annoying in Asia. Tired of the incessant approaches of these predatory creatures, they felt themselves to be 'victims' as they walked the streets of Kandy. At street level, any notion that tourism is a force for international peace and understanding is almost laughable. If the depiction of guide as predator and tourist as victim is understandable at this level of interpersonal interaction, at the 'system' level another view is possible. Profits from international tourism have a strong tendency to flow to multinational corporations and to political and economic elites in the developing nations. Seen in this perspective, and given the strategies to which the poor in the Third World have to resort to make ends meet, perhaps we need to ask again who are the real victims of international tourism. That said, however, few in the streets of Kandy would say that tourism was a bad thing, whereas wealthier people, including many involved in tourism, would wax lyrical about how foreigners were corrupting the country and destroying their culture. If international tourism in the Third World creates for many essentially demeaning roles, the truth is also that at least tourism brings some income, even if on an irregular basis. For these individuals, as for some Third World countries which have energetically pursued tourism, we must recognise the fact that they may not have any alternative.

11 Tradition, modernity and tourism in Swaziland[1]

David Harrison

Introduction

Although the social and economic contribution of international tourism to national development has clear theoretical ramifications and involves both modernisation and underdevelopment perspectives, my aim in this chapter is not so much to demonstrate the accuracy of one or other of these arguments as to offer some observations which can make consideration of the social effects of tourism in Swaziland better informed. In particular, I focus on the ambiguous status of 'tradition', which simultaneously legitimates the existing political structure and provides a crucial theme in selling the tourist industry, thus contributing to the process of 'modernity'.

The Kingdom of Swaziland is a small, land-locked country with a population of some 700,000 people. Situated between the Republic of South Africa and Mozambique, it has been crucially affected by the social and political conflicts of the region. A member of the South African Customs Union (SACU) and the Rand Monetary Area (RMA), the country is economically dependent on the Republic which, not surprisingly, is Swaziland's major trading partner.

Throughout the 1980s, the main problem of the Swazi economy was to keep pace with population growth which, over the period 1976–86, averaged 3.2 per cent per annum (Department of Economic Planning and Statistics, 1987, p. 31). In general, the economy has moved in fits and starts. Approximately two-thirds of its export income is derived from sugar, fertilizer and wood pulp, and imports are mainly accounted for by machinery and transport equipment, manufactured goods, mineral fuels and chemicals and chemical products. Swaziland is predominantly agricultural, with some 80 per cent of its population in rural areas, and agriculture contributes almost 25 per cent to the GDP. However, efforts to diversify the economy have had some success and, in 1986, the share of manufacturing in the GDP virtually matched that of the agricultural sector. In addition, since political independence in 1968, tourism has figured increasingly prominently in government plans and the number of visitors to the country has correspondingly increased. There is, indeed, considerable potential for tourism expansion, for Swaziland's 17,364 square kilometres contain a wide variety of scenically attractive geographical and climatic features.

In 1972, Swaziland was visited by 89,015 tourists, of whom 61 per cent were on holiday and 20 per cent were on business. By 1989 this number had risen, somewhat unevenly, to 257,997, with the proportions of holiday and business visitors at 63 per cent and 22 per cent respectively. However, the increase in numbers is not matched by increases in expenditure which, in real terms, has remained static. Most tourists come by road from the Republic of South Africa to take a short break, two or three days at most, and many stay for only one night, visiting the country to watch television programmes or sports activities which, because of international opposition to apartheid, have until recently been denied to the Republic.

The consequences of tourism

In some respects, the economic consequences of tourism in Swaziland can be stated quite clearly. By 1985, more than 2,000 workers were directly employed in hotels and restaurants, making up almost 3 per cent of the total wage earners in the Kingdom. By 1988, tourism was contributing about 3 per cent to GDP and more than 4 per cent of total exports. By 1988, most workers were Swazi, but the higher and better-paid positions in the hotels were generally occupied by foreigners.

In addition to those directly employed in hotels, numerous others also benefit from tourism, including taxi drivers, sculptors, carvers, wholesalers and retailers. However, the most widespread benefits probably accrue to rural workers, primarily women who produce handicrafts, and previous research has estimated that about a third of all households in the Kingdom have at least one individual involved in handicraft production (Russell, 1983, p. 16). Handicrafts tend to be sold by the producer, or by kinswomen, and there is also provision for government agencies to act as wholesalers. As in the Gambia, however (cf. Wagner, 1982, pp. 61 and 69), expatriate involvement has been important. In Swaziland, several foreign retailers dominate the top end of the handicrafts market.

The tourist industry is concentrated in central Swaziland, especially in the Ezulwini Valley between Mbabane and Manzini, as indicated in Figure 11.1. The bigger the hotel and the more costly its accommodation, the more likely it is to be in this corridor and the more likely it is to be foreign-owned. In July, 1987, there were 1,165 hotel rooms in Swaziland. Of these, non-Swazis owned 70 per cent and over 90 per cent of those in the Ezulwini Valley. Sun International dominated the upper sector of the industry, operating its own hotels and managing those in which the Government, or the *Tibiyo Takangwane* (an investment arm of the monarchy) have substantial interests. This hotel chain owned or operated 616 hotel beds in Swaziland, some 53 per cent of the total. More importantly, perhaps, it dominated the 'luxury' end of the market, owning or controlling 90 per cent of all hotel rooms which (at 1987 rates) cost more than 40 Emalangeni a night.[2]

As Swazi tourism expanded, new formal institutions have been developed and others have been adapted. In the private sector, the Hotel and Tourist Association is the main pressure group, and within government ministries there are departments to promote Swazi tourism and handicrafts. Co-operation between the private sector and the Swaziland National Trust Commission has led to the establishment of several game and nature reserves, considered increasingly important as tourist attractions.

Other social consequences have also followed from tourist development. Swazis have increasingly interacted with whites who, by most standards, are relatively affluent. Not all such interaction may be considered beneficial and, as shown below, increases in begging, prostitution and other forms of 'immoral' activity have been laid at the tourist door.

'Modernity' and 'tradition' are often contrasted, both by modernisation theorists,

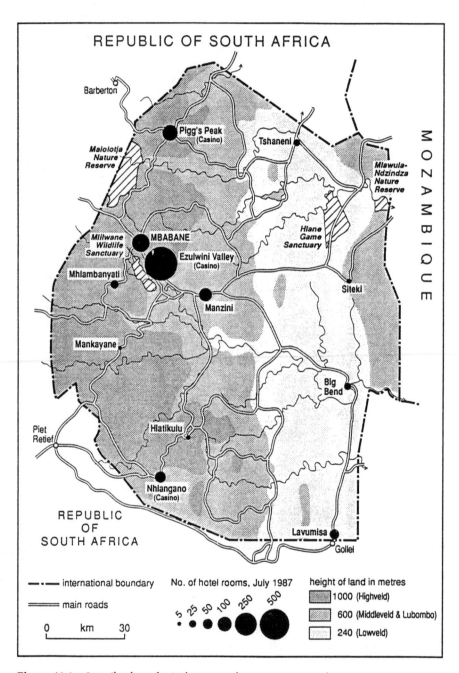

Figure 11.1   Swaziland: ecological zones and tourist accommodation, 1987

who focus on the beneficial effects of Westernisation, and their opponents, who tend to regard tradition as helpless in the face of savage attacks by modernity. Nevertheless, such positions are belied by the reality of present-day Swaziland, where 'tradition' legitimates 'modern' government and is simultaneously threatened by that same government's involvement in and support for the tourist industry. In order to substantiate such assertions, however, it is necessary, first, to detail the major political and economic institutions of Swaziland and then to indicate their relationship to the tourist industry.

The 'traditional' basis of 'modern' government

In theory, the Swazi constitution attempts to blend Swazi tradition with the features of a modern democratic society. The 'traditional' elements are described in the early ethnographies of Swaziland (Marwick, 1940; Kuper, 1947, 1961 and 1963). The King (*Ngwenyama*), as the Head of State, shared power with the Queen Mother (*Ndlovukati*) and senior princes and princesses of the royal family. Chiefs were selected by the King from the royal family, and male kin of the Queen Mother were also given important positions in the administration. The King was also assisted by *Indvunas*, the foremost of whom was equivalent to a prime minister, and by *tinyanga*, specialists in ritual. Both categories of councillor were selected from the (male) members of clans which were not part of the royal family. The King's closest advisers formed the *liqoqo*, which was, in effect, an inner council of state. Conversely, all men in the nation, including councillors, chiefs and headmen, formed the *libandla*, the Swazi National Council.

This traditional political organisation contains elements of feudalism, in that all land belongs to the Crown, with control vested in the chiefs. Clearly hierarchical, as described by anthropologists the distinctions were between aristocrat and commoner, young and old, and men and women. However, the system was undoubtedly complicated by the introduction of migrant labour at the end of the nineteenth century and work in the mines of the Republic allegedly led to a rudimentary consciousness of class (cf. Bonner, 1982, p. 211 ff). By contrast, Kuper notes that, through migrant labour, Swazi men became increasingly aware of a pan-African identity (1947, p. 23). She also stresses the role of the 'uniform of colour' in effectively segregating Europeans from Swazis, a segregation which applied both in the Republic and in Swaziland.

In these circumstances, it is unnecessary to oppose ethnicity to class. Both forms of identification may have been present. Certainly, close economic and political involvement with the Republic of South Africa crucially affected Swaziland, penetrating deep into the rural hinterland and leaving its mark on the 'traditional' organisation of Swazi homesteads (cf. Booth, 1986). At a constitutional level, too, the 'traditional' has not given way to the 'modern' in Swaziland. Rather, it has been adapted. The King remains Head of State, sharing power with the Queen Mother. Until its disbandment in 1987, the *Liqoqo* was the Council of State, in parallel to the modern Cabinet, and was chaired by a senior prince known as the Authorised Person who, in an interregnum, became Prince Regent to the Queen Mother's Queen Regent. Technically, the Swazi National Council also remains, even though the circumstances in which it might meet are unclear.

In fact, the Swazi monarchy is closely involved in the 'modern' sector of government. In 1973, five years after political independence had been gained from Britain, King Sobhuza II repealed the Westminster system and banned political parties. Since 1978, following a period of government by proclamation, a modified bicameral system has been in operation. Open (that is, not secret) elections are held every five years in forty traditional constituencies (*Tinkhundla*), every one of which is controlled by an *indvuna*, who owes his position to the King. Every *Tinkhundla* elects two members to an electoral college which, in turn, selects forty of its number to sit in the House of Assembly, where they are joined by ten of the King's appointees. The influence of the King is even more marked in the Senate, the second chamber, which is composed of twenty members, of whom half are elected by the House of Assembly and half appointed by the King. Finally, it is the King who selects the Prime Minister and members of the Cabinet. In short, even in the 'modern' sector of government, the 'traditional' monarchy is highly influential at all levels, from the nomination of *Tinkhundla* candidates, through the appointment of additional members of both chambers of parliament, up to the selection of the Prime Minister and members of the Cabinet.

The Swazi monarchy is no mere symbol. It holds real power, which is based on distinct but related sources. In the years preceding and following political independence, the monarchy purchased some of the land it had lost, through concessions made to Europeans, at the end of the nineteenth century. This land was added to the existing stock of Swazi Nation Land, held in trust by the King for the Nation, with control vested in the chiefs. As the position of *indvuna* is often held by a chief, it is these chiefs who control the *Tinkhundla* and, through the electoral college, elect members to the House of Assembly and the Senate. As already indicated, it is the King who appoints (and can dismiss) the Prime Minister and members of the Cabinet. This amounts to an impressive degree of political control.

At the economic level, and equally important, is the *Tibiyo Takangwane*, a commercial and investment company controlled by and operating to the direct benefit of the Crown (and not the Ministry of Finance) often in conjunction with foreign capital. Along with its offshoot, the *Tisuka Takangwane*, which receives mineral and other royalties on the King's behalf, *Tibiyo* represents a real, powerful and unaccountable royal stake in the 'modern' sector of the Swazi economy.

The process through which royal control of politics and the economy was established in Swaziland has been nicely described by Macmillan, who notes:

The major peculiarity of decolonisation in Swaziland was that it was the only one of the African colonies and protectorates, with the arguable exception of Zanzibar, to come to independence as a monarchy in which real power rested with the King and a council of chiefs and elders in direct descent from those who had wielded power in the pre-colonial era (1986, p. 104).

To re-establish this 'traditional' power and authority, King Sobhuza II, who led Swaziland into independence, had to re-interpret Swazi tradition so that the colonial administration and his own people accepted him and his descendants as legitimate rulers of an independent state. According to Macmillan, over three decades the King and his allies, including such social anthropologists as Hilda Kuper, were able to establish the claims of the monarchy not only against the British, but also against an increasingly proletarianised work force, a growing Swazi intelligentsia, and pressures from elsewhere. The battle was not easy and, *inter alia*, involved the creation of national (as opposed to mission) schools and a revival of the age-graded regimental system, institutions through which King Sobhuza II and his allies could control the socialisation of the young. However, by the late 1950s, class divisions and foreign influence seemed to threaten the monarchy:

In the eyes of the 'traditionalists', the unity of their nation was now threatened as never before by emerging class divisions, and by an influx of aliens who were in competition with the Swazi for jobs, women, and space in the increasingly crowded Swazi Nation areas. At the same time, the inflow of educated black South Africans to key posts, especially in education, seemed to present more forcefully than before the risk of an alien intelligentsia not only monopolising good jobs, but also 'subverting' or 'indoctrinating' – both words were used – Swazi youth (Macmillan, 1986, p. 115).

According to Macmillan, the new threat from organised labour and African nationalism led King Sobhuza II into an alliance with white settlers and international business interests. This alliance took Swaziland into the period of political independence and beyond. During this period, too, political parties briefly appeared, including one led by the King, only to be banned by Parliament, on his direction, in 1979. They were replaced, in effect by the *Tinkhundla*, allegedly a traditional Swazi institution. However, as Macmillan remarks:

It was clear that 'traditional', in this context, meant anything but old or inherited. It was as it had been so often in the past, a disguise for something thoroughly new and intended to keep power in the hands of a small section of the population (1986, pp. 121–2).

The process Macmillan describes as leading to 'the triumph of tradition' is essentially political, a quite deliberate attempt by the monarchy and its supporters over a long period to retain power in the face of competing claims from within and from outside Swaziland. There is no need to fully accept his argument (or the implicit definition of ideology as a tool for the ruling class) to recognise that, in Swaziland, 'traditional' institutions were re-formulated by King Sobhuza II and his supporters specifically to define Swazi nationhood and the political and economic place of the royal family within the newly-independent society.

It should be emphasised that the Swazis have not directly engaged in the invention of tradition, noted in other parts of colonial Africa and elsewhere, where 'tradition' has been manufactured to confer what might be regarded as a spurious authenticity on either a colonising power or a new ruling class (cf. Hobsbawn and Ranger, 1983). However, states may frequently attempt to control and manipulate custom for their own benefit, or in the interests of a wider 'unity', and this may lead to an increased focus on performance and display, perhaps exacerbated by tourism (cf. Acciaioli, 1985, 158–9).

As Macmillan points out, it was necessary for King Sobhuza II and his allies to revive many practices which had fallen into disuse under the British:

In the first 20 or so years of British administration there can, however, be no doubt that Swazi institutions decayed. The chiefs were stripped of most of their judicial functions; the age-grade or regimental system declined in the face of the competing demands of taxation and labour migration; and massive land alienation created further problems of jurisdiction for chiefs, most of whom were left in reserves while many of their followers remained on white farms. . . .

It should, however, be noted that the major Swazi ceremony, the *Ncwala*, a ritual of kingship and first-fruits ceremony, could not be fully performed between 1899 and 1920 owing to the absence of the King, and Sobhuza's initial *Ncwala* in 1921 was in itself something of a revival (Macmillan, 1986, pp. 106–107).

In effect, King Sobhuza II and his allies revived and interpreted Swazi tradition, for the colonial power and for the Swazi people. In so doing, they provided a package which legitimated the constitutional position of the monarchy and laid the functions for its political and economic dominance in the period following political independence. Importantly, as part of this process, there was an increasing focus on Swazi culture, a revival of interest in Swazi ceremonies and the promotion of Siswati as the national language. In effect, the monarchy became both the guardian and the epitome of Swazi culture. The King and the nation were one.

This section should not be regarded as a mere excursion into political economy. Tradition – revived, interpreted, even manipulated – is the basis of the Swazi constitution and its monarchy, and the monarchy is symbolically, politically and economically dominant. However, a focus on 'tradition' is also a key feature of Swazi tourism, which many Swazi consider responsible for the introduction or exacerbation of unwelcome elements of 'modernity'. For them, at least, 'tradition' and 'modernity' are in direct conflict. And as the monarchy is heavily involved in the tourist industry, its position may be considered decidedly ambiguous.

Tourism and the monarchy

As noted above, the Swazi monarchy occupies a key position in the 'modern' political order and in the Swazi economy. The Government, dominated by the monarchy, is involved in tourism through its various ministries. In particular, the Division of Tourism, a part of the Ministry of Commerce, Industry, Mines and Tourism, supervises the activities of the Swaziland Tourism Development Company, which operates Government shareholdings in the Protea Peak Casino Hotel (100 per cent) and the Nhlangano Sun Hotel (49 per cent), which also has a casino. These hotels, situated away from the popular Ezulwini Valley, represent major Government investments and both are operated by Sun International. The involvement of the monarchy in tourism, however, is not restricted to its investment through government institutions. Its own investment agency, the *Tibiyo Takangwane*, has a 39 per cent interest in the other Swazi operations of Sun International, the major transnational hotel chain in southern Africa which, as described above, dominates the Swazi tourist industry. And among its numerous other investments, *Tibiyo* owns the Swazi National Airline. Together, these give the monarchy, whether through the Government or its private investment agency, a colossal stake in the tourist industry. Its position may be legitimated by 'tradition' but, through its involvement in tourism, it also has a substantial interest in 'modern' trends and, as a consequence, in the packaging and selling of Swazi 'tradition'.

The growth of 'modernity'

If it assumed that 'modernity' is what is currently considered as 'up-to-date', and development is regarded as change which is in some respects 'progressive', it should be evident that they are not synonymous (cf. Harrison, 1988, pp. 153–156). Certainly, in Swaziland it is commonly felt that foreign influences tend to corrupt the young – a view held over several decades and not restricted to Swaziland. For many older Swazis, alcoholic drink, drugs and discotheques amount to decadence and depravation, and are seen as being encouraged by tourism.

In Swaziland, discotheques are the preserve of the young and provide a setting where interaction between young Swazis and non-Swazis is most likely. In addition, alcohol is consumed, thus increasing the 'disreputable' nature of this form of social activity. Most of the larger hotels have discotheques and set out to attract young Swazis, especially in mid-week and periods of the year when the tourist trade is slack.

Equally contentious among some Swazis are the three casinos that now exist in Swaziland (all of which have some Government or royal investment). The amount won on the jackpot on the fruit machines is regularly published in the newspapers, and it is felt that, whilst foreigners may 'play the machines', such behaviour is immoral if carried out by Swazi, who are likely to have less money to spend on gambling (and who, it is sometimes suggested, might be more inclined to become addicted to the activity).[3]

If Swazi men were considered most likely to gamble, it was young Swazi women who, in other respects, were held to be more inclined to adopt other 'foreign' patterns of behaviour. In particular, women who wear trousers, especially jeans, attract considerable hostility, which is regularly aired in newspaper articles:

There is a man at the bus rank . . . who takes it upon himself to enforce law and order where bus queues are concerned. . . . The person he picked on was an attractive teen-age girl wearing a pair of trousers. He hit her on her face and shoulders and would have had a field day if he had not been stopped by young men. . . . Other women rushed to form a line, chuckling to themselves, saying complacently, 'That's what you get from wearing trousers'. . . .

In another incident, a young woman wearing trousers was waiting for a bus and hitching at the same time on the road from Ngwenya. Four or five army vehicles drove by and stopped. One of the soldiers got off and asked her why she was wearing trousers. He then slapped her, climbed back into his truck and they all drove off.

Time and time again, the matter is brought up in parliament. Should there be a ban on women wearing trousers? The matter came up in 1979 and there was a motion against it in the House of Assembly (the lower house). The matter was again brought up last year by one of the MPs. At the time it was said that the matter would have to be taken to the Tinkhundla.

The reason the MP gave for wanting trousers to be banned was that it lowered Swaziland as a nation if the women wore trousers (and men permed their hair).

One of the reasons why there was some reluctance to ban trouser wearing was the fear that tourists, as in the case of Malawi, might be chased away from coming into the country if they were not free to wear what they wanted. Then the issue came up of banning trousers for local women. In essence, Swazi nationals. Unfortunately, this would lead to an apartheid-like situation . . .

Some government officers will not allow a smart looking woman wearing even a business-like pants-suit into their ministries. Does what she is wearing limit her ability to do a job? (Gcinaphi Dlamini, in the *Times of Swaziland*, 21st July, 1987)

One tourist official I interviewed said that he did not wish Swaziland to become like Malawi and ban tourists if they came in jeans or similar clothing. When that happened, the tourist industry declined. However, he stressed that Swazi women *knew* that such clothing was wrong, especially if they were married, and he would not allow women in his office to wear such clothes, even if it were cold. What they did at home was a different matter. (Indeed, there have been times when such strictures have also been applied to white women in Swaziland; I know of at least two cases of white women being banned from entering government offices because they were wearing trousers).

It would be a serious mistake to regard the issue of dress as trivial and numerous issues are raised in this debate. Obviously, one element is the authority of Swazi men over 'their' women, especially young women, who feel that they should be able to wear clothes of their own choosing. In defying (male) authority in such matters, women lay themselves open to several linked accusations. First, they are usurping male roles. Secondly, they are emulating tourists, and thirdly, they are engaging in 'immoral' behaviour. In fact, their 'immorality' – for which they may suffer public admonition and humiliation – consists in defying Swazi tradition. The wearing of jeans by a young woman thus takes on considerable symbolic significance. The fact that such attire is often associated with having a good time at discotheques, at which drinking also occurs, is simply seen as further evidence of moral degeneracy.

For many Swazis, 'modernity' in its various manifestations is clearly something of a problem. The fact that some young women want to wear trousers, especially jeans, is clearly not due entirely to the development of tourism. Swazi citizens visit the Republic, and in Swaziland there is open access to magazines and journals with details of European and North American fashions. Furthermore, many white visitors to Swaziland, whose behaviour local people are said to be emulating, are not holiday tourists at all; instead, they are in the Kingdom to work, often for the United Nations and other international agencies, and their arrival can be seen as part and parcel of a much longer and more complex exposure to 'Westernisation'. Such 'demonstration effects', which have been noted elsewhere (cf. de Kadt, ed., 1979, pp. 64–66), and which have been described as instruments of 'slow torture' (Turner and Ash, 1975, p. 198) do not arise from tourism alone. True, they have often been considered detrimental to members of the 'host' society, but such a perspective implies that 'traditional' patterns of behaviour are both static and morally preferable, a viewpoint which, to say the least, is somewhat contentious, if not downright patronising.

In some respects, it would be surprising if discotheques were not popular in Swaziland and, although hotels undoubtedly provide opportunities for young Swazis to enjoy Western dancing, this applies as much to hotels owned and operated by Swazis as to those operated by expatriates. Swaziland is not isolated from the rest of the world and, with or without tourism, such influences will be brought to bear on its traditions, young people and established authorities. Government or crown ownership of some of the hotels offering gambling, drinking and discotheques to the young of Swaziland merely highlights the dilemma. Indeed, it is probably the larger and more expensive hotels which try hardest to control access to alcohol. For class reasons, if for no other, they desire to protect their largely white residents from unlimited exposure to members of Swazi society. It is left to the cheaper, Swazi-owned hotels and bars to cater for the rest of the population.

What remains true is that such 'modern' activities are more likely to appeal to the young than the middle-aged or the elderly, and that the young are exposed most to those foreign influences which prevail in tourist establishments throughout Swaziland. Equally, young or single whites from the Republic who visit Swaziland may be more likely to reject the constraints of their own, racially-divided society than their (older) compatriots who stay in the better hotels. The former's motives for visiting may not always be to everyone's taste, and in Swaziland there is a small but evident incidence of prostitution. It is not a new phenomenon, and is neither 'modern' nor a new form of social contact, but it has undeniably been associated with the arrival of Europeans in Swaziland.

Prostitution

It is often argued that tourism in the Third World encourages prostitution and other forms of immorality (cf. Wolfers, 1974, pp. 70–72; Turner and Ash, 1975, pp.

230–231). Indeed, it has been alleged that gambling, pornographic films and 'prostitution across the colour line became the cornerstones of Lesotho's and Swaziland's tourist attractions' (Crush and Wellings, 1987, p. 101).

However, in the case of Swaziland, at least, such an assertion is highly questionable. This is not to say that, in Swaziland, prostitution (defined as payment specifically for sexual services) does not exist. It was already considered a problem in the late 1930s, when the young were allegedly being alienated from Swazi traditions and corrupted by increased European influence and urbanisation (cf. Marwick, 1940, p. 301). By the mid-1950s, such social problems were considered sufficiently pressing for the colonial government to set up a Commission to investigate why they were occurring, and in 1956 it reported, arriving at very similar conclusions. (Commission to Investigate Juvenile Delinquency and Allied Problems, 1956). At that time, however, the men involved were considered to be Swazi migrant workers returning from mines of the Republic.

In 1970, prostitution was the subject of yet another report, (Committee on Juvenile Delinquency, Sexual Morality and the Maintenance of Illegitimate Children), which covered much the same ground as the 1956 report, again blaming increasing urbanisation and the breakdown of social control, especially in the urban areas. However, it was then noted that prostitution was centred around a few specified hotels and, despite somewhat contradictory evidence, most of the women's clients were considered to be from outside Swaziland.

The situation was unchanged by the mid-1980s. However, the scale of prostitution in Swaziland is difficult to quantify. Published figures are rare and unhelpful, and the police are known to allocate this kind of offence a low priority. In addition, newspaper reports tend to sensationalise the issue. After all, it is 'good copy'. In April, 1984, the *Weekend Observer* carried out a 'three week investigation' and broadcast its findings under the banner headline, 'SEX FOR SALE'. It suggested that most of the women involved were dropouts from school, and quoted one as earning E200 a night from South Africans spending a public holiday in the Kingdom:

'For every shot, I charge the white man and other foreigners E30 and when it means spending a night with them in their hotel rooms, then the amount doubles,' she said (*Weekend Observer*, 28th April, 1984).

White and black tourists alike were quoted as being shocked at the immorality in Swaziland, and the opinions of the Vice-Chancellor of the University of Swaziland and the Anglican Bishop were sought. However, no estimate of the number of prostitutes operating in Swaziland was attempted and, by contrast, a spokesman for the police was more cautious:

From the legal point of view there is 'nothing' like prostitution in Swaziland ... He said when more women are found in drinking places enjoying themselves, it is assumed they are prostitutes (*Weekend Observer*, 28th April, 1984).

Interestingly, in a companion article of the same issue, 'Why do local girls fall for Shangaans?', the paper quoted Swazi men asserting that the women wanted money and a good time, which they could obtain more easily from *Shangaans* (foreigners):

But two senior workers in the hotel industry, both of them women, had different views: 'The Shangaans have that tender care. They know how to look after a woman and they know what a woman is, unlike our local guys, who only know how to booze.' (*Weekend Observer*, 28th April, 1984).

What seems to be at issue is not prostitution, where sexual services are provided specifically in return for financial gain, but an alleged preference of some Swazi women for foreigners. As in previous reports, the distinction is frequently ignored. It must also be recognised that such stereotypes are not unique to Swaziland. They exist in many societies where more wealthy, allegedly high status men from outside come into contact with local women. Much the same kind of accusation is levelled at women in other less developed countries and, indeed, was commonly directed at British women who became involved with American GIs during the Second World War.

The view that prostitution in Swaziland is increasing may be common but it is not universally held and, for reasons already provided, is difficult to prove. From the available evidence, the government appears to tread carefully. It is aware that tourists bring with them customs, habits and wants which, according to some criteria, are less than wholesome. Drinking alcohol, dancing at discotheques, the wearing of trousers by young women, using drugs, mixing with foreigners and prostitution are part of a pattern which, it should be noted, reflects almost entirely on the behaviour of women. Young men were rarely criticised for adopting 'foreign' ways. However, officials were reluctant to formally restrict the behaviour of young Swazis, and not that of tourists, on the grounds that they would be seen to operate double standards, a consideration which, by contrast, apparently did not apply at informal levels of social control. 'The man in the street' was far more willing to persuade the woman in the street to conform to traditional norms.

To argue that immorality has actually increased with Westernisation is quite different and requires a series of assessments and value judgements which would be out of place in this context. What has happened is that colonialism and Westernisation have introduced and often imposed changes to which Swazi society has had to respond. In one way or another, 'tradition' has been threatened. In the final section, I suggest that one response has been to package this tradition for the benefit of tourists whilst quite consciously attempting to preserve it from other forms of attack.

Tradition and tourism in Swaziland

Tradition is not a fixed entity. As suggested earlier, the monarchy deliberately adapted Swazi tradition for its own purposes, and in so doing was not unique. However it is defined, 'tradition', is eminently adaptable. This is perhaps especially the case when it is being portrayed by the tourist industry.

When Swaziland is advertised as a tourist venue, its traditions are emphasised, whether or not the publicity emanates from the private sector or government. We learn that in Swaziland

ANCIENT TRADITIONS MINGLE WITH UP-TO-THE-MINUTE AMENITIES: Swaziland is a fascinating blend of contrasts and contradictions, old traditions mingling with 20th-century technology . . . and the conservative and tradition-loving people are proud to wear their national dress of which feathers, skins, cow-tails and brilliant colours are such a memorable feature (Swaziland Chamber of Commerce, 1987, pp. 94–5).

In the same publication, tourists are advised that the arts and crafts of Swaziland are one of the ways in which 'the culture and traditions of the Swazi people are kept alive' (Swaziland Chamber of Commerce, 1987, p. 101).

In a sense, this is indeed the case. Material artefacts, whether produced for decoration or everyday use, for sale or for the producer, are tangible reflections and expressions of culture. However, it must be recognised that many of the allegedly 'traditional' items produced for sale to tourists have only recently been introduced into Swaziland. As the above publication recognises, the grass woven by rural women into baskets and mats is a traditional material but the items themselves have little to do with Swaziland, and much to do with what it is hoped the tourists will buy. They are the 'curios' regarded by visitors, in Russell's words, as 'authentic evidence of their journey to foreign parts' (Russell, 1983, p. 25).

A similar argument might be made for carvers and sculptors. The skills exercised by Swazis currently engaged in the production of such items have been acquired relatively recently and cannot really be described as 'traditional'. The National Handicraft Training Centre, for instance, is a recent institution, quite specifically set up to develop skills appropriate for the tourist market. Early in 1987, it entertained two visiting experts on handicrafts and tourism. According to a newspaper report:

They are from the EEC. They are Mr Ray Joyce, an expert on tourism and Mr Donald Wiels on handicraft. Mr Mkhonta, Principal Secretary for Commerce, Industry and Tourism, said the EEC wants Swaziland to spell out the needs of the two sectors, and therefore sponsored the tour of the two men. Mr Mkhonta said recently the Ministry advertised the posts of three experienced people within the two sectors. Two of them will be seconded to handicrafts while the third will go to tourism.

We have advertised the post of a handicraft designer who will help us design our handicrafts for sale in the outside market. We think that if we can get somebody experienced, especially from Europe, we would be in a better chance to know how the Europeans want our products to look like (*Times of Swaziland*, 14th May, 1987).

The carved animals and busts of human figures so common throughout Swaziland are examples of how Swazis view tourist demand. They are part and parcel of what Africa is supposed to be. So, too, are the 'traditional' dances performed in the more expensive hotels, and the animals in the game parks, preferably viewed from comfortable surroundings, might also be regarded as performers, equally 'stage managed' for the benefit of tourists.

This may appear a somewhat cynical representation of the tourist industry, and such stage management is certainly not confined to Swaziland. It can also be argued that the production of any tourist artefact, indeed all tourist art, contains elements of performance, and that even the most obvious item of 'airport art' is the product of a highly complex tourist art system, through which 'the expectations of consumers are typified, mirrored, and represented to them by others' (Jules-Rossette, 1984, p. 226). According to this perspective, the meaning of a product to all those involved in an apparently simple transaction is no easy matter to determine. The product itself is the result of a series of symbolic exchanges.

This is undoubtedly the case. However, cultural exchanges are collective as well as individual and both performer and audience may subscribe to social stereotypes, which then become part of the exchange. This point may be illustrated by reference to promotional material issued by the Tourist Division of the Swazi government. In July, 1987, it produced two posters advertising Swaziland, both of which focused on 'traditional' Swazi culture. One pictures a Swazi woman in traditional costume. She is young and bare-breasted, and her costume, a beaded apron and woollen tassels, is colourful and revealing. Such pictures must be seen in the context of other coverage of 'African' affairs, where 'the native' is similarly portrayed – for example, in postcards from South Africa and other colonies in the 1920s and 1930s, as well as many European news items on recent African political events. For many Swazis, such costumes are regarded as being quite different from the allegedly provocative forms of dress worn by some young Swazi women at discotheques.[4] For whites, at whom this promotional literature is directed, and who will have been socialised into specific racial stereotypes, the distinction might not be so clear. Preconceptions of another kind might also be involved in 'reading' the second picture, of three Swazi men, again in traditional costume. Carrying knobkerries, wearing skirts, with skins around their waists and beads across their chests, the men are indeed 'picturesque'. The commentary in the official tourist guide, in which several such pictures appear, provides additional information:

Present-day Swazis delight in their customs and traditions. Swazis dress in colourful costume, Emahiya, the women wearing the traditions[sic] beehive hairstyle – Sicholo. Swazi warriors carry shields, knobsticks, spears and battleaxes as part of their dress. These are some of the outward signs of a deeply-rooted social system, unique in Africa (Swaziland Tourist Office, undated, p. 2).

In fact, as even a casual visitor to Swaziland discovers, such costumes are worn only on special occasions. The Swaziland Tourist Office, a government institution, is packaging and selling Swazi tradition. The message it is conveying to potential tourists, mostly whites from the Republic of South Africa, is that Swaziland is a country of exotic people, with unfamiliar customs and colourful costumes, which is locked in the past. Once again, we have returned to the 'picturesque occupants' of Swaziland, noted by John Buchan early this century (1903, p. 132).

In presenting the above images, the Swaziland Tourist Office is doing no more than similar organisations in other less developed countries. Indeed, its approach is recommended by many consultants to the industry:

Reason enough for foreign tourists to come to Swaziland from afar to discover and have a look at 'Africa at its best' . . . Reason enough to consider this country as a whole to be a 'Nature and Heritage Reserve'. So a future tourism management should do its best to create favourable conditions for visitors to witness, hear and experience the uniqueness of Swaziland. Any sidestep from traditional and national lifestyle would be fatal (G. Conradi, Tourism Manager and Consultant, 'Tourism rediscovers paradise', *Observer*, Swaziland, 6th April, 1985).

The logical conclusion of this policy is to consider the entire country a showpiece, a living, moving, breathing storehouse of tradition. In fact, if Macmillan is correct in his analysis of the development of 'traditionalism' in Swaziland, such a development would fit perfectly with the prevailing political ideology which, nevertheless, has prevented neither the Swazi Government nor the royal family from increasingly participating in numerous sectors of a modern economy.

At its worst, focus on tradition as a selling point can lead to parody. Consider the following advertising feature in the in-flight magazine of the national airline, owned by *Tibiyo Takangwane*, the monarchy's investment arm, and designed to attract conference tourists to the Royal Swazi Sun Hotel, in which it has a substantial interest:

The Royal Swazi Sun has a reputation for organising special evenings which are built around a particular 'theme' . . . Suggestions include: 'Out of Africa' evening – using the Swazi village in the grounds of the hotel, we can have lamb or ox on the spit, Swazi musicians and singers, huge fires and flares for lighting effects – a different type of evening for those of us who live in cities and towns.

As the conference organiser went on to explain,

I remember when one big insurance company asked for this theme and delegates really entered into the spirit of the evening, dressing up in Swazi costumes or safari suits. One guy actually hired a gorilla suit in Johannesburg and brought it with him. This is the kind of crowd we really enjoy working for (Royal Swazi National Airways, June/July, 1987, p. 13).

Although tradition may be packaged and sold by the Swazi authorities to increase tourism, it is no mere marketing device. On 19th May, 1987, Pastor Phil Dacre of the Rhema Church, an evangelical sect, was arrested for sedition and detained under the law (designed to combat terrorism and political unrest) which allowed the authorities to commit him to prison for up to sixty days without trial. His offence was to write pamphlets criticising, on religious and moral grounds, features of the traditional Incwala kingship and first fruits ritual. Dacre was subsequently joined in detention by another pastor, the church's administrator, and the General Manager of the company which printed the pamphlets. In July, the sixty-day period was renewed, and Dacre's first appearance in court was set for 21st September, 1987, four months after his initial arrest.[5]

His arrest, under a law which can only be described as draconian, indicates a revival of opposition on the part of mission churches to some Swazi traditions, an opposition which, according to Macmillan, was 'discreetly dropped' in the late 1960s. (1986, p. 121). It also supports Macmillan's argument for the importance of 'traditionalism' in Swazi politics. Not even pastors are allowed to rock the boat in paradise.

Conclusions

In Swaziland, the monarchy is dominant. As Head of State, the King controls the electoral process, appointing and dismissing leading government officials, and indirectly controlling all government investments. As monarch, he has a constitutional power base and direct control over his subjects through the chiefs, who hold and allocate Swazi Nation Land on his behalf. He also controls the royal finances and has a major stake in the country's economy, often in partnership with foreign capital. Government and the crown have increasingly invested in tourism, especially the hotel sector, normally in partnership with the Sun International chain of hotels, which dominates Swazi tourism.

Overall, the political and economic dominance of the monarchy is legitimated by 'tradition', re-interpreted by King Sobhuza and his allies in the years preceding independence and later enforced by further changes in the constitution in the post-independence period. And when the role of such tradition is questioned, the full power of the state is exercised and critics are charged with sedition. In short, it is 'tradition' or, at any rate, the appeal to tradition, which both established and continues to reinforce the 'modern' Swazi state.

However, the involvement of the state and *Tibiyo Takangwane* in tourism has also made the monarchy party to the presentation, packaging and selling of Swazi tradition to attract tourists to the country. In such circumstances, 'tradition' becomes an advertising gimmick, presenting potential tourists (mainly white South

Africans) with exotic people in colourful costumes and spectacular ceremonies, thus reinforcing what many would regard as an unfavourable stereotype of Swazi society. To add to the contradiction, it is also possible to see tourism as but part of a continuing process of 'modernisation', which for decades has allegedly undermined the authority of (male) traditional Swazi rulers over the young and (especially) over women, introducing forms of behaviour and dress into the country which are considered to threaten the traditional Swazi way of life.

In Swaziland (as elsewhere) 'tradition' and 'modernity' are not polar opposites. Furthermore, the relationship of tourism to tradition and modernity is in no sense straightforward. For the Swazi government, tourism may be a mixed blessing. Arguably, its power is based on a successful appeal to tradition and yet, in its support for and investment in tourism, it may be encouraging a continued process of modernisation which ultimately will exoticise and undermine the foundation of its legitimacy.

When a country opens its doors to international tourism, its traditions (however marketable) are going to be changed, if not threatened. And it is the young, both 'visitor' and 'host', who will be in the forefront of 'culture contact' and who will be the most susceptible to change. In Swaziland, this process did not start with international tourism; it commenced with the first arrival of the Europeans and has continued ever since. What tourism has done, as it has done elsewhere, is to emphasise the contrast between tourist and 'host' and reinforce the process. In Swaziland, so close to and dependent on the Republic of South Africa, it is unlikely that this pattern can be reversed.

Notes

1. Fieldwork in Swaziland in July and August, 1987, was part of a visit funded by the British Council. I am grateful to Don Funnell and Ieuan Griffiths, colleagues at the University of Sussex, and to members of the Social Science Research Unit, University of Swaziland, for comments on a more comprehensive report on this research (cf. Harrison, 1990). Sue Rowland was good enough to provide the map and Malcolm Crick commented on an earlier draft.
2. The value of the Emalangeni, the currency of Swaziland, is equal to that of the South African Rand, to which it is directly linked.
3. It was my *impression*, and that of Crush and Wellings (1987, p. 103), that male Swazis, perhaps employed by the casino, were considered to be most 'at risk', tending to spend their earnings gambling rather than on their wives and families.
4. Nevertheless, an amused King Sobhuza II made no concessions to a white visitor's discomfort when she was shocked by the traditional costumes and 'arrogant yet enticing' deportment of young Swazi women dancers: 'They dance to excite the warriors,' said Sobhuza (Packer, 1953? pp. 169–170).
5. Up to the time of writing, I have been unable to discover the outcome of these proceedings.

Bibliography

Acciaioli, G., 1985, 'Culture as Art: From Practice to Spectacle in Indonesia', *Canberra Anthropology*, 8 (1 and 2), pp. 148–172.

Agora: Furusato ga Kuzurerul Rizōto Hō to Watashi-tachi, No. 65, 1991, 10th August.

Ahmed, S.A., 1986, 'Perceptions of the Socio-economic and Cultural Impact of Tourism in Sri Lanka', *Canadian Journal of Development Studies*, 7 (2): 239–255.

Allard, L., 1989, 'Statistical Measurement in Tourism', in Witt, S. and Moutinho, L., eds., *Tourism Marketing and Management Handbook*, Prentice Hall, New York and London, pp. 419–24.

Allcock, J. and Przeclawski, eds, 1990, 'Tourism in Centrally-planned Economies', *Annals of Tourism Research*, 17 (1).

Alleyne, F.W., 1984, 'Comment on Bélisle's "Tourism and Food Production in the Caribbean"', *Annals of Tourism Research*, 11 (3): 519–22.

de Alwis, A., 1980, *Tourism: The Greatest Movement for World Peace and Understanding*, Ceylon Tourist Board, Colombo.

Almagor, U., 1985, 'A Tourist's Vision Quest in an African Game Preserve', in Cohen, E., ed., 'Tourist Guides: Pathfinders, Mediators, and Animators,' *Annals of Tourism Research* (Special Issue), Vol. 12 (1): 31–47.

American Automobile Association, 1990, *Bahamas, Bermuda, Caribbean*, AAA, Heathrow, Florida.

AMPO Japan–Asia Quarterly Review: Special Issue on Official Development Aid, 1990, 21 (4).

AMPO Japan–Asia Quarterly Review: Special Issue on Resort Development, 1991, 22 (4).

Anglo–American Caribbean Commission, (A–ACC), 1945, *Caribbean Tourist Trade: A Regional Approach*, A–ACC, London.

Archer, B., 1977, *Tourist Multipliers: the State of the Art*, University of Wales Press, Cardiff.

Archer, B., 1984, 'Economic Impact: Misleading Multiplier', *Annals of Tourism Research*, 11 (3): 517–8.

Archer, B., 1987, *The Bermudian Economy: An Impact Study*, Ministry of Finance, Bermuda (May).

Archer, B., 1989, 'Tourism and Island Economies: Impact Analyses', in Cooper, C., ed., *Progress in Tourism, Recreation and Hospitality Management: Volume One*, Belhaven, London, pp. 125–34.

Archer, E., 1985, 'Emerging Environmental Problems in a Tourist Zone: The Case of Barbados', *Caribbean Geography*, 2 (1): 45–55.

Arguello Salazar, M., 1988, 'Preoccupación por Baja en al Turismo', in *Actualidad Turística* (San José) 2:1 (15).

Aronson, G., 1990, *Israel, Palestinians, and the Intifada: Creating the Facts on the West Bank*, Kegan Paul International, London.

Arrow, K.J., 1975, 'Vertical Integration and Communication', *Bell Journal of Economics*, 6 (1): 173–183.

Asahi Shinbun 'Enjo' Shuzaihan, 1985, *Enjo Tojō Koku Nippon*, Asahi Shinbunsha, Tokyo.

Asia Travel Trade, 1977 (August), Supplement 2.

Asia Travel Trade, 1984 (January), 'Sri Lanka After the Riots'.

Asia Travel Trade, 1980 (October), 'Nepal Market Probe'.

Asia Travel Trade, 1990 (July/August), 'China in Crisis': 6–21.

Asiaweek, 1989, 'Open Doors, Empty Rooms', 22nd September: 70–74.

Attanayake, A., Samaranayake, H.M.S., and Ratnapala, N., 1983, 'Sri Lanka', in Pye, E.A. and Lin, T., eds, *Tourism in Asia: The Economic Impact*, Singapore, Singapore University Press, pp. 241–351.

Awanohara, S., 1975, 'Protesting the Sexual Imperialists', *Far Eastern Economic Review*, 87 (21st March): 5–6.

Azicri, M., 1988, *Cuba: Politics, Economy and Society*, Frances Pinter, London.

Bach, Q.V.S., 1987, *Soviet Economic Assistance to the Less Developed Countries*, Oxford University Press, Oxford.

Bachmann, P., 1988, *Tourism in Kenya: A Basic Need for Whom?*, Peter Lang, Berne.

Bacon, W., 1987, 'Sex in Manila for Profits in Australia', *Times on Sunday*, 19th April: 21–24.

Balasubramanyam, V.N., 1980, *Multinationals and the Third World*, Trade Policy Research Centre, London.

Banco Nacional de Cuba, Comité Estatal de Estadísticas, *Cuba: Quarterly Economic Report*, Havana.

Bangkok Post, 10th February, 1989.

Bangkok Post, 12th August, 1989.

Barang, M., 1988, 'Tourism in Thailand', *South*, December: 72–73.

Barclay, J., 1990, 'Castro's Revolution of Restoration', *The Independent*, 12th December.

Baretje, R., 1982, 'Tourism's External Account and the Balance of Payments', *Annals of Tourism Research*, 9 (1): 57–67.

Barnett, T., 1988, *Sociology and Development*, Hutchinson, London.

Bar-on, R., ed, 1982, *Survey of Tourists and Residents Departing by Air, 1979/80* (Special Series No. 686), Central Bureau of Statistics, Jerusalem.

Barry, K., 1984, *Female Sexual Slavery*, New York University Press, New York.

Beekhuis, J., 1981, 'Tourism in the Caribbean: Impacts on the Economic, Social and Natural Environments', *Ambio*, 10, 325–31.

Beijing Review, 1989, (July) 'Hotels Suffer Heavy Losses': 43.

Bélisle, F.J., 1983, 'Tourism and Food Production in the Caribbean', *Annals of Tourism Research*, 10 (4): 497–513.

Bélisle, F.J., and Hoy, D.R., 1980, 'The Perceived Impacts of Tourism by Residents: A Case Study in Santa Marta, Columbia', *Annals of Tourism Research*, 7 (1): 83–101.

Ben-Arieh, Y., 1984, *Jerusalem in the 19th Century*, Yad Izhak Ben Zvi Institute, New York.

Benvenisti, M., 1976, *Jerusalem: The Torn City*, Isratypeset, Jerusalem.

Benvenisti, M., 1984, *The West Bank Data Project: A Survey of Israel's Policies*, American Enterprise Institute for Public Policy Research, Washington.

Benvenisti, M. and Khayat, S., 1988, *The West Bank and Gaza Atlas*, West Bank Data Project/Jerusalem Post, Jerusalem.

Berger, P., Berger, B. and Kellner, H., 1974, *The Homeless Mind*, Penguin, Harmondsworth.

van den Berghe, P., 1980, 'Tourism as Ethnic Relations: A Case Study of Cuzco, Peru', *Ethnic and Racial Studies*, 3 (4): 375–392.

Bhatia, A.K.,1986 (4th edition), *Tourism Development: Principles and Practices*, Sterling Publishers, New Delhi.

Bird, B., 1989, *Langkawi – From Mahsuri to Mahathir: Tourism for Whom?* Institute of Social Analysis (INSAN), Kuala Lumpur.

Birnbaum, S., ed; 1988, *Birnbaum's Caribbean, 1989*, Houghton Mifflin, Boston.

Blanco, S., 1990, 'Coup Sends Philippines Back to Square One', *Asia Travel Trade*, February: p. 9.

Blasier, C., 1983, *The Giant's Rival: The USSR and Latin America*, University of Pittsburgh Press, Pittsburgh.

Blumberg, R.L., 1978, 'The Political Economy of the Mother–Child Family Re-visited', in

Marks, A., and Römer, R., eds, *Family and Kinship in Middle America and the Caribbean*, University of the Netherlands and the Department of Caribbean Studies, Royal Institute of Linguistics and Anthropology, Leiden, pp. 526–75.

Blume, H., et al., n.d., *Baedeker's Caribbean, including Bermuda*, Baedeker, Stuttgart.

Boissevain, J., 1977, 'Tourism and Development in Malta', *Development and Change*, 8: 523–38.

Boissevain, J., and Inglott, P.S., 1979, 'Tourism in Malta', in de Kadt, E., ed, *Tourism: Passport to Development?*, Oxford University Press, New York and Oxford, pp. 265–84.

Bonner, P., 1983, *Kings, Commoners and Concessionaires: The Evolution and Dissolution of the Nineteenth-Century Swazi State*, Cambridge University Press, Cambridge.

Boo, E., 1990, *Ecotourism: The Potentials and the Pitfalls, Vols 1 and 2*, World Wildlife Fund, Washington, DC.

Booth, A., 1986, 'Homestead, State and Migrant Labour in Colonial Swaziland', in Daniel, J. and Stephen, M.F., eds, *Historical Perspectives on the Political Economy of Swaziland: Selected Articles*, Social Science Research Unit, University of Swaziland, Kwaluseni, Swaziland, pp. 17–50.

Böröcz, J., 1990, 'Hungary as a Destination', *Annals of Tourism Research*, 17 (1): 19–35.

Bosakova, V., 1987, 'Relaciones entre Checoslovaquia y Cuba', *Economía y Desarrollo*, 101: 38–59.

Bote Gomez, V., Sinclair, M.T., Sutcliffe, C.M.S. and Valenzuela Rubio, M., 1989, 'Vertical Integration in the British/Spanish Tourism Industry', *Leisure, Labour and Lifestyles: International Comparisons; Tourism and Leisure: Models and Theories*, Proceedings of the Leisure Studies Association Second International Conference, Conference Papers, No. 39, Vol. 8, Part 1: 80–96.

Bowman, G., 1989, 'Fucking Tourists: Sexual Relations and Tourism in Jerusalem's Old City', *Critique of Anthropology*, 9 (2): 73–93.

Bowman, G., 1991, 'The Mirror of God: The Image of the Holy Land in the Pilgrimages of the Various Christianities', in Sallnow, M. and Eade, J., eds, *Contesting the Sacred: The Anthropology of Christian Pilgrimage*, Routledge, London: pp. 98–121.

Box, B. and Cameron, S., eds, 1990, *Caribbean Islands Handbook, 1991*, Travel and Trade Publications, Bath.

Boynton, L.L., 1986, 'The Effects of Tourism on Amish Quilting Design', *Annals of Tourism Research*, 13 (3): 451–65.

Brett, E.A., 1987, 'States, Markets and Private Power in the Developing World: Problems and Possibilities', in Dearlove, J. and White, G., eds, *IDS Bulletin* (Sussex, Institute of Development Studies), 18 (3): 31–7.

Britton, R., 1979, 'The Image of the Third World in Tourism Marketing', *Annals of Tourism Research*, 6 (3): 318–29.

Britton, S., 1982, 'The Political Economy of Tourism in the Third World', *Annals of Tourism Research*, 9 (3): 331–358.

Britton, S., 1987a, 'Tourism in Pacific Island States: Constraints and Opportunities', in Britton, S. and Clarke, W.C., eds, *Ambiguous Alternative: Tourism in Small Developing Countries*, University of the South Pacific, Suva, pp. 113–39.

Britton, S., 1987b, 'Tourism in Small Developing Countries: Development Issues and Research Needs', in Britton, S. and Clarke, W.C., eds, *Ambiguous Alternative: Tourism in Small Developing Countries*, University of the South Pacific, Suva, Fiji, pp. 167–87.

Bromley, R., 1979, 'Who Are the Casual Poor?' in Bromley, R. and Gerry, C., eds, *Casual Work and Poverty in Third World Cities*, Wiley and Sons, Chichester, pp. 3–23.

Brown, M., 1980, 'Spectacular Growth in the Filipino Marriage Market', *Sydney Morning Herald*, 3rd September: 10.

Brundenius, C., 1984, *Revolutionary Cuba: The Challenge of Economic Growth with Equity*, Westview Press, Boulder.

Bryden, J., 1973, *Tourism and Development: A Case Study of the Commonwealth Caribbean*, Cambridge University Press, New York.

Brydon, L. and Chant, S., 1989, *Women in the Third World: Gender Issues in Rural and Urban Areas*, Edward Elgar, Aldershot.

Buchan, J., 1903, *The African Colony: Studies in the Reconstruction*, William Blackwood and

Sons, Edinburgh and London.

Burley, N. and Symanski, R., 1981, 'Women Without: An Evolutionary and Cross-cultural Perspective on Prostitution', in Symanski, R., ed, *The Immoral Landscape: Female Prostitution in Western Societies*, Butterworths, Toronto, pp. 239–273.

Butler, R.W., 1980, 'The Concept of a Tourism Area Cycle of Evolution: Implications for Management of Resources', *Canadian Geographer* 24 (1): 5–12.

Calder, S., 1990, *Traveller's Survival Kit: Cuba*, Vacation Work, Oxford.

Capablanca, E., 1985, 'La Habasna Vieja: Anteproyecto de Restauracion', *Cuidad y Territorio*: 63–64, 57–63.

Carciofi, R., 1983, 'Cuba in the Seventies', in White, G. et al, eds, *Revolutionary Socialist Development in the Third World*, Wheatsheaf, Brighton, pp. 193–233.

Caribbean Tourism Research Centre (CTRC), 1976, *Economic Impact of Tourism*, CTRC, Barbados.

Caribbean Tourism Research and Development Centre (CTRC), 1988, 'Caribbean Tourism – Economic Development', *Tourism Management*, June: 155.

Caribbean Tourism Organisation (CTO), 1990, *Caribbean Tourism Statistical Report, 1989*, CTO, Christchurch, Barbados.

Carlton, D.W., 1979, 'Vertical Integration in Competitive Markets Under Certainty', *Journal of Industrial Economics*, 27 (3): 189–209.

Casson, M., 1987, *The Firm and the Market*, Basil Blackwell, Oxford.

Castillo, R., 1981, *Santiago de Cuba*, Editorial Orbe, Havana.

Caves, R.E. and Jones, R.W., 1981, (Third Edition) *World Trade and Payments*, Little, Brown and Co., Boston.

Center for Solidarity Tourism, 1989, 'Impacts of Tourism in the Philippines, *Contours* 4 (2): 29.

Central Bank of Kenya, 1989, *Economic Report*, Central Bank of Kenya, Nairobi.

Central Bank of Sri Lanka, 1987, *Review of the Economy, 1987*, Central Bank, Colombo.

Central Bureau of Statistics, 1984, 1989, *Economic Survey*, C.B.S., Ministry of Planning and Development, Nairobi.

Ceylon Tourist Board, 1982a, *Annual Statistical Report*, Colombo.

Ceylon Tourist Board, 1982b, *Welcome to Sri Lanka*, July–August–September, Colombo.

Chafets, Ze'eo, 1989, 'Fear and Loathing in Israel', *U.S. News and World Report*, July 10th, 36–38.

Chandrakala, S., 1989, *The Impact of Tourism on India's Environment*, Equations, Bangalore.

Chant, S., 1984, 'Las Olvidadas: A Study of Women, Housing and Family Structure in Querétaro, Mexico', Unpublished Ph.D. dissertation, Department of Geography, University College, London.

Chant, S., 1991a, *Women and Survival in Mexican Cities: Perspectives on Gender, Labour Markets and Low-Income Households*, Manchester University Press, Manchester.

Chant, S., 1991b, 'Sexo, Migración y Estrategias de Supervivencia en los Hogares de Bajos Ingresos: En Busca de las Causas del Crecimiento Urbano en Guanacastre', in *Geoísmo* (Universidad de Costa Rica/Instituto Geográfico Nacional, San José) 3:2 (forthcoming).

Chesney-Lind, M. and Lind, I.Y., 1986, 'Visitors as Victims: Crimes Against Tourists in Hawaii', *Annals of Tourism Research*, 13 (2): 167–91.

Chow, W.S., 1988, 'Open Policy and Tourism Between Guangdong and Hong Kong', *Annals of Tourism Research*, 15 (2): 205–218.

Chuah, F., Chuah, L.D., Reid-Smith, L., Rice, A. and Rowley, K., 1987, 'Does Australia have a Filipana Brides Problem?', *Australian Journal of Social Issues*, 22 (4): 573–583.

Clad, J., 1990, 'Gasping for Breath', *Far Eastern Economic Review*, 8th March: 25–26.

Claire, R., and Cottingham, J., 1982, 'Migration and Tourism: An Overview', in Inter-cultural Studies Information Service (ISIS), *Women in Development: A Resource Guide for Organisation and Action*, ISIS Women's International and Communication Service: 205–215.

Cleverdon, R., 1979, *The Economic and Social Impact of Tourism in Developing Countries*, The Economist Intelligence Unit Ltd, London.

Cliffe, L. and Seddon, D., 1991, 'Africa in a New World Order', *Review of African Political*

Economy, 50, March: 3–11.

Coase, R.H., 1937, 'The Nature of the Firm', *Economica* (New Series), 4 (16): 386–405.

Cockburn, R., 1988a, 'The Geography of Tourism, Part I: The East', *The Geographical Magazine*, 60 (3): 2–5.

Cockburn, R., 1988b, 'The Geography of Tourism, Part II: The West', *The Geographical Magazine*, 60 (4): 44–47.

COCODERA (Comisión Co-ordinadora del Desarrollo de la Desembocadura del Rió Ameca), 1980, *Programa de Ordenacion de la Zona Conurbada de la Desembocadura del Rió Ameca*, Puerto Vallarta.

Coffey, B., 1991, 'Investment Incentives as a Means of Encouraging Tourism in Latin America: The Case of Costa Rica', Department of Geography, State University of New York College at Geneseo (mimeo).

Cohen, E., 1971, 'Arab Boys and Tourist Girls in a Mixed Jewish–Arab Community', *International Journal of Comparative Sociology*, 12 (4): 217–233.

Cohen, E., 1974, 'Who is a Tourist? A Conceptual Clarification', *Sociological Review*, 22 (4): 527–53.

Cohen, E., 1979, 'A Phenomenology of Tourist Experiences', *Sociology*, 13 (2): 179–201.

Cohen, E., 1982a, 'Jungle Guides in Northern Thailand: The Dynamics of a Marginal Occupational Role', *Sociological Review*, 30 (2): 236–266.

Cohen, E., 1982b, 'Thai Girls and Farang Men: The Edge of Ambiguity', *Annals of Tourism Research*, 9 (3): 403–428.

Cohen, E., 1985, 'The Tourist Guide: The Origins, Structure and Dynamics of a Role', in Cohen, E., ed, 'Tourist Guides: Pathfinders, Mediators, and Animators', *Annals of Tourism Research*, (Special Issue) Vol. 12 (1): 5–29.

Cohen, E., 1986, 'Lovelorn Farangs: The Correspondence Between Foreign Men and Thai Girls', *Anthropological Quarterly*, 59 (3): 115–127.

Cohen, E., 1988a, 'Authenticity and Commoditization in Tourism', *Annals of Tourism Research*, 15 (3): 371–386.

Cohen, E., 1988b, 'Tourism and AIDS in Thailand', *Annals of Tourism Research*, 15 (4): 467–486.

Cohen, E., 1989a, '"Primitive and Remote": Hill Tribe Trekking in Thailand', *Annals of Tourism Research*, 16 (1): 30–61.

Cohen, E., 1989b, 'Alternative Tourism: A Critique', in Singh, T.V., et al., eds, *Towards Appropriate Tourism: The Case of Developing Countries*, Peter Lang, Frankfurt and Berne, pp. 127–42.

Comité Estatal de Estadísticas, Annually, *Anvario Estadístico de Cuba*, Havana.

Comité Estatal de Estadísticas, Annually, *Cuba en Cifras*, Havana.

Comité Estatal de Estadísticas, Annually, *Guía Estadística*, Havana.

Commission of Christian Pilgrims, 1984, *Annals 1984*, Editiones Christianae, Jerusalem.

Commission to Investigate Juvenile Delinquency and Allied Problems in Swaziland, 1956, *Report*, Government Printer, Mbabane, Swaziland.

Committee on Juvenile Delinquency, Sexual Morality and the Maintenance of Illegitimate Children in the Urban Areas of Swaziland, 1970, *Report*, Government Printer, Mbabane, Swaziland.

Costa Rica Guide (December, 1988), Guide Castro: San José.

Cottingham, J., 1981, 'Sex Included', *Development Forum*, 9 (5): 16.

Craik, J., 1991, *Resorting to Tourism: Cultural Policies for Tourist Development in Australia*, Allen and Unwin, Sydney.

Crick, M., 1989, 'Representations of International Tourism in the Social Sciences: Sun, Sex, Sights, Savings and Servility', *Annual Review of Anthropology*, 18: 307–344.

Crompton, J., 1979, 'Motivations for Pleasure Vacation', *Annals of Tourism Research*, 6 (4): 408–24.

Crush, J. and Wellings, P., 1983, 'The Southern Africa Pleasure Periphery, 1966–1983', *Journal of Modern African Studies*, 21 (4): 673–698.

Crush, J. and Wellings, P., 1987, 'Forbidden Fruit and the Export of Vice: Tourism in Lesotho and Swaziland', in Britton, S. and Clarke, W.C., eds, *Ambiguous Alternative: Tourism in*

Small Developing Countries, The University of the South Pacific, Suva, Fiji, 91–112.

Crystal, E., 1989, 'Tourism in Toraja (Sulawesi, Indonesia)', in Smith, V.L., ed, *Hosts and Guests: The Anthropology of Tourism*, University of Pennsylvania Press, Philadelphia, pp. 139–68 (First published 1978 by Basil Blackwell, Oxford).

Cuba Tourist Newsletter, (CTN), National Institute of Tourism, Havana.

Curtin, V. and Sobers, A., 1988, *Caribbean Tourism Statistical Report, 1987*, Caribbean Tourism Research Centre, Christ Church, Barbados.

D'Amore, L.J., 1988, 'Tourism: a Vital Force for Peace', *Annals of Tourism Research* 15 (2): 269–270.

Dann, G.M.S., 1981, 'Tourism Motivation: An Appraisal', *Annals of Tourism Research*, 8 (2): 187–219.

Davidson, D., 1985, 'Women in Thailand', *Canadian Women's Studies*, 16 (1): 16–19.

Davies, R., 1979, 'Informal Sector or Subordinate Mode of Production?' in Bromley, R. and Gerry, C., eds, *Casual Work and Poverty in Third World Cities*, Wiley and Sons, Chichester, 87–104.

Davis, D., 1978, 'Development and the Tourist Industry in Third World Countries', *Society and Leisure* 1 (2): 301–22.

Day, R., 1989, 'China's Numbing Blitz Strangles Tour Market', *Asia Travel Trade*, July/ August: 6–8.

Debbage, K.G., 1990, 'Oligopoly and the Resort Cycle in the Bahamas', *Annals of Tourism Research*, 17 (4): 513–27.

Department of Economic Planning and Statistics, 1987, *Economic Review and Outlook*, Government of Swaziland, Mbabane.

Diehl, J., 1989, 'Israeli Agents, Disguised as Tourists, "Shoot Arabs"', *Guardian Weekly*, 27th August, London.

Din, K.H., 1982, 'Tourism in Malaysia: Competing Needs in a Plural Society', *Annals of Tourism Research*, 9 (3): 453–80.

Din, K.H., 1989, 'Islam and Tourism: Patterns, Issues and Options', *Annals of Tourism Research*, 16 (4): 542–643.

Dogan, H., 1989, 'Forms of Adjustment: Sociocultural Impacts of Tourism', *Annals of Tourism Research*, 16 (2): 216–236.

Duffield, B.S., 1982, 'Tourism: The Measurement of Economic and Social Impact', *Tourism Management*, December, 1982: 248–255.

Duncan, W.R., 1986, 'Castro and Gorbachev: Politics of Accommodation', *Problems of Communism*, 35 (2): 45–57.

Dunn Ross, E.L. and Iso-Ahola, S.E., 1991, 'Sightseeing Tourists' Motivation and Satisfaction', *Annals of Tourism Research*, 18 (2): 226–37.

Dunning, J.H., 1979, 'Explaining Changing Patterns of International Production: In Defence of the Eclectic Theory', *Oxford Bulletin of Economics and Statistics*, 41 (3): 269–295.

Dunning, J.H. and McQueen, M., 1982, 'Multinational Corporations in the International Hotel Industry', *Annals of Tourism Research* 9 (1): 69–90.

Economist, 1990, *The World in 1991*, Economist Publications, London.

Economist Intelligence Unit (EIU), 1986, *International Tourism Report 2*, EIU, London, 69–79.

Economist Intelligence Unit (EIU), 1991, *Mexico: Country Profile, 1990–1*, Economist Intelligence Unit, London.

Edgell, D.L., 1990, *Charting a Course for International Tourism in the 1990s: An Agenda for Managers and Executives*, Department of Commerce, Washington DC.

Edwards, A., 1985, *International Tourism Forecasts to 1995*, The Economist Publications Ltd, London.

Edwards, A., 1991, *European Long Haul Travel Market: Forecasts to 2000*, Economist Intelligence Unit, London.

Ekachai, S., 1990, *Behind the Smile: Voices of Thailand*, Thai Development Support Committee, Bangkok.

Elliott, J., 1983, 'Politics, Power and Tourism in Thailand', *Annals of Tourism Research*, 10 (4): 377–393.

Elson, D. and Pearson, R., 1981, 'The Subordination of Women and the Internationalisation of Factory Production' in Young, K., et al., eds, *Of Marriage and the Market*, CSE Books, London, pp. 144–66.

Emmanuel, A., 1972, *Unequal Exchange: A Study in the Imperialism of Trade*, Monthly Review Press, New York and London.

Enloe, C., 1989, *Bananas, Beaches and Bases: Making Sense of International Politics*, University of California Press, Berkeley, Los Angeles.

Ennew, J., 1986, *The Sexual Exploitation of Children*, Polity Press, Cambridge.

Ericsson, L., 1980, 'Charges Against Prostitution: An Attempt at a Philosophical Assessment', *Ethics*, 90: 335–366.

Erisman, H.M., 1983, 'Tourism and Cultural Dependency in the West Indies', *Annals of Tourism Research*, 10 (3): 337–361.

Erisman, H., 1985, *Cuba's International Relations: The Anatomy of a Nationalistic Foreign Policy*, Westview Press, Boulder.

Evans, N., 1979, 'The Dynamics of Tourism Development in Puerto Vallarta', in de Kadt, E., ed, *Tourism: Passport to Development?* Oxford University Press, New York and Oxford: 305–321.

Evans-Pritchard, D., 1989, 'How "They" see "Us": Native American Images of Tourists', *Annals of Tourism Research*, 16 (1): 89–105.

Fagen, R., 1978a, 'Cuba and the Soviet Union', *The Wilson Quarterly*, 2 (1): 69–78.

Fagen, R., 1978b, 'A Funny Thing Happened on the Way to the Market: Thoughts on Extending Dependency Ideas', *International Organisation*, 32 (1): 287–300.

Farver, J.A.M., 1984, 'Tourism and Employment in the Gambia', *Annals of Tourism Research*, 11 (2): 249–65.

Fernand-Laurent, J., 1985, *Activities for the Advancement of Women: Equality, Development and Peace*, Department of International Economic and Social Affairs, United Nations, New York.

Fideicomiso Puerto Vallarta, 1985, *Cuaderno Básico de Estadisticas*, Puerto Vallarda.

Fielder, M., 1991, 'Limited Burmese Days', *Weekend Guardian*, 9th November, p. 27.

Finney, B.R. and Watson, K.A., eds, 1975, *A New Kind of Sugar: Tourism in the Pacific*, East–West Center, Honolulu.

Fish, M., 1984a, 'Deterring Sex Sales to International Tourists: A Case Study of Thailand, South Korea and the Philippines, *International Journal of Comparative and Applied Criminal Justice*, 8 (2): 175–186.

Fish, M., 1984b, 'On Controlling Sex Sales to Tourists: Commentary on Graburn and Cohen', *Annals of Tourism Research*, 11 (4): 615–617.

Fisher, H. and Bar-on, R., 1983, *Pilgrimage Promotion, 1983*, Mimeographed handout for Jerusalem Conference, 31st May–6th June, Israel Ministry of Tourism, Jerusalem.

Fletcher, J.E., 1989, 'Input–Output Analysis and Tourism Impact Studies', *Annals of Tourism Research*, 16 (4): 515–29.

Foster-Carter, A., 1976, 'From Rostow to Gunder Frank: Conflicting Paradigms in the Analysis of Underdevelopment', *World Development*, 4 (3): 167–80.

Francisco, R., 1983, 'The Political Impact of Tourism Dependence in Latin America', *Annals of Tourism Research*, 10 (3): 363–376.

Frank, A.G., 1991, 'No Escape from the Laws of World Economics', *Review of African Political Economy*, 50:21–32.

Fraser, P.D. and Hackett, P., 1985, *Caribbean Economic Handbook*, Euromonitor, London.

Frater, J., 1982, 'Farm Tourism in England and Overseas', *Research Memorandum 93*, Centre for Urban and Regional Studies, Birmingham.

Fujiwara, M., 1991, 'Resort Act: Panacea for the Construction Industry', AMPO, *Japan–Asia Quarterly Review: Special Issue on Resort Development* 22 (4): 37–40.

GAO Reports and Testimony, 'Aviation Security: Training Standards Needed for Extra Security Measures at Foreign Airports', December, 1989: 21–22.

Gartner, W.C. and Holecek, D.F., 1983, 'Economic Impact of an Annual Tourism Industry Exposition', *Annals of Tourism Research*, 10 (2): 199–212.

Gay, J., 1985, 'The Patriotic Prostitute', *The Progressive*, 49 (3): 34–36.

Gayle, D., 1986, *The Small Developing State: Comparing Political Economies in Costa Rica,*

Singapore and Jamaica, Gower, Aldershot.

Gébler, C., 1988, *Driving Through Cuba: An East–West Journey*, Hamish Hamilton, London.

Geertz, C., 1973, 'Religion as a Cultural System' in Geertz, C., *The Interpretation of Culture: Selected Essays*, Basic Books, New York: pp. 87–125.

Getino, O., 1990, *Turismo y Desarrollo en América Latina*, Noriega Editores, Editorial Limusa, México.

Giarelli, A., 1981, 'End of "Sex Tours"', *World Press Review*, October: 21.

Go, F., 1988, 'Key Problems and Prospects in the International Hotel Industry', *Travel and Tourist Analyst*, No. 1, pp. 27–49.

Godínez, O., J.M. 1988, 'El ICT Espera en el Quirófano, *Actualidad Turística* (San José) 2 (1): 32–3.

Goonatilake, S., 1978, *Tourism in Sri Lanka*, People's Bank of Sri Lanka, Colombo.

Goldstein, C., 1991, 'Asian Hotels Slowly Recover from Gulf War Jitters: Balmy Weather Ahead', *Far Eastern Economic Review*, 11th April, pp. 42–4.

Gormsen, E., 1988, 'Tourism in Latin America – Spatial Distribution and Impact on Regional Change', *Applied Geography and Development*, 32: 65–80.

Graburn, N.H.H., 1983, 'Tourism and Prostitution', *Annals of Tourism Research*, 10 (3): 437–42.

Graburn, N.H.H., 1984, 'The Evolution of Tourist Arts', *Annals of Tourism Research*, 11 (3): 393–419.

Graburn, N.H.H., 1989, 'Tourism: the Sacred Journey', in Smith, V., ed, *Hosts and Guests: The Anthropology of Tourism*, (second edition) University of Pennsylvania Press, Philadelphia, pp. 21–36 (first edition published in 1978 by Basil Blackwell, Oxford).

Graburn, N.H.H. and Jafari, J., 1991, eds, 'Tourism Social Science', *Annals of Tourism Research*, 18 (1).

Granma Weekly Review (GWR), Havana.

Gravette, A.G., 1988, *Cuba: Official Guide*, Macmillan Caribbean, London.

Greenberg, P.S., 1989, 'Hong Kong Isn't China, But It's Being Shunned as if It Were', *Kansas City Star*, 10th September, 5K.

Greenwood, D., 1972, 'Tourism as an Agent of Change: A Spanish–Basque Case', *Ethnology*, XI (1): 80–91.

Greenwood, D., 1989, 'Culture by the Pound: An Anthropological Perspective on Tourism as Cultural Commoditization', in Smith, V.L., ed, *Hosts and Guests: The Anthropology of Tourism*, (second edition), University of Pennsylvania Press, Philadelphia, pp. 171–85 (first published 1978 by Basil Blackwell, Oxford).

Gugler, 1980, '"A Minimum of Urbanism and a Maximum of Ruralism": The Cuban Experience', *International Journal of Urban and Regional Research*, 4 (4): 516–535.

Haddad, H. and Wagner, D., 1985, *All in the Name of the Bible: Selected Essays on Israel, South Africa and American Christian Fundamentalism*, Palestine Human Rights Campaign, Chicago.

Halebsky, S. and Kirk, J., 1990, *Transformation and Struggle: Cuba Faces the 1990s*, Praeger, New York.

Halebsky, S. et al., 1991, *Cuba's Struggle for Development: Dilemmas and Strategies*, Westview, Boulder.

Hall, C., 1985, *Costa Rica: A Geographical Interpretation in Historical Perspective*, Westview, Boulder, Colorado.

Hall, C.M., 1989a, 'Impact of the America's Cup on Fremantle, Western Australia: Implications for the Hosting of Hallmark Events', in Welch, R., ed, *Geography in Action*, Department of Geography, University of Otago, Dunedin: 74–80.

Hall, C.M., 1989b, 'The Politics of Hallmark Events', in Syme, G.J., Shaw, B.J., Fenton, D.M. and Mueller, W.S., (eds), *The Planning and Evaluation of Hallmark Events*, Avebury, Brookfield, USA, 219–241.

Hall, C.M., 1991, *Tourism in Australia: From Susceptible to Sustainable Development*, Longman Cheshire, South Melbourne.

Hall, D.R., 1981a, 'External Relations and Current Development Patterns in Cuba', *Geography*, 66 (3): 237–240.

Hall, D.R., 1981b, 'Town and Country Planning in Cuba', *Town and Country Planning*, 50 (3): 81–3.

Hall, D.R., 1984, 'Foreign Tourism under Socialism: The Albanian "Stalinist" Model', *Annals of Tourism Research*, 11 (4): 539–555.

Hall, D.R., 1989, 'Cuba', in Potter, R.B., ed., *Urbanization, Planning and Development in the Caribbean*, Mansell, London, 77–113.

Hall, D.R., 1990a, 'Eastern Europe Opens its Doors', *Geographical Magazine*, 62 (4): 10–15.

Hall, D.R., 1990b, 'Stalinism and Tourism: A Study of Albania and North Korea', *Annals of Tourism Research*, 17 (1): 36–54.

Hall, D.R., ed, 1991, *Tourism and Economic Development in Eastern Europe and the Soviet Union*, Belhaven, London.

Halsell, G., 1988, *Prophesy and Politics: Militant Evangelists on the Road to Nuclear War*, Lawrence Hill and Co., Westport.

Hamberg, J., 1986, 'The Dynamics of Cuban Housing Policy', in Bratt, R. et al., eds, *Critical Perspectives on Housing*, Temple University Press, Philadelphia, 586–624.

Hamilton-Smith, E., 1987, 'Four Kinds of Tourism', *Annals of Tourism Research*, 14 (3): 332–44.

Hammond, N., 1991, 'Nations unite to put Mayan past on the world tourist map', *The Times*, 27th June: 20.

Handley, P., 1991, 'Thai Resort Shows How Not to Develop: Wish You Were Here', *Far Eastern Economic Review*, 28th November, p. 54.

Hannerz, U., 1969, *Soulside: Inquiries into Ghetto Culture and Community*, Columbia University Press, New York.

Harrell-Bond, B., 1978, ' "A Window on an Outside World": Tourism as Development in the Gambia', *American Universities Field Staff Reports*, No. 19, American Universities Field Staff, Hanover.

Harris, Kerr, Forster and Co., 1967, *Ceylon Tourism Plan*, Hawaii.

Harrison, D., 1988, *The Sociology of Modernization and Development*, Unwin Hyman, London.

Harrison, D., 1990, 'Tourism in Swaziland', *Research Paper 29*, Social Science Research Unit, University of Swaziland, Kwaluseni, Swaziland.

Hawkesworth, M., 1984, 'Brothels and Betrayal: On the Functions of Prostitution', *International Journal of Women's Studies*, 7 (1): 81–91.

Henderson, J., 1990, *The Caribbean*, Cadogan Books, London.

Henry, S., 1982, 'The Working Unemployed: Perspectives on the Informal Economy and Unemployment', *Sociological Review*, 30 (3): 460–477.

Hirschman, A., 1975, 'Policymaking and Policy Analysis in Latin America: A Return Journey', *Policy Sciences*, 6: 385–402.

Hirst, D., 1977, *The Gun and the Olive Branch: the Roots of Violence in the Middle East*, Faber and Faber, London.

Hobsbawn, E. and Ranger, T., eds, 1983, *The Invention of Tradition*, Cambridge University Press, Cambridge,

Hoivik, T. and Heiberg, T., 1980, 'Centre–Periphery Tourism and Self-Reliance', *International Social Science Journal*, 32 (1): 69–98.

Holden, P., Horlemann, J., and Pfäfflin, eds, 1985, *Tourism, Prostitution, Development: Documentation*, Ecumenical Coalition on Third World Tourism (ECTWT), Bangkok.

Hollander, P., 1981, *Political Pilgrims: Travels of Western Intellectuals to the Soviet Union, China and Cuba, 1928–1978*, Oxford University Press, Oxford.

Hong, E., 1985, *See the Third World While it Lasts*, Consumers Association of Penang, Penang.

Huertas Alpizar, T., 1988, 'Beneficios del Turismo', *Actualidad Turística* (San José), 2 (1): 10.

Hulme, D. and Turner, M., 1990, *Sociology and Development: Theories, Policies and Practices*, Harvester Wheatsheaf, New York and London.

Hunt, D., 1989, *Economic Theories of Development: An Analysis of Competing Paradigms*, Harvester Wheatsheaf, New York and London.

Hurtado, M.E., 1989, 'Cuba Loses its Inhibitions', *South*, 106: 16–17.

Hymer, S.H., 1976, *The International Operations of National Firms: A Study of Direct Investment*, M.I.T. Press, Cambridge, Mass.

Iida, T., 1974, *Enjo Suru Kuni, Sareru Kuni*, Nikkei Shinsho, Tokyo.

India Today, 1989, 'Sri Lanka: Island in Turmoil', 30th September: 20.

Inoue, R., 1991, 'An Army of Japanese Tourists', *AMPO: Japan–Asia Quarterly Review: Special Issue on Resort Development*, 22 (4): 2–10.

Instituto Costarricense de Turismo (ICT), 1989, *Papagayo Gulf Project*, San José.

International Monetary Fund (IMF), 1990, *International Financial Statistics*, IMF, Washington DC.

Ishigami, E., 1991, 'Japanese Business in ASEAN Countries: New-industrialisation or Japanisation?' *IDS Bulletin*, 22 (2): 21–28.

ISIS (Inter-cultural Studies Information Service), 1979, 'Tourism and Prostitution', special issue of *International Bulletin*, 13, International Feminist Collective, Rome.

ISIS (Inter-cultural Studies Information Service), 1984, 'Prostitution: Who Pays?', *Women's World*, 3, World International Cross-Cultural Exchange: 4–5.

Israeli Central Bureau of Statistics, 1988, *Statistical Abstract of Israel, 1988*, Central Bureau of Statistics, Jerusalem.

Izurieta, C., 1982, 'Empresas Extranjeras, Producción Bajo Licencia y Formas Oligopolicas en la Industria Manufactera en Costa Rica', *Revista de Ciencias Sociales*, 24: 33–46.

James, P., ed, 1990, *Technocratic Dreaming: Of Very Fast Trains and Japanese Designer Cities*, Left Book Club, Melbourne.

Jamison, B. and Jamison, C.A., 1990, *Best Places to Stay in the Caribbean*, Houghton Mifflin, Boston.

Jenkins, C.L. and Henry, B.M., 1982, 'Government Involvement in Tourism in Developing Countries', *Annals of Tourism Research*, 9 (4): 499–521.

Jennett, C. and Stewart, R.G., eds, 1987, *Three Worlds of Inequality: Race, Class and Gender*, Macmillan, Melbourne.

Jommo, R.B., 1987, *Indigenous Enterprise in Kenya's Tourism Industry*, Institut Universitaire d'Études du Développement, Geneva.

Jones, D.R.W., 1986, 'Prostitution and Tourism', in J.S. Marsh, ed, *Canadian Studies of Parks, Recreation and Tourism in Foreign Lands*, Occasional Paper 11, Department of Geography, Trent University, Peterborough, 241–248.

Jones, M., 1986, *A Shady Place for Shady People: The Real Gold Coast Story*, Allen and Unwin, Sydney.

Jud, D.G., 1974, 'Tourism and Economic Growth in Mexico since 1950', *Inter-American Affairs*, 28: 19–43.

Judge, J., 1989, 'The Many Lives of Old Havana', *National Geographic*, 176 (2): 278–300.

Jules-Rosette, B., 1984, *The Messages of Tourist Art: an African Semiotic System in Comparative Perspective*, New York and London, Plenum Press.

Jurgensen, O., 1987, 'Tourism and Prostitution in South-east Asia', *The Manitoba Social Science Teacher* 14 (1): 5–12.

de Kadt, E., ed, 1979, *Tourism: Passport to Development?*, Oxford University Press, New York and Oxford.

de Kadt, E., 1990, 'Making the Alternative Sustainable: Lessons from Development for Tourism', *Discussion Paper*, No. 272, Institute of Development Studies, University of Sussex, January.

Kapferer, B., 1988, *Legends of People, Myths of State: Violence, Intolerance and Political Culture in Sri Lanka and Australia*, Smithsonian Institution Press, Washington.

Katz, S., 1985, 'The Israeli Teacher-Guide: The Emergence and Perpetuation of a Role', in Cohen, E., ed, 'Tourist Guides: Pathfinders, Mediators and Animators', *Annals of Tourism Research* (Special Issue), 12 (1): 49–72.

Kelly, N., 1991, 'Tourism: Counting the Cost', *Far Eastern Economic Review*, 18th July: 44.

Kennedy, J., Russin, A. and Martínez, A., 1978, *The Impact of Tourism Development on Women: A Case Study of Ixtapa-Zihuatanejo*, Draft Report for Tourism Projects Department, World Bank, Washington.

Kent, N., 1975, 'A New Kind of Sugar', in Finney, B.R. and Watson, K.R., eds, *A New Kind of Sugar: Tourism in the Pacific*, East–West Center, Honolulu, pp. 169–80.

Khan, H., Chou, F.S. and Wong, E.C., 1990, 'Tourism Multiplier Effects on Singapore', *Annals of Tourism Research*, 17 (3): 408–418.

Kincaid, J., 1988, *A Small Place*, Virago Press, London.

Kitching, G., 1985, 'Politics, Method and Evidence in the "Kenya" Debate', in Bernstein, H. and Campbell, B.K., eds, *Contradictions of Accumulation in Africa: Studies in Economy and State*, Sage, Beverly Hills, California, 115–51.

Kohn, T., 1988, 'Island Involvement and the Evolving Tourist', paper presented at First Conference on Anthropology of Tourism, Group for Anthropology in Policy and Practice (GAPP), Roehampton Institute, 22nd–23rd April.

Korea Church Women United, 1983, *Kisaeng Tourism: A Nation-wide Survey Report on Conditions in Four Areas – Seoul, Pusan, Cheju, Kyongju*, Research Material Issue No. 3, Korea Church Women United, Seoul.

Kousis, M., (1989), 'Tourism and the Family in a Rural Cretan Community', *Annals of Tourism Research*, 16 (3): 318–332.

Krause, W. and Jud, D.G., with Hyman, J., 1973, *International Tourism and Latin American Development*, Bureau of Business Research, Graduate School of Business, University of Texas at Austin.

Krippendorf, J., 1987, *The Holiday Makers: Understanding the Impact of Leisure and Travel*, Heinemann, Oxford.

Kuji, T., 1991, 'The Political Economy of Golf', AMPO, *Japanese–Asia Quarterly Review: Special Issue on Resort Development*, 22 (4): 47–54.

Kuper, H., 1947, *The Uniform of Colour: A Srudy of White–Black Relationships in Swaziland*, Witwatersrand University Press, Johannesburg.

Kuper, H., 1961, first published 1947, *An African Aristocracy: Rank Among the Swazi*, Oxford University Press, London and New York.

Kuper, H., 1963, *The Swazi: An African Kingdom*, Rinehart and Winston, New York and Chicago.

Lall, S., 1974, 'Less Developed Countries and Private Foreign Direct Investment: A Review Article', *World Development*, 2 (4 and 5): 43–48.

Lamont-Brown, R., 1982, 'The International Expansion of Japan's Criminal Brotherhood', *Police Journal*, 55 (4): 355–359.

Lane, C. et al, 1990, 'Brezhnev with a Beard', *Newsweek*, 6th August: 32–3.

Lanfant, M-F., 1980, 'Tourism in the Process of Internationalisation', *International Social Science Journal*, 32 (1): 14–43.

Latham, J., 1989, 'The Statistical Measurement of Tourism', in Cooper, C.P., ed, *Progress in Tourism, Recreation and Hospitality Management*, Volume One, Belhaven, London. pp. 55–76.

Lea, J., 1981, 'Changing Approaches towards Tourism in Africa: Planning and Research Perspectives', *Journal of Contemporary African Studies*, 1 (1): 19–40.

Lea, J., 1988, *Tourism and Development in the Third World*, Routledge, London.

Lee, G., 1987, 'Tourism as a Factor in Development Co-operation', *Tourism Management*, 8 (1): 2–19.

Lee, W., 1991, 'Prostitution and Tourism in South-East Asia', in Redclift, N. and Sinclair, M.T., eds, *Working Women: International Perspectives on Gender and Labour Ideology*, Routledge, London and New York: 79–103.

Lélé, S.M., 1991, 'Sustainable Development: A Critical Review', *World Development* 19 (6): 607–21.

LeoGrande, W.M., 1979, 'Cuban Dependency: A Comparison of Pre-revolutionary and Post-revolutionary International Economic Relations', *Cuban Studies*, 9 (2): 1–28.

Lewis, J.P. and Kapur, D., 1990, 'An Updating Country Study: Thailand's Needs and Prospects in the 1990s', *World Development*, 18 (10): 1363–1378.

Lewis, W.A., 1954, 'Economic Development with Unlimited Supplies of Labour', *Manchester School* 22 (2): 139–191.

Lewis, W.A., 1958, 'Unlimited Supplies of Labour: Further Notes', *Manchester School*, 26 (1): 1–32.

Lickorish, L.J., 1988, 'Travel Megatrends in Europe to the Year 2,000', *Annals of Tourism Research*, 15 (2): 270–1.

Liebow, E., 1967, *Tally's Corner: A Study in Negro Streetcorner Men*, Little, Brown and Co., Boston.

Lim, L., 1983, 'Capitalism, Imperialism and Patriarchy: The Dilemma of Third World

Women Workers in Multinational Factories', in Nash, J., et al., eds, *Women, Men and the International Division of Labour*, State University of New York, Albany, New York., pp. 70–91.

Lin, T. and Sung, Y., 1984, 'Tourism and Economic Diversification in Hong Kong', *Annals of Tourism Research*, 11 (2): 231–47.

Ling, C.Y., 1991, 'Malaysia: For Only a Select Few', *AMPO: Japan–Asia Quarterly Review: Special Issue on Resort Development*, 22 (4): 32–3.

Little, I.M.D., 1982, *Economic Development: Theory, Policy and International Relations*, Basic Books, New York.

Lowenthal, D., 1976, 'The Return of the Non-native: New Life for Depopulated Areas', in Kosinski, L.A. and Webb, J.W., eds, *Population at Microscale*, New Zealand Geographical Society, pp. 143–8.

Lustick, I., 1980, *Arabs in the Jewish State: Israel's Control of a National Minority*, University of Texas Press, Austin.

MacCannell, D., 1973, 'Staged Authenticity: Arrangements of Social Space in Tourist Settings', *American Journal of Sociology*, 79 (3): 589–603.

MacCannell, D., 1976, *The Tourist: A New Theory of the Leisure Class*, Macmillan, London.

McCormack, G., 1991a, 'The Price of Affluence: The Political Economy of Japanese Leisure', *New Left Review*, No. 188, July–August, pp. 121–34.

McCormack, G., ed, 1991b, *Bonsai Australia Banzai: Multifunctionpolis and the Making of a Special Relationship with Japan*, Pluto Press, Sydney.

McDowall, D., 1989, *Palestine and Israel: The Uprising and Beyond*, I.B. Tauris, London.

MacFarquhar, E., 1989, 'China Prepares for the Bitter Harvest', *U.S. News and World Report*, 10th July: 34–35.

McGee, T., 1979, 'The Poverty Syndrome: Making Out in a Southeast Asian City', in Bromley, R. and Gerry, C., eds, *Casual Work and Poverty in Third World Cities*, Wiley and Sons, Chichester, 45–68.

Machlis, G. and Burch, W., 1983, 'Relations Between Strangers: Cycles of Structure and Meaning in Tourist Systems', *Sociological Review*, 31 (4): 666–92.

Mackay, L., 1987, 'Tourism and Changing Attitudes to Land in Negril, Jamaica', in Besson, J. and Momsen, J., eds, *Land and Development in the Caribbean*, Macmillan, London, pp. 132–52.

McKean, P.F., 1989, 'Towards a Theoretical Analysis of Tourism: Economic Dualism and Cultural Involution in Bali', in Smith, V.L., ed, *Hosts and Guests: The Anthropology of Tourism* (second edition), University of Pennsylvania Press, Philadelphia, pp. 119–38 (first edition published in 1978 by Basil Blackwell, Oxford).

Mackie, V., 1988, 'Division of Labour: Multinational Sex in Asia', in McCormack, G and Sugimoto, Y., eds, *Modernization and Beyond: The Japanese Trajectory*, Cambridge University Press, Cambridge, pp. 218–32.

McManus, J., 1990, 'Cashing in on the Caribbean', *South*, 116: 55–6.

Macmillan, H., 1986, 'Swaziland: Decolonisation and the Triumph of "Tradition"', in Daniel, J. and Stephen, M.F., eds, *Historical Perspectives on the Political Economy of Swaziland: Selected Articles*, Social Science Research Unit, University of Swaziland, Kwaluseni, Swaziland, 104–125.

MacNaught, T.J., 1982, 'Mass Tourism and the Dilemmas of Modernization in Pacific Island Communities', *Annals of Tourism Research*, 9 (3): 359–81.

Mandel, E., 1978, *Late Capitalism*, Verso, London.

Manor, J., 1984, ed, *Sri Lanka: In Change and Crisis*, Croom Helm, London.

Marwick, B.A., 1940, *The Swazi: An Ethnographic Account of the Natives of the Swaziland Protectorate*, Cass, London.

Masouda, T., 1984, *A Report on the Social and Professional Subjugation of Arab Guides of Jerusalem and the West Bank who are Members of the Union of Tourist Guides of the City of Jerusalem*, Arab Studies Society, Statistics Section, Jerusalem. (In Arabic.)

Mathieson, A. and Wall, G., 1982, *Tourism: Economic, Physical and Social Impacts*, Longman, Harlow.

Matsui, Y., 1987a, 'The Prostitution Areas in Asia: An Experience', *Women in a Changing*

World, 24 (November): 27–32.

Matsui, Y., 1987b, 'Japan in the Context of the Militarisation of Asia', *Women in a Changing World*, 24 (November): 7–8.

Matthews, H.G., 1978, *International Tourism: A Political and Social Analysis*, Schenkman Publishing Company, Cambridge.

Matthews, H.G., 1990, 'Review of the Politics of Tourism in Asia', *Annals of Tourism Research*, 17 (2): 323–325.

May, R.J., 1975, 'Tourism and the Artefact Industry in Papua New Guinea', in Finney, B.R. and Watson, K.A., eds, *A New Kind of Sugar: Tourism in the Pacific*, East–West Center, Honolulu, pp. 125–32.

M'Bow, A.M., 1985, 'Campana Internacional para la Salvaguarda de la Plaza Vieja de la Habana', *Ciudad y Territorio*, 63–4: 65–71.

Meijer, W.G., 1989, 'Rucksacks and Dollars: The Economic Impact of Organized and Non-organized Tourism in Bolivia', in Singh, T.V., et al., eds, *Towards Appropriate Tourism: the Case of the Developing Countries*, Peter Lang, Frankfurt and Berne, pp. 227–49.

Mendis, E.D.L., 1981, *The Economic, Social and Cultural Impact of Tourism on Sri Lanka*, Christian Workers Fellowship, Colombo.

Mesa-Lago, C., 1981, *The Economy of Socialist Cuba: A Two Decade Appraisal*, University of New Mexico Press, Albuquerque.

Meyer, W., 1988, *Beyond the Mask*, Verlag breitenbach Publishers, Saarbrücken, Fort Lauderdale.

Milne, S.S., 1987, 'Differential Multipliers', *Annals of Tourism Research*, 14 (4): 499–515.

Mingmongkol, S., 1981, 'Official Blessings for the "Brothel of Asia"', *Southeast Asia Chronicle*, 78: 24–25.

Mitchell, J.F., 1972, 'To Hell with Paradise: A New Concept in Caribbean Tourism', Address at Caribbean Travel Association Press Conference, Haiti, 21st September. It is reprinted in Mitchell, J.F., 1989, *Caribbean Crusade*, Concepts Publishing, Waitsfield, Vermont, pp. 177–82.

Moeran, B., 1983, 'The Language of Japanese Tourism', *Annals of Tourism Research*, 10 (1): 93–108.

Momsen, J.H., 1985, 'Tourism and Development in the Caribbean', *Mainzer Geographische Studien*, 26: 25–36.

Momsen, J.H., 1986, 'Linkages Between Tourism and Agriculture: Problems for the Smaller Caribbean Economies', Seminar Paper No. 45, University of Newcastle upon Tyne, Dept. of Geography, October.

Monk, J. and Alexander, C.S., 1986, 'Free Port Fallout: Gender, Employment, and Migration on Margarita Island', *Annals of Tourism Research*, 13 (3): 393–413.

Morris, A., 1987, *South America*, (third edition), Hodder and Stoughton, London.

Morris, B., 1987, *The Birth of the Palestinian Refugee Problem, 1947–1949*, Cambridge University Press, Cambridge.

Moynihan, M., 1989, 'Tibet's Agony', *The New Republic*, 10th November: 10–11.

Murai, Y., ed, 1989, *Musekinin Enjo Taikoku Nippon*, Tokyo, JICC Shuppankyoku.

Murai, Y., 1991, 'Bali: Tourists, Tuna and ODA', *AMPO: Japan–Asia Quarterly Review: Special Issue on Resort Development*, 22 (4): 28–31.

Naibavu, T. and Schutz, B., 1974, 'Prostitution: Problem or Profitable Industry?, *Pacific Perspective*, 3 (1): 59–68.

Nash, D., 1989, 'Tourism as a Form of Imperialism', in Smith, V.L., ed, *Hosts and Guests: The Anthropology of Tourism*, (second edition), University of Pennsylvania, Philadelphia, pp. 37–52 (first published in 1978 by Basil Blackwell, Oxford).

Nason, J.D., 1984, 'Tourism Handicrafts, and Ethnic Identity in Micronesia', *Annals of Tourism Research*, 11 (3): 421–49.

Nayyar, D., 1988, 'Some Reflections on the Uruguay Round and Trade in Services', *Journal of World Trade Law*, 22 (5): 34–47.

Noda, M., 1991, 'The Crossing of Japanese ODA and Resort Development: Investing in Mal-Development', *AMPO: Japan–Asia Quarterly Review: Special Issue on Resort Development*, pp. 34–6.

Noronha, R., 1979, 'Paradise Revisited: Tourism in Bali', in de Kadt, E., ed, *Tourism: Passport to Development?*, Oxford University Press, Oxford and London, pp. 177–204.

Novak, V., 1989, 'Hawaii's Dirty Secret', *Common Cause Magazine*, November–December: 11–27.

Nunez, T., 1963, 'Tourism, Tradition and Acculturation: "Weekendismo" in a Mexican Village', *Ethnology* II (3): 347–52.

Obeyesekere, G., 1984, 'The Origins and Institutionalisation of Political Violence' in Manor, J., ed, *Sri Lanka: In Change and Crisis*, Croom Helm, London.

O.E.C.D., 1989, *Tourism Policy and International Tourism in O.E.C.D. Member Countries*, OECD, Paris.

Oglethorpe, M.G., 1984, 'Tourism in Malta: A Crisis of Dependence', *Leisure Studies*, 3 (2): 141–61.

O'Grady, A., 1990, *The Challenge of Tourism*, Ecumenical Coalition on Third World Tourism (ECTWT), Bangkok.

O'Grady, R., 1981, *Third World Stopover*, World Council of Churches, Geneva.

Oi, W.Y. and Hurter, A.P., 1965, *Economics of Private Truck Transportation*, William C. Brown, Dubuque, Iowa.

O'Malley, J., 1988, 'Sex Tourism and Women's Status in Thailand, *Loisir et Societe*, 11 (1): 99–114.

O'Neill, H., 1984, 'HICs, MICs, NICs and LICs: Some Elements in the Political Economy of Graduation and Differentiation', *World Development*, 12 (7): 693–712.

Ong, A., 1985, 'Industrialisation and Prostitution in Southeast Asia', *Southeast Asia Chronicle*, 96: 2–6.

Ong, A., 1987, *Spirits of Resistance and Capitalist Discipline: Factory Women in Malaysia*, State University of New York, Albany, New York.

Pacific Travel News, 1984, March: 42–48 and 12–25.

Packenham, R.A., 1986, 'Capitalist Dependency and Socialist Dependency: The Case of Cuba', *Journal of InterAmerican Studies and World Affairs*, 28 (1): 59–92.

Packer, J., 1953, *Apes and Ivory*, Eyre and Spottiswoode, London.

Parnwell, M.J.G., 1992, 'Tourism and Rural Handicrafts in Thailand', in Hitchcock, M., King, V.T. and Parnwell, M.J.G., eds, *Tourism in South-east Asia: Theory and Practice*, Routledge, London.

Parnwell, M.J.G., and Khamanarong, S., 1990, 'Rural Industrialisation and Development Planning in Thailand', *Southeast Asian Journal of Social Science*, 18 (2): 1–28.

Parsons, T., 1964, 'Evolutionary Universals in Society', *American Sociological Review*, 29 (3): 339–57.

Peake, R., 1989, 'Swahili Stratification and Tourism in Malindi Old Town, Kenya', *Africa*, 59 (2): 209–20.

Pearce, D., 1989, *Tourist Development*, Longman, Harlow (Second edition).

Peppelenbosch, P. and Tempelman, G., 1989, 'The Pros and Cons of International Tourism in the Third World', in Singh, T.V., Theuns, L.H. and Go, F.M., eds, *Towards Appropriate Tourism: The Case of Developing Countries*, Peter Lang, Frankfurt and Berne, pp. 23–34.

Perez, L.A., 1973–4, 'Aspects of Underdevelopment: Tourism in the West Indies', *Science and Society*, 37 (4): 473–480.

Perez, L.A., 1975, 'Tourism in the West Indies', *Journal of Communications*, 25 (2): 136–43.

Pérez-López, J.F., 1986, 'The Economics of Cuban Joint Ventures', *Cuban Studies*, 16: 181–207.

Pérez-López, J.F., 1987, 'Cuban Oil Re-exports: Significance and Prospects', *Energy Journal*, 8: 1–16.

Pérez-López, J.F., 1988a, 'Cuban Hard-currency Trade and Oil Re-exports', in Roca, S.G., ed, *Socialist Cuba: Past Interpretations and Future Challenges*, Westview, Boulder, 123–158.

Pérez-López, J.F., 1988b, 'Cuban–Soviet Sugar Trade: Price and Subsidy Issues', *Bulletin of Latin American Research*, 7: 123–147.

Perkins, R. and Bennet, G., 1985, *Being a Prostitute: Prostitute Women and Prostitute Men*, George Allen and Unwin, Sydney.

di Perna, P., 1979, *The Complete Travel Guide to Cuba*, St. Martin's Press, New York.

Peterson, L., Ed, 1990, *Fodor's 91 Caribbean*, Fodor's Travel Publications, New York and London.

Philippine Women's Research Collective, 1985, *Filipinas for Sale: An Alternative Report on Women and Tourism*, Philippine Women's Research Collective, Quezon City.

Phillips, A., 1977, 'The Concept of Development', *Review of African Political Economy*, 8: pp. 7–20.

Phongpaichit, P., 1981, 'Bangkok Masseuses: Holding Up the Family Sky', *Southeast Asia Chronicle*, 78: 15–23.

Phongpaichit, P., 1982, *From Peasant Girls to Bangkok Masseuses*, Women, Work and Development 2, International Labour Office, Geneva.

Picard, M., 1990, '"Cultural Tourism" in Bali: Cultural Performances as Tourist Attractions', *Indonesia*, 49: 37–74.

Pi-Sunyer, O., 1979, 'The Politics of Tourism in Catalonia', *Mediterranean Studies*, 1 (2): 29–30.

Pi-Sunyer, O., 1989, 'Changing Perceptions of Tourism and Tourists in a Catalan Resort Town', in Smith, V.L., ed, *Hosts and Guests: The Anthropology of Tourism*, (second edition), University of Pennsylvania Press, Philadelphia, pp. 187–199 (first published in 1978 by Basil Blackwell, Oxford).

Place, S.E., 1991, 'Nature Tourism and Rural Development in Tortuguero', *Annals of Tourism Research*, 16 (2): 186–201.

Poon, A., 1987, 'Information Technology and Innovation in Caribbean Tourism: Implications for the Caribbean Tourist Industry', unpublished D. Phil. thesis, University of Sussex.

Poon, A., 1989, 'Competitive Strategies for a "New Tourism"', in Cooper, C.P., ed., *Progress in Tourism, Recreation and Hospitality Management*, Belhaven, London, pp. 91–102.

Poon, A., 1990, 'Flexible Specialisation and Small Size: the Case of Caribbean Tourism', *World Development*, 18 (1): 109–23.

Potter, R.B., 1983, 'Tourism and Development: The Case of Barbados, West Indies', *Geography*, 68: 44–50.

Price, N., 1988, *Behind the Planter's Back*, Macmillan, London and Basingstoke.

van Raaij, W.E., and Francken, D.A., 1984, 'Vacation Decisions, Activities and Satisfactions', *Annals of Tourism Research*, 11 (1): 101–12.

Rajotte, F., 1987, 'Safari and Beach-resort Tourism: the Costs to Kenya', in Britton, S. and Clarke, W.C., eds, *Ambiguous Alternative: Tourism in Small Developing Countries*, University of South Pacific, Suva, pp. 78–90.

Rann, H. and Geide, P., 1985, *Hildebrand's Travel Guide: Cuba*, K+G, KARTO=GRAFIK Verlagsgesellschaft, Frankfurt am Main.

Redclift, M., 1984, *Development and the Environmental Crisis: Red or Green Alternatives?*, Methuen, London.

Redclift, M., 1987, *Sustainable Development: Exploring the Contradictions*, Routledge, London and New York.

Reynoso y Valle, A., and De Regt, J.P., 1979, 'Growing Pains: Planned tourism Development in Ixtapa-Zihuatanejo', in de Kadt, E., ed, *Tourism: Passport to Development?*, Oxford University Press, New York and Oxford, pp. 113–134.

Richter, L.K., 1980, 'The Political Uses of Tourism: A Philippine Case Study', *Journal of Developing Areas*, 14 (January): 237–257.

Richter, L.K., 1982, *Land Reform and Tourism Development: Policy Making in the Philippines*, Schenkman, Cambridge.

Richter, L.K., 1989, *The Politics of Tourism in Asia*, University of Hawaii Press, Hawaii.

Richter, L.K. and Richter, W.L., 1985, 'Policy Choices in South Asian Tourism Development', *Annals of Tourism Research*, 12 (2): 201–217.

Richter, L.K. and Waugh, W.L. Jr., 1986, 'Terrorism and Tourism As Logical Companions', *Tourism Management*, 7 (4) December: 230–238.

Ridenour, R., 1990, 'Double Trouble with Dollars', *South*, 116: 48–9.

Riley, P.J., 'Road Culture of International Long-term Budget Travellers', *Annals of Tourism Research*, 15 (3): 313–28.

Ritchie, J.E., 1975, 'The Honest Broker in the Cultural Market Place', in Finney, B.R. and

Watson, K.A., eds, *A New Kind of Sugar: Tourism in the Pacific*, East–West Center, Honolulu, pp. 49–58.

Rix, A., 1990, *Japan's Aid Programme: A New Global Agenda*, AIDAB, Canberra.

Roca, S.G., 1988, 'Cuba's International Economic Relations in the Late 1980s', in Roca, S.G., ed, *Socialist Cuba: Past Interpretations and Future Challenges*, Westview, Boulder, 101–22.

Rodenburg, E.E., 1980, 'The Effects of Scale in Economic Development: Tourism in Bali', *Annals of Tourism Research*, 7 (2): 177–96.

Roebuck, J. and MacNamara, P., 1973, 'Ficheras and Free-lancers: Prostitution in a Mexican Border City', *Archives of Sexual Behaviour*, 2 (3): 231–244.

Rogers, J.R., 1989, 'Clear Links: Tourism and Child Prostitution', *Contours*, 4 (2): 20–22.

Romeril, M., 1989, 'Tourism – The Environmental Dimension', in Cooper, P.C., ed, *Progress in Tourism, Recreation and Hospitality Management, Vol. I*, Belhaven Press, London, pp. 103–13.

Rosen, R., 1982, *The Lost Sisterhood*, John Hopkins University Press, Baltimore.

Rowley, A., 1991, 'Investment in Real Estate Expected to Hit the Skids: Japan's Sorry Estate', *Far Eastern Economic Review*, 21st March, p. 61.

Royal Swazi National Airways, 1987, 'Hotel', *Ndiza Natsi*, 4 (18) June/July, TA Publications, Johannesburg.

Rudolph, J.D., 1985, *Cuba: A Country Study*, U.S. Government Printing Office, Washington, D.C. (Third Edition).

Runge, J., 1990, *Rum and Reggae: An Alternative Guide to the Caribbean*, Harrap-Columbus, London.

Russell, M., 1983, 'The Production and Marketing of Women's Handicrafts in Swaziland', Report of a field survey in Swaziland, January–October, for the International Labour Organisation, Social Science Research Unit, University of Swaziland, Kwaluseni, Swaziland.

Safa, H., 1981, 'Runaway Shops and Female Employment: The Search for Cheap Labour', *Signs*, 7 (2): 418–433.

Said, E., and Hitchens, C., eds, 1988, *Blaming the Victims: Spurious Scholarship and the Palestinian Question*, Verso Press, London.

Samarasuriya, S., 1982, *Who Needs Tourism? Employment for Women in the Holiday Industry of Sudugama, Sri Lanka*, Research Project: Women and Development, Colombo/Leiden.

Sampson, A., 1968, *The New Europeans*, Hodder and Stoughton, London.

Samy, J., 1975, 'Crumbs from the Table? The Workers' Share in Tourism', in Finney, B.R. and Watson, K.A., eds, *A New Kind of Sugar: Tourism in the Pacific*, East–West Center, Honolulu, pp. 111–121.

Santos, L., 1991, 'Japanese Tourism in Cebu', *AMPO Japan–Asia Quarterly Review: Special Issue on Resort Development*, 22 (4): 26–7.

Schiller, H.I., 1976, *Communication and Cultural Domination*, International Arts and Sciences Press, New York.

Schlüter, R., 1991, 'El Turismo Internacional and América Latina', *Revista Latinoamericana del Turismo* 1: 7–17.

Schmidt, C., 1979, 'The Guided Tour: Insulated Adventure', *Urban Life: A Journal of Ethnographic Research*, 8 (4): 441–468.

Schott, J.J. and Mazza, J., 1986, 'Trade in Services and Developing Countries', *Journal of World Trade Law*, 20 (3), 253–273.

Schroeder, S., 1982, *Cuba: A Handbook of Historical Statistics*, G.K. Hall and Co., Boston, Mass.

Schürmann, H., 1981, 'The Effects of International Tourism on the Regional Development of Third World Countries', *Applied Geography and Development*, 18: 80–93.

Schwab, D., ed, 1988, *Caribbean*, APA, Singapore.

Schwartz, R.D., 1991, 'Travelers Under Fire: Tourists in the Tibetan Uprising', *Annals of Tourism Research* 18 (4): 588–604.

Sealey, N.E., 1982, *Tourism in the Caribbean*, Hodder and Stoughton, London.

Secretaría de Desarrollo Urbano y Ecologia (SEDUE)/Gobierno del Estado de Jalisco, 1985, *Plan Municipal de Desarrollo Urbano: Centros de Poblacion, Puerto Vallarta*, Puerto Vallarta.

Selwyn, T., forthcoming, 'Being in Nature: Tourism and Nationalism in Israel', in Selwyn,

T., ed, *Chasing Myths*, Cambridge University Press, Cambridge.

Sentfleben, W., 1986, 'Tourism, Hot Spring Resorts and Sexual Entertainment: Observations from Northern Taiwan – A Study in Social Geography', *Philippine Geographical Journal*, 30 (Jan.–June): 21–41.

Sereewat, S., 1983, *Prostitution: Thai–European Connection: An Action-Oriented Study*, Commission on the Churches' Participation in Development, World Council of Churches, Geneva.

Seward, S. and Spinrad, B., eds, 1982, *Tourism in the Caribbean: The Economic Impact*, International Development Research Centre, Ottowa.

Sharon, M., 1983, 'The Propaganda War', *Jerusalem Post*, 14th June.

Sheahan, J., 1987, *Patterns of Development in Latin America: Poverty, Repression and Economic Strategy*, Princeton University Press, Princeton, New Jersey.

Shearman, P., 1987, *The Soviet Union and Cuba*, Royal Institute of International Affairs, London.

Shoesmith, D., 1981, 'The Fantasy Tourism Industry and Prostitution in the Philippines', *Asian Bureau Australia*, October: 4–5.

Shurma-Smith, P., 1988, 'Kinship, Identity and Second Home Ownership on the Ile aux Moines, Brittany', paper presented at the First Conference on Anthropology and Tourism, Group for Anthropology in Policy and Practice (GAPP), Roehampton Institute, 22nd–23rd April.

Sims, G.A., 1916, *The Republic of Cuba*, Banker's Loan and Securities Co., New Orleans.

Sinclair, M.T. and Tsegaye, A., 1990, 'International Tourism and Export Instability', *Journal of Development Studies*, 26 (3): 487–504.

Slater, D., 1982, 'State and Territory in Post-revolutionary Cuba: Some Critical Reflections on the Development of Spatial Policy', *International Journal of Urban and Regional Research*, 6 (1): 1–34.

Smith, J.T., 1985, 'Sugar Dependency in Cuba: Capitalism versus Socialism', in Seligson, M.A., ed, *The Gap Between Rich and Poor*, Westview, Boulder, 366–378.

Smith, V., 1988, 'Geographical Implications of "Drifter" Tourism: Borocay, Philippines'. Paper presented to the Symposium on Tourism, 13th–20th August, International Geographical Union, Christchurch, New Zealand.

Smith, V., 1989, (second edition) *Hosts and Guests: the Anthropology of Tourism*, University of Pennsylvania Press, Philadelphia. First edition published in 1978 by Basil Blackwell, Oxford.

Smith, W.S., 1988, 'The Cuban–Soviet Alliance', in Smith, W.S. and Morales Dominguez, E., eds, *Subject to Solution: Problems in Cuban–U.S. Relations*, Lynne Rienner, Boulder, pp. 1–13.

Sobers, A., et al., 1990, *Caribbean Tourism Statistical Report, 1989*, Caribbean Tourism Organization, Christ Church, Barbados.

Sorensen, J., 1990, 'An Assessment of Costa Rica's Coastal Management Program', *Coastal Management Journal*, 18 (1): 37–63.

Srisang, K., ed, 1991, *Caught in Modern Slavery: Tourism and Child Prostitution in Asia*, The Ecumenical Coalition on Third World Tourism (ECTWT), Bangkok.

Stansfield, D., 1980, 'The Mexican Tourist Industry', *Bolsa Review*, 14 (4): 226–232.

State Committee for Statistics, 1990, *The Cuban Economy in 1989*, Havana.

State Statistical Bureau of the People's Republic of China, 1990, *China: Statistical Yearbook, 1990*, China Statistical Information and Consultation Service Centre and University of Illinois at Chicago, Beijing and Illinois.

Stiglitz, J.E., 1988, *Economics of the Public Sector*, Norton, London.

Stringer, P.F., 1981, 'Hosts and Guests: The Bed and Breakfast Phenomenon', *Annals of Tourism Research*, 8 (3): 357–376.

Stronge, W. and Redman, M., 1982, 'US Tourism in Mexico: An Empirical Analysis', *Annals of Tourism Research*, 9 (1): 21–35.

Summary, R.M., 1987, 'Tourism's Contribution to the Economy of Kenya', *Annals of Tourism Research*, 14 (4): 531–40.

Susman, P., 1987a, 'Spatial Equality and Socialist Transformation in Cuba', in Forbes, D. and

Thrift, N., eds, *The Socialist Third World*, Basil Blackwell, Oxford, 250–281.

Susman, P., 1987b, 'Spatial Equality in Cuba', *International Journal of Urban and Regional Research*, 11 (2): 218–241.

Sutcliffe, C., 1985, 'Measuring the Economic Effects of Tourism on an Underdeveloped Region', in Ashworth, G.J. and Goodall, B., eds, *The Impact of Tourist Development on Disadvantaged Regions*, Geografisch Instituut, Rijksuniversiteit, Groningen, pp. 55–65.

Suzuki, N., ed, 1989, *Nihon no Keizai Kyōryoku: Tojōkoku Keizai Hatten no Shiten Kara*, Ajia Keizai Kenkyūjo, Tokyo.

Swaziland Chamber of Commerce, 1987, *Swaziland: A Review of Commerce and Industry – 1987 edition*, B and T Enterprises, Manzini, Swaziland.

Swaziland Tourist Office, u.d., *The Kingdom of Swaziland: Tourist Guide*, Jubilee Printing and Publishing, Mbabane.

Sweet, J.D., 1989, 'Burlesquing "the Other" in Pueblo Performance', *Annals of Tourism Research*, 16 (1): 62–75.

Symansk, R., 1981, *The Immoral Landscape: Female Prostitution in Western Societies*, Butterworths, Toronto.

Taylor, D., 1984, 'Cheap Thrills', *New Internationalist*, 142: 14.

Teeha, R., 1991, 'Guam: Breaking Even with Tourism or Just Breaking?', *AMPO: Japan–Asia Quarterly Review: Special Issue on Resort Development*, 22 (4): 21–2.

Teye, V., 1988a, 'Coups d'Etat and African Tourism: A Study of Ghana', *Annals of Tourism Research*, 15 (3): 329–356.

Teye, V., 1988b, 'Geographic Factors Affecting Tourism in Zambia', *Annals of Tourism Research*, 15 (4): 487–503.

Thirlwall, A.P., 1983, (Third Edition), *Growth and Development*, Macmillan, London.

Thitsa, K., 1980, *Providence and Prostitution: Image and Reality for Women in Buddhist Thailand*, Change International Reports, London.

Thuens, H.L., 1987, 'Appropriate Tourism for the Third World: A Bibliography on the Socio–Cultural Dimension: 1963–1984', *Tourism Recreation Research*, 12 (2): 55–64.

Thurot, J. and Thurot, G., 1983, 'The Ideology of Class and Tourism: Confronting the Discourse of Advertising', *Annals of Tourism Research*, 10 (1): 173–89.

Tiglao, R., 1991, 'Cebu's Business Climate is Alternative Magnet to Manila: The Other Philippines', *Far Eastern Economic Review*, 28th November, pp. 60–2.

Todaro, M.P., 1985, (Third Edition) *Economic Development in the Third World*, Longman, London.

Tokman, V., 1978, 'An Exploration into the Nature of Informal–Formal Sector Relations', *World Development* 6 (9/10): 1065–1075.

Torrents, N., 1989, *La Habana*, Editorial Destino, Barcelona.

Toye, J., 1987, *Dilemmas of Development: Reflections on the Counter-Revolution in Development Theory and Policy*, Blackwell, Oxford.

Trick, D.R., 1989, 'Oppression: The Rise and Fall of Tourism', *USA Today*, 14th November.

Truong, T.D., 1983, 'The Dynamics of Sex Tourism: The Cases of South-East Asia', *Development and Change* 14 (4): 533–553.

Truong, T.D., 1990, *Sex, Money and Morality: Prostitution and Tourism in South-East Asia*, Zed Press, London.

Tsuruoka, D., 1991, 'Malaysia Embraces Japan as its Economic Model: Look East and Up, *Far Eastern Economic Review*, 28th March, pp. 50–2.

Tucker, A., ed, *The Penguin Guide to the Caribbean, 1990*, Viking Penguin, New York.

Turner, L., 1976, 'The International Division of Leisure: Tourism and the Third World', *World Development*, 4 (3): 253–260.

Turner, L. and Ash, J., eds, 1975, *The Golden Hordes: International Tourism and the Pleasure Periphery*, Constable, London.

Turner, V. and Turner, E., 1978, *Image and Pilgrimage in Christian Culture*, Basil Blackwell, Oxford.

Tüting, L., 1989, 'Trekking Tourism in Nepal', *Tourismus und Okologie, ökozid 5*, Focus Verlag, Giessen.

Tyson, A.S., 1989, 'China Lures Investors with Political Risk Insurance', *Christian Science*

Monitor, 24th August: 4.

United Nations, *Statistical Yearbook, 1987*, U.N., New York, 1990.

United Nations Centre on Transnational Corporations, (UNCTC), 1982, *Transnational Corporations in International Tourism*, U.N., New York.

United Nations Conference on Trade and Development (UNCTAD), 1988, *Trade and Development Report, 1988*, UNCTAD, New York.

United Nations Economic, Scientific and Cultural Organisation (UNESCO), 1976, 'The Effects of Tourism on Socio–Cultural Values', *Annals of Tourism Research*, 4 (2): 74–105.

Urry, J., 1988, 'Cultural Change and Contemporary Holiday-making', *Theory, Culture and Society*, 5 (1): 35–55.

Urry, J., 1990, *The Tourist Gaze: Leisure and Travel in Contemporary Societies*, Sage, London.

U.S. News and World Report, 1984, 3rd December: 45.

U.S. News and World Report, 1989, 18th September: 18.

Uzzell, D., 1984, 'An Alternative Structuralist Approach to the Psychology of Tourism Marketing', *Annals of Tourism Research*, 11 (1): 79–99.

Var, T., Schlüter, R., Ankomah, P. and T-H Lee, 1989, 'Tourism and World Peace: The Case of Argentina', *Annals of Tourism Research* 16 (3): 431–4.

Vasconi, M.A., 1991, 'Aproximacion a la Conceptualizacion de la Geografia del Turismo', *Revista Latinoamericana del Turismo*, 1: 18–38.

Wagner, D., 1985, 'Anxious for Armageddon: Probing Israel's Political Support Among American Fundamentalists', in Haddad, H. and Wagner, D., *All in the Name of the Bible: Selected Essays on Israel, South Africa and Christian Fundamentalism*, Palestine Human Rights Campaign, Chicago.

Wagner, U, 1982, *Catching the Tourist: Women Handicraft Traders in the Gambia*, Department of Social Anthropology, University of Stockholm.

Wagner, U. and Yamba, B., 1986, 'Going North and Getting Attached: The Cases of Gambians', *Ethnos*, 51: 3–45.

Wahnschaft, R., 1982, 'Formal and Informal Tourism Sectors: A Case Study in Pattaya, Thailand', *Annals of Tourism Research*, 9 (3): 429–451.

Waters, S., 1988, 1989, 1991, *The Travel Industry Yearbook*, Child and Waters, New York.

Wheeler, T., 1987, *Sri Lanka: A Travel Survival Kit*, Lonely Planet, Melbourne.

White, G., 1987, 'Cuban Planning in the Mid-1980s: Centralization, Decentralization and Participation', *World Development*, 15 (1): 153–61.

White, K.J. and Walker, M.B., 1982, 'Trouble in the Travel Account', *Annals of Tourism Research*, 9 (11): 37–56

Whyte, W., 1955, *Street Corner Society: The Social Structure of an Italian Slum*, University of Chicago Press, Chicago.

Wihtol, R., 1982, 'Hospitality Girls in the Manila Tourist Belt', *Philippine Journal of Industrial Relations*, 4 (1–2): 18–42.

Wilkinson, P.F., 1989, 'Strategies for Tourism in Island Economies', *Annals of Tourism Research*, 16 (2): 153–77.

Williams, A.M., Shaw, G., 1988, eds, *Tourism and Economic Development: Western European Experiences*, Belhaven, London.

Williamson, O.E., 1975, *Markets and Hierarchies: Analysis and Anti-Trust Implications*, Free Press, New York.

Wilson, D., 1979, 'The Early Effects of Tourism in the Seychelles', in de Kadt, E., ed, *Tourism: Passport to Development?*, Oxford University Press, New York and Oxford: 205–236.

Withyman, M., 1985, 'The Ins and Outs of International Travel and Tourism Data', *International Tourism Quarterly*, 4: 61–7.

Witt, S.F., Brooke, M.Z. and Buckley, P.J., 1991, *The Management of International Tourism*, Unwin Hyman, London.

Wolfers, M., 1974, *Black Man's Burden Revisited*, Allison and Busby, London.

Wood, R.E., 1984, 'Ethnic Tourism, the State, and Cultural Change in Southeast Asia', *Annals of Tourism Research*, 11 (3): 353–74.

Woodward, J., 1990, 'PAN AM 103', a PBS Documentary, 23rd January.

World Bank (The International Bank for Reconstruction and Development), 1990, *World Development Report 1990*, Oxford University Press, New York.

World Tourism Organisation (WTO), 1983, *Regional Breakdown of World Tourism Statistics, 1978–82*, WTO, Madrid.

World Tourism Organisation (WTO), 1985a, *Regional Breakdown of World Travel and Tourism Statistics, 1980–84*, WTO, Madrid.

World Tourism Organisation (WTO), 1985b, *Traveller Departures and Main Destinations, 1983–1984*, WTO, Madrid.

World Tourism Organisation (WTO), 1988, *Economic Review of World Tourism*, WTO, Madrid.

World Tourism Organisation (WTO), 1990, *Yearbook of Tourism Statistics, 1989, Vols I and II*, WTO, Madrid.

World Tourism Organisation (WTO), 1991a, *Current Travel and Tourism Indicators*, WTO, Madrid, February.

World Tourism Organisation (WTO), 1991b, *Yearbook of Tourism Statistics, 1990*, Vols. I and II, WTO, Madrid.

World Tourism Organisation (WTO), 1991c, *Tourism in the Year 2000: Qualitative Aspects Affecting Global Growth – a Discussion Paper*, WTO, Madrid.

Worsley, P., 1980, *The Three Worlds: Culture and World Development*, Weidenfeld and Nicolson, London.

Worsley, P., 1984, 'One World or Three? A Critique of the World-system Theory of Immanuel Wallerstein', *Socialist Register*: 298–338.

Wright, D.L., 1975, 'Air Inclusive Tour Holiday Industry', in Stopford, J.M., Channon, D.F. and Norburn, D., eds, *British Business Policy: A Casebook*, Macmillan, London, pp. 47–55.

Yacoumis, J., 1989, 'South Pacific Tourism Promotion: A Regional Approach', *Tourism Management*, 10 (1), March: 15–28.

Yoyori, M., 1977, 'Sexual Slavery in Korea, *Frontiers: A Journal of Women's Studies*, 2 (1): 76.

Zellers, M., 1990, *1990 Caribbean*, Fielding Travel Books, New York.

Zimbalist, A., 1982, 'Soviet Aid, U.S. Blockade and the Cuban Economy', *Comparative Economic Studies*, 24 (4): 137–145.

Zimbalist, A., 1988, 'Cuba', in Paus, E., ed, *Struggle Against Dependence: Non-traditional Export Growth in Central America and the Caribbean*, Westview, Boulder, 169–92.

Zimbalist, A. and Eckstein, S., 1987, 'Patterns of Cuban Development: the First Twenty-five years', *World Development*, 15 (1): 5–22.

Index